$20.86

The Border Within

THE ECONOMICS OF IMMIGRATION
IN AN AGE OF FEAR

THE BORDER WITHIN

Tara Watson & Kalee Thompson

The University of Chicago Press   Chicago and London

The University of Chicago Press, Chicago 60637
The University of Chicago Press, Ltd., London
Published 2021
Printed in the United States of America

30 29 28 27 26 25 24 23 22 21   1 2 3 4 5

ISBN-13: 978-0-226-27022-7 (cloth)
ISBN-13: 978-0-226-27036-4 (e-book)
DOI: https://doi.org/10.7208/chicago/9780226270364.001.0001

Library of Congress Cataloging-in-Publication Data

Names: Watson, Tara, author. | Thompson, Kalee, author.
Title: The border within : the economics of immigration in an age of fear /
Tara Watson and Kalee Thompson.
Other titles: Economics of immigration in an age of fear
Description: Chicago ; London : The University of Chicago Press, 2021. |
Includes index.
Identifiers: LCCN 2021016975 | ISBN 9780226270227 (cloth) |
ISBN 9780226270364 (ebook)
Subjects: LCSH: Immigration enforcement—Economic aspects—United
States. | Illegal aliens—United States. | United States—Emigration and
immigration—Economic aspects. | United States—Emigration and
immigration—Government policy.
Classification: LCC JV6471 .W37 2021 | DDC 363.25/9370973—dc23
LC record available at https://lccn.loc.gov/2021016975

♾ This paper meets the requirements of ANSI/NISO Z39.48-1992
(Permanence of Paper).

CONTENTS

PROLOGUE

The American narrative celebrates the idea of immigrants arriving to build a better life in a land of abundance. Yet Americans have always struggled with immigration, particularly as it intersects with race, poverty, and economic opportunity. In the last couple of decades, the immigrant share of the US population has grown greater than at any time since the early twentieth century—as has the centrality of the immigration debate.

Since the year 2000, an average of a million people from all over the world have been granted legal permanent status ("green cards") in the United States each year.[1] Federal law sets annual limits on how many individuals can be legally admitted to the country, with priority given to spouses, minor children, and parents of US citizens, who collectively make up two-thirds of the annual total, as well as to people with certain in-demand professional skills. There's also a "diversity" lottery for residents of countries that don't send many people (in 2018, more than fourteen million people competed for fifty thousand slots).[2]

But many individuals are unable to immigrate legally. Even for those with fairly close family ties—the adult children of US citizens, for example—there is currently a six- to seven-year wait for would-be immigrants from most of the world. No more than 7 percent of green cards are issued to migrants coming from any given country in any given year, making it harder to legally enter from some countries than others. For an unmarried adult from Mexico with a US-citizen parent, the current wait time is more than nineteen years.[3] A less-educated

FIGURE 1. Foreign-born population in the United States, 2017

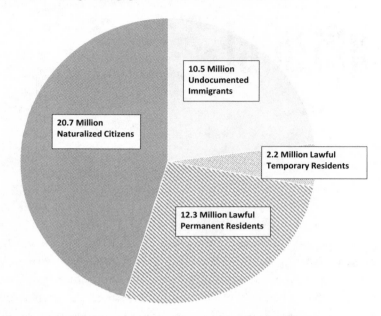

10.5 Million
Undocumented
Immigrants

20.7 Million
Naturalized Citizens

2.2 Million Lawful
Temporary Residents

12.3 Million Lawful
Permanent Residents

Note: Pew estimates adjust for undercount and therefore differ slightly from official Census Bureau estimates.
Source: Pew Research

resident of Mexico without relatives in the United States typically cannot expect any route to legal immigration in their lifetime. Though the current political rhetoric often calls for newcomers to simply "wait in line," this sentiment reflects a misunderstanding of our immigration system. For many would-be immigrants, there is no line.

Millions of people are determined to come to the US even in the absence of a legal pathway, of course, and many of them succeed. Almost a quarter of the foreign-born population now living in the United States, and more than 40 percent of all noncitizens, are in the country without legal status (see figure 1).[4] Of the 10.5 million undocumented residents, about half crossed the border illegally, while the rest arrived on a temporary visa and stayed after it expired.

Concerns about the scale of immigration and the fact that so many immigrants live in the US without authorization has prompted a desire for policy action. Many US citizens are concerned about immigrants taking American jobs, using social services, and committing crime, though—as we discuss later in this book—these concerns for the most part do not align with the evidence on immigration's impacts. Some anti-immigrant sentiment is rooted in racism and fear of demographic change. As the number of undocumented immigrants living in the United States has increased substantially over recent decades, so too have enforcement efforts.

There are three main approaches to reducing the number of undocumented immigrants in the United States. One is to prevent unauthorized immigration through aggressive border control. Fears about terrorism and the drug trade add further impetus to secure the border. Indeed, advanced technology and expanded manpower in recent decades have greatly enhanced border security. Though increased security is also evident along the US border with Canada, most of the enforcement effort has been focused at the southern border.

Today, it is much more expensive to cross the southern border with the help of a paid guide than it was in the past (the estimated cost nearly tripled from $1,500 in 2010 to $4,100 in 2015, and in 2017 John Kelly, then head of the Department of Homeland Security, bragged that enforcement efforts had pushed up smuggling fees even higher).[5] It is also more physically dangerous—as well as riskier in terms of the likelihood, and consequences, of being caught.

Border enforcement both directly and indirectly impacts the number of long-term residents within the United States. Somewhat ironically, expanded enforcement efforts at the border have led some unauthorized residents to become more deeply rooted in their American communities. The relatively porous border of the past meant that migration was often temporary, and fluidly responsive to economic conditions in both the US and in immigrants' home countries. Now, given the risks and expense of border crossing, those who choose to come to America without legal status are more often those who hope to settle here. Once in the US, many migrants do not dare return to their country of origin even for a visit, for fear that they will not be able to reenter. Ties with family in the country of origin are weakened. America becomes home.

Border control tends to dominate both the resources spent and conversation about enforcement, but interior enforcement is a second important policy lever. Interior enforcement efforts focus on arresting and removing immigrants already living in the United States. A third set of policies, also sometimes considered part of interior enforcement, makes the United States less attractive to both existing and would-be immigrants by limiting work opportunities and reducing access to public benefits. All three approaches aim to deter future migration by raising the costs and reducing the benefits of making the decision to come to the United States.

This book focuses particularly on interior enforcement, which has distinct characteristics. Unlike border control, which most often affects those who do not yet live in the United States, interior enforcement frequently targets those who are long-term residents with families. Whereas border control tends to be a fairly blunt policy instrument, interior enforcement can be tailored to meet the goals of a given presidential administration, especially in an environment without robust legislation governing the issue.

One administrative approach is to focus on a narrow set of objectives such as removing immigrants who present a public safety risk and making it more difficult for unauthorized immigrants to work in the formal sector. These goals can be achieved in a way that is transparent and systematic and includes due-process protections. Alternatively, an administration can choose a high-visibility and capricious approach, making it clear that any undocumented immigrant is at risk of deportation regardless of personal circumstance. As we illustrate in this book, directing resources in this way does not achieve stated objectives like reducing crime or discouraging workplace competition, but does sow fear and confusion in immigrant communities.

Aggressive interior enforcement impacts a wide range of economic behaviors, often in ways that go beyond the explicit text or ostensible goals of the policy. In the legal context, the term "chilling effect" is used to describe the impact of legal actions that deter individuals from exercising their rights without formally curtailing those rights. In the 1965 Supreme Court case *Lamont v. Postmaster General*, Chief Justice William Brennan argued that requiring individuals to sign up at the post office if they wished to receive communist literature constituted a chilling effect on freedom of speech.[6]

The enforcement of immigration policy can likewise generate chilling effects. A construction worker fearing deportation may stay quiet about an unsafe structure; an undocumented mother may decide not to enroll her citizen child in a publicly available health insurance program. Chilling effects indirectly influence the economic decision-making, educational outcomes, and health of immigrants—and are heightened when enforcement is highly visible and seemingly arbitrary in its implementation. And the consequences of enforcement extend beyond immigrants themselves, affecting American citizens living in immigrant families as well as the broader American society.

In the following pages, we investigate the costs of aggressive interior enforcement tactics in both human and economic terms. We also look at the effectiveness of these policies in achieving their purported goals. Though the ostensible goals of interior enforcement might be to improve public safety and reduce workplace competition, the evidence suggests that the current approach does more to engender a sense of uncertainty and vulnerability among immigrants than it does to achieve those ends.

*   *   *

The concept of "illegal immigration" dates to 1875. Though some states started to restrict immigration after the Civil War, the federal government placed no restrictions on immigration itself in the first century of nationhood. It wasn't until 1875 that the Page Act—fueled by concerns about Asian immigration in the western part of the country—regulated immigration for the first time. The act prohibited the immigration of forced laborers from China and Japan, women identified as potential prostitutes (in practice excluding nearly all Chinese women), and convicts. Soon after, the 1882 Chinese Exclusion Act banned all Chinese laborers from immigrating and the 1888 Scott Act made it illegal for Chinese laborers to return to the United States if they left. In *Chae Chan Ping v. United States*, a Chinese worker challenged the Scott

FIGURE 2. Percentage of US population born outside the US, 1850–2017

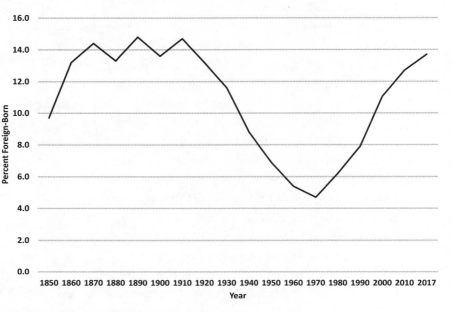

Source: US Census Bureau and Pew Research

Act when he was refused reentry to the United States, and the Supreme Court sided with the government, in 1889 officially deeming the restriction of immigration to be a federal power.

Even as further immigration restrictions were passed in the late nineteenth century, there was no effort to deter the entry of healthy Europeans to the United States. Immigrants provided essential labor for the rapidly growing nation. "Already in the restrictions enacted in the 1880s could be seen the emerging divisions between those who saw immigrants as a drain on social resources or unfair competitors in the labor market," Sacramento State historian Patrick Ettinger writes, "and those who saw immigrants as vital resources for the industrial economy."[7]

In 1900, as now, around 14 percent of the US population was foreign born (see figure 2).[8] The late 1800s and early 1900s witnessed a pronounced shift in migration from northern and western Europe to that from other parts of Europe (see figure 3), and the political rheto-

FIGURE 3. Regions of origin of the foreign-born population, 1850–2017

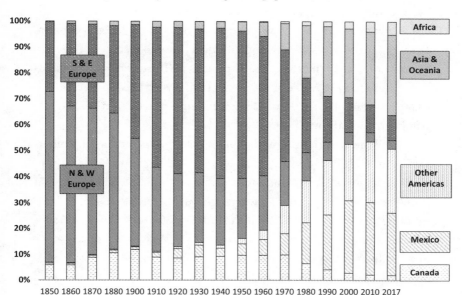

Note: 1890 data unavailable.
Source: Authors' analysis of Census and American Community Survey data

ric concerning the changing face of immigration was strikingly similar to some of the uglier sentiments heard today.[9]

The restrictionist approach took hold during World War I, with a series of laws culminating in the Immigration Act of 1924. Nonprofessional immigrants admitted annually from any Eastern Hemisphere country were limited to 2 percent of the population of residents from that country living in the United States as of the 1890 census, with further restrictions on Asian immigration. The 1890 benchmark favored northern and western Europeans and made it difficult for others—notably Italians and eastern European Jews—to find safe haven in the United States. Interestingly from today's vantage point, no explicit quotas were imposed on immigration from the Western Hemisphere, which at that time was dominated by immigration from Canada.

The quota system introduced in the 1920s served as the governing framework for four decades. Though the quotas didn't apply to Western Hemisphere migrants, Depression-era concerns about jobs led hundreds of thousands of Mexicans working in the US to be repatriated, in some cases forcibly. The United States also experimented with a massive initiative for Mexican guest workers, the Bracero program, from 1942 to 1964, with significant efforts to make sure workers returned home after their short-term contracts. The quota policy and informal targeting of Mexican workers gradually led to an America with many fewer immigrants. By 1960, fewer than 6 percent of US residents had been born abroad.[10]

But by the civil rights era, the quota system was seen as an embarrassment, with President Lyndon Johnson calling it "un-American in the highest sense."[11] The Immigration and Nationality Act of 1965, also known as the Hart-Cellar Act, changed the orientation of the legal immigration system. It did limit the number of visas from each hemisphere — including, for the first time, from the Western Hemisphere — and limited immigrants from any given country in the Eastern Hemisphere to twenty thousand, but the new system significantly broadened access for would-be immigrants from Asia and Africa. It also established a preference system prioritizing family relationships and professional skills. Immediate relatives of US citizens were not subject to the country-based limits, which some predicted would allow for ample European migration, quelling the fears that the ethnic makeup of the country would change. This 1965 framework largely remains in effect, with the family-based approach to immigration the central feature of the system today.

Those hoping that immigration would continue to be dominated by people from Europe would soon be disappointed. In the 1970s, world economic realities combined with the liberalized immigration rules led to influxes of immigrants from Asia, Central America, and — especially — Mexico. The family-based approach amplified those inflows over the subsequent decades, and legal immigration was supplemented by many family members who came to the US "without papers." Today's immigrants are mostly from Mexico, Central and South America, and Asia, with a smaller but growing population from Africa (see figure 3). New inflows from Mexico have declined substantially since the Great Recession of 2007–08, whereas Central American

FIGURE 4. Distribution of foreign-born population across states, 1980 and 2017

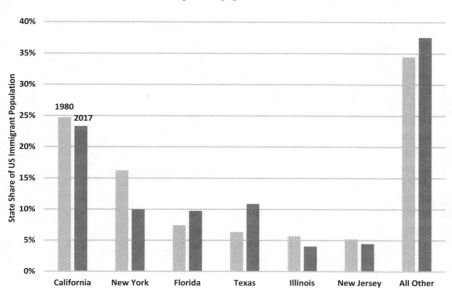

Source: Authors' analysis of Census and American Community Survey data

migration has been more dominant. The number of immigrants — and the intensity of the immigration debate — is now greater than at any time since the early twentieth century.

As immigration started to rise again in the 1970s, most immigrants lived in six states: California, New York, Florida, Texas, Illinois, and New Jersey. But in the past few decades, the immigrant population has substantially expanded into places that were not previously considered immigrant destinations. California and New York still have high immigrant populations, but they are attracting a smaller share of the foreign born than before (see figure 4). At the same time, many southern states witnessed enormous growth in their foreign-born populations relative to historical norms. Between 1980 and 2017, for example, North Carolina went from 1.7 percent foreign born to 8.9 percent, and Georgia from 2.1 percent to 11.2 percent. Nevada saw its foreign-born population grow from 7.8 percent to 21.2 percent of the whole over the same time period.[12] This expansion has prompted fears of economic, demo-

FIGURE 5. Estimated undocumented population (millions), 1990–2017

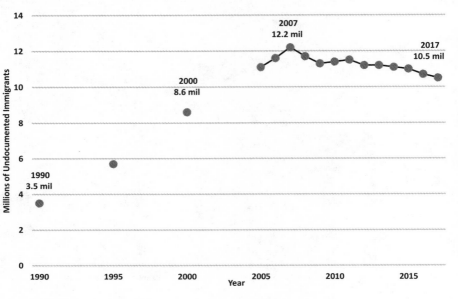

Source: Pew Research

graphic, and social upheaval, and renewed calls for an America that looks more like the America of the past.

*   *   *

According to estimates produced by the Pew Research Center, the unauthorized population in the US grew from 3.5 million in 1990 to a historical peak of 12.2 million in 2007. Since the Great Recession, that number has gradually declined, reaching 10.5 million as of 2017, as shown in figure 5.[13]

Increasingly, the undocumented population is made up of long-term US residents. An estimated two-thirds of the total undocumented population has been in the US for more than ten years.[14] Many unauthorized adults (about 14 percent) are married to an American citizen or lawful permanent resident, and the majority of undocumented parents have at least one US-citizen child. Like many countries, the United States has birthright citizenship; children born in the US are born citizens, regardless of the immigration status of their parents.

FIGURE 6. Undocumented population by region of origin, 2017

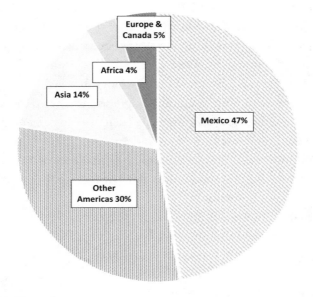

Source: Pew Research

About 7 percent of *all* children now living in the United States live with at least one unauthorized parent. That's 5.1 million kids, 4.1 million of them US citizens themselves.[15] These family ties mean there is no neat separation between the undocumented community and the rest of the population; immigration policies directly impact US citizens as well.

What do we know about the national origins of the current undocumented population? The largest group, about five million individuals, were born in Mexico. They represent 47 percent of those living in the United States without papers as of 2017 (just a few years earlier, over 50 percent of unauthorized immigrants were from Mexico; see figure 6).[16] Another 18 percent come from Central America, especially the "Northern Triangle" countries of El Salvador, Guatemala, and Honduras; and 12 percent were born in the Caribbean or South America. About 14 percent of undocumented immigrants are originally from Asia.

Given that so many undocumented immigrants are from Mexico and Central America, it's no surprise that many enter the country across the 1,954-mile border between the US and Mexico, sometimes legally on a tourist or work visa but more often surreptitiously. A tiny percentage cross illegally over the Canadian border or are otherwise smuggled to US shores. Most other undocumented migrants arrive by air on tourist or work visas, which they then overstay. The Department of Homeland Security estimates that 497,000 individuals with temporary visas in the 2019 fiscal year were still in the country without status by December 2019, a figure that only includes those who originally arrived by air or sea.[17] The Center for Migration Studies, a pro-migrant think tank based in New York, estimates that over 60 percent of all new unauthorized residents in 2016 arrived on a visa rather than entering without inspection.[18] This fact places an upper limit on the potential effectiveness of border enforcement alone in limiting the growth of the undocumented population.

The majority of undocumented immigrant adults are employed, though most work in low-income jobs. The nonprofit Migration Policy Institute estimates that 26 percent of undocumented residents live in a family whose annual income is below the federal poverty level ($26,200 for a family of four in 2020 dollars).[19]

Not surprisingly, there is a degree of uncertainty in employment numbers for undocumented immigrants. A disproportionate number of immigrants are engaged in informal "under-the-table" work—as gardeners, nannies, handymen, and housekeepers—that may not be captured in administrative data and surveys. In fields where the data are relatively reliable, though, they reveal that several million undocumented workers are not exactly laboring "in the shadows." The US Department of Agriculture reports that fully half of all hired farmworkers in the United States were unauthorized as of 2014–2016, for example.[20] More than two million undocumented immigrants work in retail and service jobs, 1.2 million work in construction, and 940,000 in manufacturing.[21] Undocumented immigrants are entrenched in both formal and informal sectors of the American workforce—so much so that 74 percent work in occupations deemed during the global coronavirus pandemic to be "essential critical infrastructure," according to the Center for Migration Studies.[22]

In many ways, unauthorized immigrants go about their business like ordinary Americans, often with a tacit "don't ask don't tell" agreement among employers, landlords, educators, neighbors, social service workers, and immigrants themselves. Their day-to-day lives may not appear so different from those of their citizen neighbors and friends.

But the threat of enforcement shapes the lives of the undocumented — where they live, how they get to work, whether they visit the doctor when they get sick. The capricious nature of the enforcement system only adds to the sense of uncertainty. Immigrants who have been in the US for decades live with the fear that they could be uprooted at any moment, or that their own misstep or simple bad luck could derail plans and destroy dreams for the people they love most. Lives are undone, or not, at the whim of the police officer who pulls someone over for a missing taillight.

* * *

As the population of undocumented immigrants in the US has increased, so too has the national focus on enforcement. In 1986, the United States spent about $1 billion to enforce immigration laws. As of 2020, the Department of Homeland Security devotes over a third of its $88 billion annual budget to divisions with responsibility for immigration issues.[23] A 2013 Migration Policy Institute study found that the United States spends more on its immigration enforcement agencies than on all of its other principal criminal federal law enforcement agencies combined.[24] That was even before Trump, before talk of a $5 billion wall.

The largest of the immigration agencies is Customs and Border Protection (CBP), with a 2020 budget of about $17.4 billion and almost sixty-two thousand employees. CBP is charged with maintaining the integrity of the nation's boundaries and ports of entry. Immigration and Customs Enforcement (ICE), primarily responsible for internal enforcement, has over twenty-one thousand employees and a 2020 budget of about $8.4 billion. A third agency, US Citizenship and Immigration Services (USCIS), adds $4.1 billion and another nineteen thousand–plus workers.[25] USCIS provides immigration and citizenship benefits and is responsible for implementing DACA, or Deferred

Action for Childhood Arrivals, President Obama's 2012 executive order to protect so-called Dreamers, unauthorized immigrants who arrived as children.

The three agencies combined cost about $30 billion a year. By some metrics, this combined $30 billion is a small number. The social security budget is around $1 trillion a year and the defense budget $700 billion. But immigration enforcement spending now exceeds that of other important federal law enforcement programs. The US Coast Guard budget is around $12 billion annually, the FBI spends about $10 billion, and the Drug Enforcement Agency (DEA) budget is under $3 billion.[26] Immigration enforcement (CBP, ICE, and USCIS combined) costs each American around $90 per year, more than the Coast Guard, FBI, and DEA combined.

What do we get for this money? Much of it is spent at the border and — despite the political rhetoric about hordes of immigrants easily streaming in — the southern border is far more secure than it was a decade or two ago. Today, there is a wall or fencing along 700 of the 1900 miles separating the US from Mexico. Old walls have been built taller and stronger. Drones and military-style surveillance have become the norm. Substantially more manpower is devoted to border security.

Less pronounced in the public imagination is the more than $8 billion per year the country spends on *interior* (or internal) enforcement. In large part, these funds go to employing the twenty-one thousand immigration officers who track down immigrants living or working without authorization in the United States, and to funding the detention centers that hold tens of thousands of immigrants as their cases proceed.

* * *

In this book, we assess the costs of internal immigration enforcement — that which takes place after immigrants have established lives in the United States. What are our policies, and how much do we spend to implement them? What are the human costs of the current regime for undocumented immigrants and their families? What are the economic costs for individual families and the larger society when a bread-winner is deported? How do the so-called chilling effects associated with ramped-up enforcement impact the way that immigrants interact with the education system, the healthcare system, and other social services? What liberties do all Americans sacrifice when aggressive enforcement policies are put in place within the borders of the United States?

We also evaluate the potential benefits of interior enforcement. What are the possible fiscal and social advantages of having fewer undocumented immigrants in the United States? How does unauthorized immigration shape the economy? Does aggressive enforcement deter future illegal migration?

This book is divided into three parts. Part 1 is focused on the impact immigrants have on the job market, and the US economy more broadly. In part 2, we focus on the policy of enforcement, including the history of the lawmaking that has brought us to current rules and realities. In part 3, our focus shifts to taxes, healthcare, crime, education, and other social services, and we look at how the undocumented population impacts and is impacted by each.

As we progress through discussions of the economics and policy of immigration, it's easy to get lost in the statistics. To help emphasize the real-world impacts of immigration policy, we also tell the stories of six immigrant families, each of which includes at least one undocumented member. Our hope is that sharing these stories will help to elucidate how sometimes-abstract policy decisions play out on the ground.

In part 1, where we talk about jobs, we introduce these families and their stories of arrival in the United States, including the forces that brought them to particular destinations and the methods by which they found employment. In order to understand the impacts of interior enforcement, it's critical to first understand the role unauthorized immigrants play in the economy and society. Because many studies do not distinguish between documented and undocumented immigrants, we also examine the impact of immigration overall on the labor market.

In part 2, as we explain the enforcement regime and how it has evolved over time, we tell the stories of how the undocumented members of these six families have been caught up in the enforcement system in recent years — and the impact those interactions have had on their own lives and, in many cases, on their loved ones.

In part 3, we address immigrants' impact on and interaction with other key social systems in the US: healthcare, welfare, tax, criminal justice, and education. The stories describe how many of the families continued on with a new type of "normal" after enforcement actions interrupted once-everyday routines.

We began this project before the current wave of national obsession with illegal immigration. In 2013 and 2014, author Tara Watson released a pair of academic papers, one on the impact local enforcement has on immigrant mobility, the other on the effect of enforcement on immigrants' willingness to enroll in health insurance. The research investigated the "chilling effects" of immigration enforcement policies, meaning the indirect impacts caused by fear and confusion, rather than by policy changes in and of themselves. The evidence makes clear that aggressive enforcement can have wide-ranging consequences, like deterring immigrants from enrolling their eligible citizen children in public health insurance. Enforcement does not appear to induce many undocumented immigrants to leave an area, but the stress and uncertainty of the enforcement environment does affect how immigrants navigate daily life.

At the time we started this project, it was President Barack Obama who was known derogatorily in many circles as the "Deporter-in-Chief." The extreme rhetoric and tactics ushered in by the Trump presidency — young immigrant children forcibly separated from their parents, National Guard troops deployed to the southern border, a monthlong government shutdown prompted by a standoff over building a multibillion-dollar wall — were scarcely imaginable.

Even before the hyperpoliticization of the last few years, we recognized that summarizing the evidence on broad economic impacts of illegal immigration — and attempting to tell a representative sample of immigrant stories — would be a daunting undertaking. We intentionally tried to limit the challenge before us by focusing on interior enforcement, as opposed to border enforcement, which is generally covered in more depth elsewhere. Despite the barrage of media attention on the Trump administration's horrific family separation policies and substandard conditions in detention centers and overcrowded border camps, our focus remained on enforcement actions away from the border, those affecting immigrants living in the US long-term.

And though it is often difficult in the data to separate the impacts of unauthorized immigration from those of legal immigration, we tried to zero in on the impacts of undocumented immigration — as opposed to the impact of legal immigrants who have become US citizens, are on that path, or are working legally in the US on visas. For this reason, the stories we tell in this book are all those of undocumented immigrant families or mixed-status families (meaning families in which an undocumented individual is married to a US citizen or has citizen children). Likewise, though undocumented people from all over the globe are living and working in the US, Mexican and Central American families are the primary subject of contemporary policy debates — and, often, political vitriol. Of the six families we profile in this book, four have one or more family members born in Mexico. One family is originally from Guatemala, and one from South Korea.

We connected with these families in various ways. None were known to us before our reporting for this project began in late 2014. In several cases, initial introductions were provided by members of local immigrant groups. In a couple of cases, the introductions came about through our own personal friends or friends of friends. In all cases, there was at least one initial, extended in-person interview. Most follow-up interviews happened by phone over a span of several years. Though most of the families were initially interviewed with the understanding that their real names would be used in this book, we later decided — together with the individuals profiled — to change the names of the majority of families given the more threatening enforcement environment that developed after we began our research. In several cases, we have also changed a small number of other identifying details in order to better protect our subjects' identities.

A note about language: Throughout this book, we use the term "immigrant" to mean any foreign-born person residing in the US, regardless of their citizenship status or legal status. We favor the terms "undocumented" or "unauthorized" to describe those immigrants living in the United States without legal status, but also occasionally use "illegal immigrant" if a source or subject uses that term themselves. (Until the mid-1990s, "illegal alien" was the common usage for most US politicians and publications. Today, the use of "illegal alien" immediately identifies a speaker as anti-immigrant to those on the liberal end of the political spectrum, while the rejection of the seemingly matter-of-fact term "illegal" is somewhere between eye-roll-inducing and infuriating to those on the conservative end. In 2013, the Associated Press banned its reporters from using "illegal immigrant," advising writers to rephrase sentences to avoid such labels; "an immigrant who entered the country illegally" is okay.[27] A larger number of media organizations have since instituted a narrower ban, discouraging reporters from referring to unauthorized immigrants as "illegals," when used as a noun — the idea being that no person is illegal; it is the act of immigrating that's illegal.)

*   *   *

Many US-born Americans have strong feelings about immigration. Some see today's immigrants as little different from their own ancestors: hardworking strivers whose vitality is crucial to the economic — and demographic — future of the country. Such people may feel deep empathy for the newcomer's struggle, respect for the immigrant work ethic — as well as, in some cases, a personal gratefulness of a sort for the ways that immigrant labor makes their own lives easier. Immigration is celebrated as a source of diversity and cultural vibrancy. Other native-born Americans see immigrants, and particularly those who come to the US without authorization, as job stealers, people who are upping competition, deflating wages, and making it harder for those who are already here to make a good living. They may fear that immigrants are driving up the crime rate and expanding the welfare state — or simply upending, in unsettling ways, what these critics view as traditional cultural norms. Such people may yearn for a stronger rule of law, pointing out that we have laws on the books that dictate who is allowed to live in the country, and the fact that these laws are so often disregarded weakens the rule of law more generally. They may long for stiffer penalties for those who live and work in the United States without permission.

With this book, we set out to help clarify the reality behind many of the most common concerns related to unauthorized immigration, as well as to present a handful of illustrative stories of the real people whose very lives have become embroiled in one of the country's most divisive political issues. We find that many—though not all—of the common arguments supporting a more aggressive enforcement regime are rooted in misperceptions about the impacts undocumented immigrants have on the economy and American society. We also document the high human and economic costs and questionable efficacy of today's enforcement regime. Our hope is that a close, methodical look into the issue of interior enforcement and the lives it affects can offer guidance for a more humane and effective immigration policy in the near future.

PART ONE

ARRIVALS

Nevada, 2005

When Jorge Ramirez left for the US border in 2005, he'd never been outside his small town in the northeast part of Mexico State. When he was growing up his father worked in masonry and his mother sold food in the local street markets. He was the only one of four brothers to graduate from high school, but without money or connections attending university was out of the question, he says. Through his early twenties Jorge worked as a door-to-door salesman, peddling everything from books to knives to mirrors to watches. He was twenty-four when he decided to leave home and head north.

Jorge knew just one person in the United States, a friend who was living and working near Las Vegas, Nevada. In Mexico, Jorge was living at home with his parents, and worrying about their medical bills. "All my family, they are self-employed, everybody live day by day," he says. "My parents are getting old and I know that they cannot support their life, so that's why I had to try to come to US and try to support my family."

He paid $1,500 to a coyote—a guide who makes an illicit business of orchestrating illegal border crossings—and came over the border with a group of five men near Sonora, Arizona. He brought nothing with him but clothes and water. "I figured out it's kind of like a chain," Jorge says of the system of coyotes and lesser "guias" (guides) that shuttle migrants across vast expanses of borderland desert, often sheltering them in a series of safe houses. "You talk to the first person and you are blind after that. You don't know what's going on, you just have to follow." Jorge's crossing took close to two weeks. "I don't know how I can explain this," he says, sitting in the comfortable living room of his own home in Washington State nine years later. "I know it's not good. I know I did bad, but it's just that I have to do it for my family."

Jorge made it to Las Vegas, and moved in with his friend, who helped him to buy a fake social security card and then to get a job at his own workplace, a local Wendy's fast-food restaurant. They started Jorge on the fries, making $5.75 an hour. He generally worked forty to fifty hours a week, sometimes on twelve-hour shifts that ended at 2:00 in the morning. Despite his low salary, the money was significant to Jorge's family. Every week he would go to Western Union and wire most of his paycheck back to Mexico. "That was a huge, huge difference for my family," Jorge says. "I can really support and pay for medical bills that I couldn't [pay for] in Mexico."

Within a couple of months, Jorge was moved to burger preparation, then to cashier.

The store manager told him he could easily rise to manager if he improved his English. All but a couple of the employees at the restaurant were Latino, Jorge says, and though it was never discussed openly, Jorge assumed that many of the others were undocumented as well. "To be honest, I think they know. The managers, they know, but nobody wants to take those jobs," he says. "It's hard to find people who want to work for that money."

Jorge was a standout employee. Within a couple months he got a raise—to $6 an hour. The manager didn't tell him in advance, he just waited until Jorge opened the first paycheck reflecting the tiny bump.

"Hey! Did you see your check?" he asked Jorge.

"Yeah."

"I gave you a raise! You're a good worker."

"Right. Thank you!" Jorge said.

"I mean, it's not really a lot of money, but that made me feel good," he recalls.

Immigrants at Work

The labor market is central to the debate about immigration in America. Are immigrants good or bad for the US economy? How do immigrants impact the job prospects of native workers? How do they affect the prices of goods and services? These questions lie at the crux of many disagreements about the ideal level of immigration and the best approach to enforcement. We devote part 1 of this book to the question of immigrants in the labor market. We start by discussing immigration regardless of legal status, about which there is much more information, and then turn to unauthorized immigration specifically.

Most immigrants come to the United States to work. There's a reason that migration tends to go from poor countries to rich ones. Simply put, migrants want to earn more than they can at home. Yes, some immigrants are motivated to come to the United States to take advantage of healthcare and social supports, or to give their children the opportunity to go to better schools in America.[1] Others come to flee violence or persecution, or to live with a spouse or child. But the consensus among economists is that the primary motivator for migration is jobs. Ironically, as a 2006 review piece by Gordon Hanson at the University of California, San Diego notes, the higher wages in the United States are such an obvious driver of migration that there are relatively few studies on the topic.[2]

Perhaps the best evidence that jobs are a primary motivator for migration is that immigrants' actions are strongly influenced by employment opportunities. For instance, one 1999 study found that when Mexican wages decreased by 10 percent, apprehensions at the US border—a measure of attempts at unauthorized migration—increased 6 to 8 percent over the next few months.[3] It's also true that US employment opportunities matter: Following the recent Great Recession, for example, the unauthorized population dropped from an estimated 12.2 million to 10.5 million.[4]

One recent study shows that individual-level economic prospects matter as well. Matching US census and administrative records, researchers Randall Akee of the University of California, Los Angeles and Maggie R. Jones of the US Census Bureau follow a cohort of immigrants who arrived in the United States between 2005 and 2007.[5] (Because of the researchers' reliance on administrative earnings records, the sample is employed in the formal sector and skews toward documented immigrants.) When immigrants first arrive, their earnings are 30 to 40 percent below that of similarly aged US-born workers in the state. Their wages gradually increase over time. The average earnings of immigrants who stay in the United States (or, at least, of those who stayed until the study concluded in 2015) converge to those of the native born by 2012. By contrast, those immigrants who eventually leave the country experience relative wage declines in the year or two just before they leave the United States. Though this pattern isn't definitive, especially since the researchers can't rule out that some immigrants absent from the administrative data still live in the United States, it certainly suggests that immigrants stick around for good wages and leave when opportunities dry up.

Once in the US, immigrants move to where the jobs are. As we discuss in more detail later in part 1, less-educated US-born men don't move much in response to a local economic downturn, but Mexican-born men are very responsive to such downturns, leaving areas that are struggling and finding areas of growth within the United States.[6] Internal migration within the US is further support for the notion that immigrants tend to be driven by work opportunities.

We also know—and will discuss more extensively in part 3—that low-income immigrants are less likely to qualify for and take advantage of social services than low-income Americans. Most programs exclude undocumented immigrants, and many require five years of legal residency before documented immigrants are eligible. But even among eligible immigrants, participation rates are lower than those for comparable native-born Americans. Most immigrants arrive knowing they will need to work to support themselves, and labor-force participation rates of foreign-born men (especially undocumented men) well exceed those of the native born. Immigrants are also less likely to commit crime than the US born, as we discuss at length in part 3.

All of these facts point to the same conclusion: The primary motivator for migration to the United States is the work opportunities. While there are some immigrants who move mainly to flee violence, to join loved ones, or to take advantage of the safety net, they are in the minority. This means that policy efforts to reduce access to public programs or to raise the fear of deportation are unlikely to have a major impact on the number of immigrants living in the United States. Immigrants, including unauthorized immigrants, will continue to live and work in the United States as long as there are good work opportunities available.

Washington State, 2006

Jorge Ramirez had been working at the Nevada Wendy's for seven months when he heard about a construction job in Washington State. A contractor who had been hired to do the stucco work on a new outdoor shopping mall was looking for laborers. Jorge had been doing some stuccoing work on the side in Nevada and soon several Mexican guys he knew from the area decided to head north together.

The company arranged the lodging, which by Jorge's standards was incredibly expensive: $300 a week for a hotel room. The first month the work went smoothly but then the contractor ran out of money. "When he realize he doesn't have enough money to finish the job he just left," Jorge says. The workers were stiffed out of their second month's pay. Lena Graber, an immigration attorney in California who has volunteered at workers' rights clinics, says this scenario is shockingly common: "It will blow your mind how much people work and don't get paid." Under-the-table work, particularly, she notes, leaves undocumented workers with "total vulnerability to discrimination and poor treatment by employers—as well as just insecurity and lower wages."

Despite the way the job ended, Jorge had realized he liked the plastering work. He started just walking around to construction sites, going up to the man who seemed to be in charge, and asking for work. "I met a very good guy," Jorge says. "He gave me an opportunity for one week and after one week he say that I should stay with him." Jorge ended up working for the man, a small-business owner who was himself an immigrant from eastern Europe, for almost four years, and learning every side of the stucco business. He enjoyed the work but eventually the businessman, too, encountered financial problems. Once again, Jorge wasn't paid for his last couple months of work. Since he was working illegally, going to the authorities didn't occur to him as an option. But he doesn't hold a grudge against his old boss. "I got experience from him and I am very grateful because he was a great boss," Jorge says. "I learned a lot from him. I know he didn't pay me but he wasn't a bad person."

Jorge had been able to get a driver's license soon after he arrived in Washington. The state was one of the first to allow undocumented immigrants to get licenses, a policy that gained public support in part because of the argument that it would be impossible to harvest the state's large apple crop if undocumented immigrants were unable to drive to and in the orchards. Jorge had been driving in Nevada, too — there was no other way to get to and from his fast-food job. But he did so illegally. The practice was common, he says, and the cops weren't that strict. During the time he lived in Nevada in 2005 and 2006, he never heard of a person being arrested after a traffic stop simply for not having a license. The one time he got pulled over it was for making an illegal turn. "They ask me for my license and insurance," he says. "And so I have insurance. I didn't have a license." The cop handed him a ticket for $250. "That kind of hit me hard. But I don't want to get in any trouble so I paid right away."

Immigrants' Impact on the Labor Market

Since immigrants are mainly in the US to work, it's natural to wonder how they affect the labor market. Many Americans believe that immigration is overall quite harmful to US residents. A 2015 Pew Research Center survey revealed that while 45 percent of Americans believed that immigrants were making society better in the long run, 37 percent believed that they were making it worse.[7] No surprise: There is a stark divide between political parties, and it predates Trump's election. In the same 2015 survey, 53 percent of Republicans said immigrants make society worse, compared to just 24 percent of Democrats. When asked specifically about the economy, those polled had an even more negative view of immigrants: 71 percent of Republicans and 34 percent of Democrats said that immigrants were making the economy worse.

A larger proportion of Democrats, 38 percent, were under the impression that immigrants were making the economy better, a belief that just 12 percent of Republicans shared.

It might seem obvious to a student of basic economics that immigrants would harm the earnings prospects of US-born workers. After all, a standard supply-and-demand graph would suggest that more workers competing for the same jobs would tend to reduce wages. But as many economists have argued in recent decades, the truth is more complicated. Immigrants increase the supply of workers, but also stimulate demand for products and services. And firms sometimes react to the availability of immigrant labor in surprising ways. The upshot is that theoretical models offer a less clear prediction about how immigrants affect the labor market than one might think.

To get a better handle on the question, economists look to the data. They typically use large, nationally representative data sets from the Bureau of Labor Statistics and the Census Bureau; these data sets do a fairly good job of including interview responses from both authorized and unauthorized immigrants even though they do not distinguish between these.[8] (The major surveys ask respondents about their citizenship status but do not ask the legal status of noncitizens for fear that the question would lead to incomplete survey response. The decennial census does not ask about citizenship at all in its own very limited survey.) As a result, much of what we know about how immigrants affect the labor market applies to immigrants or noncitizens collectively, regardless of legal status.

What do the data show? Most researchers find that the overall effect of immigration on employment and wages for Americans is small, and perhaps even positive. But the weight of the evidence also suggests less-educated Americans face adverse consequences from immigration. In particular, American-born workers without a high school degree, disadvantaged minorities, and previous waves of immigrants most directly compete with new migrants, and these same groups of people may lose jobs or face lower wages due to immigration.

Some economists believe these negative effects of immigration are quite large for the most disadvantaged. Other research finds smaller effects, and the size of the impact for this group is a matter of ongoing

debate. A related concern is that by introducing competition that reduces wages for the most disadvantaged US-born workers, and by adding new immigrant workers who tend to cluster at the bottom end of
the earnings distribution, immigration may exacerbate the rising income inequality that has been observed in the US since the 1970s.

The perspective on the wage question has evolved considerably in
recent decades. In the 1970s, prominent researchers like Barry Chiswick, an economist who spent most of his career at the University of
Illinois at Chicago and now teaches at George Washington University,
found little adverse impact of immigration.[9] By the 1980s, there was
pushback by George Borjas, a Cuba-born economist who became a
dominant voice in the field.[10] Borjas's work is informed in part by the
rising number of immigrants and the changing composition of the immigrant population: Between 1970 and 2000, the fraction of the foreign
born from Europe or Canada fell from 68 percent to 21 percent, while
immigration from Mexico, Central America, and Asia increased.[11]

Borjas also noted the changing education levels of immigrants relative to US natives. Though immigrants in the early twentieth century
often lacked education, they weren't very different in that respect from
most US-born workers of that time. But the profile for today's immigrants looks very different from that for the native born. Immigrants
are concentrated at both the high end and the low end of the earnings
distribution, and they work disproportionately in specific occupations:
high-tech STEM fields at the high end and manual/physical jobs at the
low end.

The biggest shock to supply in the recent past has been in the low-
education group. In 1980, immigrants represented roughly 11 percent
of people without a high school degree aged twenty-five to sixty-four
years. That number was 46 percent by 2000.[12] The change results
from both the arrival of more new immigrants without much education and from rising high school graduation rates among the US born.
Figure 7 shows the distribution of education for foreign-born and US-
born individuals between the ages of twenty-five and sixty-four, and
demonstrates that immigrants are overrepresented among those with
advanced degrees, particularly among naturalized citizens. Immigrants
are also highly represented among those at the bottom of the educa-

FIGURE 7. Education by nativity and citizenship

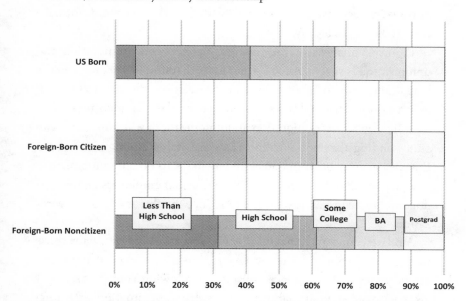

Source: Authors' calculations using American Community Survey data from a sample of individuals ages 25–64

tion distribution, with 31 percent of noncitizens lacking a high school degree. With immigration increasing the supply of less-educated workers, it stands to reason that US-born workers with similarly low levels of education might suffer.

Worker Protections

In addition to the increase in supply of less-educated workers, some research suggests a secondary reason that immigrants might reduce wages: union bargaining. Immigrants are less likely to be unionized, and legal protections are weak for unauthorized immigrants trying to organize. One landmark example involved Jose Castro, a Mexican immigrant who presented false papers in 1988 to work at Hoffman Plastics, running the machines that "mix and cook" custom chemical compounds used by other businesses.[13] Castro and several coworkers were laid off in 1989 — in violation of labor law — after supporting union activities. A 2002 Supreme Court decision, *Hoffman Plastics v. National*

Labor Relations Board, ruled that Castro could not receive $66,591 in back pay because as an undocumented worker he could not have earned the wages legally.

Rigorous analysis of the relationship between immigration and unionization is sparse. A 1994 paper finds that immigrants weaken the bargaining power of labor unions, presumably by offering a viable non-union option for employers.[14] More recent research identifies a less clear link between immigration and unionization, with one European study finding that unionization rates are stable among native-born Europeans even as immigrants are less likely to be union members.[15] The jury is still out, but some activists fear that employers choose undocumented workers specifically to reduce the threat of labor organization.

A related concern is that immigrant workers — and especially those that are unauthorized — enjoy fewer protections when it comes to safety issues and workplace complaints, allowing companies to get away with substandard labor practices. In these situations, the mission of the Department of Labor (DOL) is at odds with that of Immigration and Customs Enforcement (ICE). To pursue action, DOL relies on whistleblowing and cooperation from workers affected by firm abuses, but unauthorized workers are unlikely to come forward for fear of being deported.

The case of Delmer Joel Ramirez Palma, an undocumented immigrant born in Honduras, is the type of story that encourages other unauthorized workers to keep quiet. As a thirty-eight-year-old who had lived in the United States for two decades, Ramirez Palma was employed in 2019 as a metal worker in the construction of a new Hard Rock Hotel in New Orleans. According to his lawyers, he complained to supervisors several times about safety issues while working on the project, the *New York Times* reported. One day in October 2019, the eighteen-story structure partially collapsed, killing three of Ramirez Palma's colleagues.

Ramirez Palma had been trying to change his immigration status since 2011. In 2016, he had been given temporary relief as a caretaker for his autistic son, but subsequently lost several appeals. Two days after the 2019 collapse, Ramirez Palma was arrested by ICE and, after several weeks in detention, was deported to Honduras. ICE claimed that Ramirez Palma had lost his final appeal the week before the incident, and that the timing of the arrest was coincidental. Still, according to his wife who remains in the country, the event was enough to deter other unauthorized workers from participating in the Occupational Safety and Health Administration's ongoing investigation into the hotel collapse.[16]

What Might Have Been

How does one go about investigating the impact of immigrants on the US labor market? The fundamental question for many studies is what would have happened if there had been fewer immigrants since 1970. (That year is often used as a starting point for analysis because it is a historical low point in the fraction of US residents who were foreign born.) We can never observe this parallel universe—what economists call the counterfactual—so researchers instead need to make educated guesses based on theory and data.

The two dominant approaches in the literature have been cross-city comparisons (comparing cities with large and small immigrant inflows) and cross–skill group comparisons (comparing Americans who are more directly competing with migrants for jobs to those not facing such competition). A 2006 *New York Times Magazine* profile[17] of George Borjas of the Harvard Kennedy School and his primary intellectual rival, UC Berkeley economist David Card, highlights how these two different approaches—both trying to answer the same question—yield starkly different conclusions about the impact of immigrants on native job opportunities.

Card, a Canadian who is also known for his work demonstrating that, contrary to standard economic theory, raising the minimum wage does not cost fast-food jobs, has done influential work on immigration by comparing cities. Card's work has inspired a large literature exploiting the fact that immigrants are unevenly distributed across cities and states. Miami, Florida, consists of 62 percent foreign-born residents, while fewer than 1 percent of residents of Billings, Montana, are foreign born.[18] Comparing native wages in immigrant-dense areas to those in immigrant-sparse areas might give researchers some idea of the effect of immigration on wages. As it turns out, American wages are higher in immigrant-dense cities, and wages rise faster in places with more immigrant inflows, suggesting perhaps that there is no adverse impact of immigration on native wages.

But not so fast. Miami and Billings are not particularly similar. It's well known that immigrants tend to be attracted to growing, high-wage areas. Perhaps high wages are responsible for the presence of more immigrants, rather than immigrants causing high wages. Is it the chicken or the egg?

Economists use a variety of sophisticated techniques to address this critical issue. These techniques typically involve some predetermined or random element that partially influences where immigrants settle. For example, Card and many others have used historical settlement patterns to establish where immigrants of a particular country-of-origin group are likely to put down roots.[19] In 1970, a third of Mexican immigrants to the United States lived in the Los Angeles area and less than 2 percent of Portuguese immigrants did. More than a third of Portuguese immigrants lived in the Providence, Rhode Island/New Bedford, Massachusetts, area, whereas almost no Mexican immigrants had put down roots there.[20]

Overall growth of Mexican immigration in the following decades affected Los Angeles more than Providence, and we would expect this to have been true even if the two cities had faced similar economic conditions. If, instead, there had been rapid increases in Portuguese immigration, Providence would have seen a greater surge in its overall foreign-born population. By analyzing changes in migration patterns — stemming both from historical immigrant settlement locations and from the size of new inflows to the US from different countries — researchers can predict the extent to which immigration to different cities can be attributed to reasons other than current local economic conditions.[21]

Using this "enclave approach" and similar strategies, researchers compare growth in wages of US natives living in areas that were destined to experience rapidly increasing immigration because of historical settlement patterns (like Los Angeles) to those that were not (like

Providence). Analysis implies that a 10 percent increase in immigration (stemming from these predetermined factors) likely reduces wages by perhaps 1 or 2 percent for those native workers in similar occupations, relative to other cities.[22] It's interesting to note that most studies do not separately identify the effects of an increase as opposed to a decrease in immigration; typically, they compare cities with large influxes of immigrants to those with smaller influxes.

One historical example does look at the wage impacts of contractions in immigration brought about by the restrictive immigration policies of the 1920s. Researchers Ran Abramitzky, Philipp Ager, Leah Platt Boustan, Elior Cohen, and Casper W. Hansen studied how cities that were more affected by the restrictions (because they had more immigrants from eastern and southern Europe, for example) fared compared to those who were less affected. Surprisingly, the wages of native-born workers did not increase following the reductions in immigration — they declined slightly or stayed the same.[23]

Using an alternative quasi-random determinant of immigration, Federal Reserve Bank of Dallas labor economist Pia Orrenius and Madeline Zavodny, then of Agnes Scott College, looked at how the awarding of spousal green cards in a local area affects wages of the native born.[24] (In 2018, about 270,000 green cards were issued to spouses of US citizens, about a quarter of all people becoming legal permanent residents in that year.)[25] Compared to other immigrants, those who get a green card because they are married to a US citizen are less likely to choose a location within the United States based on their own work opportunities — they are more likely to be a secondary earner and to locate based on their spouse's prior decisions. When a lot of immigrant spouses enter a local labor market, native wages in manual occupations like blue-collar production jobs and farm labor show a modest decrease of 0.8 percent, but the researchers find "no evidence of adverse wage impacts on medium- and high-skilled native workers."

In another attempt to take advantage of noneconomic factors driving migration decisions, Card looked at an unusual immigration event known as the Mariel boatlift.[26] A sudden decision by Fidel Castro in 1980 to allow emigration created an exodus of roughly 125,000 Cuban migrants to the US, about half of whom settled in Miami. The labor supply in Miami increased by 7 percent almost overnight. This event provided a remarkable opportunity to investigate the short-run impact of immigration. If immigrants increased the labor supply in Miami, shouldn't wages have fallen there compared to other cities with fewer immigrants? Surprisingly, relative to a group of comparison cities, Card found virtually no impact on native wages following the Mariel boatlift.

Similarly, in a 2016 analysis of Danish data (Scandinavian countries are known for their amazing data!), Mette Foged of the University of Copenhagen and UC Davis economist Giovanni Peri examine the effects of a refugee dispersal policy that placed migrants according to somewhat random factors.[27] Here, the analysis shows *positive* effects on native wages in the same types of occupations, including sales, services, and machine operations. The authors explain these surprising findings by showing that natives move to better-paying occupations — ones that are more complex, require stronger communication skills, and have less of a manual component — after immigrants arrive.

All told, the area-based approach paints a fairly rosy picture of immigration. Studies tend to find that immigrants strengthen the local labor market overall, and that there are at most small negative impacts on those most directly competing with the newly arrived workers. It is in part because of this body of evidence that many economists have a more positive view of immigration than the general public.

Not everyone is satisfied by this local-market-based method of analysis, however. Borjas makes the case that even if one bases one's analysis on migration decisions of immigrants that are not economically motivated — thereby solving the chicken-and-egg problem noted above — it is still misleading to compare across cities. Why? Because what happens in one city affects others. US-born workers are less mobile than immigrants, but they do tend to slowly migrate toward high-wage, low-rent cities. In the postwar period, for example, California was a center of economic growth and attracted many Americans from the Northeast, South, and Midwest. This migration would likely have continued, Borjas argues, were it not for the large influx of post-1970 immigrants pushing down wages and pushing up rents in the Golden State. Wages are not lower in California than in other places, but they are lower than they would be in the absence of immigration, Borjas maintains. With less immigration, a US-born factory worker might be living in California today and earning a high wage, rather than working in the Midwest where the cost of living is lower. The impact of immigration on the midwestern worker is potentially amplified when the factory moves to take advantage of cheap immigrant labor in another part of the US.

The key insight is that the true impact of immigration is not only felt by residents of the cities where immigrants live, but by Americans across the country, particularly those who work or would otherwise work in the same types of jobs as immigrants. As an alternative to the city-based approach, Borjas has focused on looking at age- and education-based "skill" groups nationwide — comparing the wages of those who didn't complete high school who are ten, twenty, or thirty years out of school, for example. In a 2003 paper titled "The Labor Demand Curve is Downward Sloping,"[28] Borjas looks across education and experience groups rather than geographic regions, concluding that immigration does have a significant downward impact on wages of the native born. He finds that immigration caused native-born Americans who didn't finish high school an overall wage loss of 5 percent over the 1980s and 1990s, a real-life deficit of $1,200 a year per worker, on average. The adverse effect immigrants have on the most disadvantaged groups as estimated by this method is triple the size that one would generate just focusing on local labor markets. "To many economists as well as lay folk, Borjas's findings confirmed what seemed intuitive all along: add to the supply of labor, and the price goes down," journalist Roger Lowenstein wrote in the *New York Times*.

In a 2010 paper, Borjas, University of Chicago economist Jeffrey Grogger, and Gordon H. Hanson of the University of California, San Diego use the national skill-group idea to specifically examine the impact of immigration on less-educated Black men across the United States.[29] Their analysis was inspired by the following incident, which took place in Stillmore, Georgia, in 2006 and was described in the *Wall Street Journal* the following January: "After a wave of raids by federal immigration agents on Labor Day weekend, a local chicken-processing company called Crider Inc. lost 75 percent of its mostly Hispanic 900-member workforce. The crackdown threatened to cripple the economic anchor of this fading rural town. But for local African Americans, the dramatic appearance of federal agents presented an unexpected opportunity. Crider suddenly raised pay at the plant. An advertisement in the weekly Forest-Blade newspaper blared 'Increased Wages' at Crider, starting at $7 to $9 an hour—more than a dollar above what the company had paid many immigrant workers."[30]

Comparing across education and age groups nationally, the authors find that wage effects for native-born Black and white men are roughly the same. New immigrant arrivals increasing the workforce by 10 percent (for example, one million young, less-educated immigrants arriving in a country of ten million young, less-educated workers) leads to roughly a 3 percent decline in wages for those existing workers, regardless of race. However, Black men, who are more likely than whites to directly compete with immigrants, are also more likely to lose their jobs altogether. The same 10 percent immigration change is associated with almost 6 percent of Black men losing their jobs.

These estimates and others using similar national-level approaches have been criticized by Card and others because other important factors also affect less-educated Americans over time. No good benchmark exists for what would have happened over the past half-century in the absence of immigration. Factors like the growth of international trade, the adoption of new technology, and the declining real value of the minimum wage are all partially responsible for the hard times faced by the lowest-earning Americans. Borjas' more recent work with renowned labor economist Richard Freeman suggests the displacement effects of a robot used in manufacturing are much larger than those of a foreign-born worker.[31] Other research suggests that growth in trade with China was responsible for a quarter of job losses in manufacturing between 1990 and 2007.[32] In other words, even without immigration, less-educated American workers would be struggling. The question is how much of that struggle is explained by rising immigration.

Painesville, Ohio, 2000

Eduardo Lopez borrowed the money for the coyote from his mom. She had left their hometown in the central Mexican state of Guanajuato for northern Ohio in the winter of 1998. Eduardo was fifteen at the time, and still in high school. He finished school at seventeen and married his girlfriend, Elena; just a few months later, the young couple started the journey north. There was a lot of violence and corruption in his small town, Eduardo says, and he didn't have the money for further schooling. The future he saw for himself at home was bleak.

Eduardo and Elena each paid the smuggler $1,600. The trip took a day and a half. They spent one night on the Mexican side of the Arizona border, then walked about six hours through the desert. It wasn't too strenuous, Eduardo says. There were plenty of rests. The coyote's fee included plane tickets from Phoenix to Cleveland. It was before 9/11 and there was little airport security. As Eduardo recalls, he and Elena boarded the plane without showing any ID.

At that time, people from Guanajuato had already been migrating to Ohio for a decade or more. The draw was jobs, mostly in northern Ohio's plant nurseries. The industry had thrived in the mild growing climate adjacent to Lake Erie for over a century, and it employed thousands of people. Increasingly those people were Mexicans. Nursery owners like Mark Gilson of Gilson Gardens in Perry, Ohio, had come to depend on immigrant labor. When he was a kid and his grandparents and then his parents ran the farm, Puerto Rican workers were common at the regions' nurseries, Gilson says. By the 1980s, there was an increase in the Latino labor supply and by the early 2000s about half of Gilson's workforce was made up of Mexicans. A couple of his top guys had been there since the 1980s. "You find a good worker in a small business and the first thing you do is hire their brothers and their sisters and their cousins," Gilson says. "And that's what we did." He'd always put up "help wanted" signs in his own retail store, and still hired college students on summer break and what he calls "locally grown" workers—especially to staff the retail space where English-language skills were required. But when needed, he'd hang fliers in the local Mexican grocery. "The Mexicans are reliable," Gilson says. "They tend to find a way to get to work. They tend to work out daycare problems easier. They don't work crazy fast, but they're steady. So that makes them just dependable."

For the first couple of months after they arrived in Ohio, Eduardo and Elena lived with Eduardo's mother, but as soon as they'd saved up a little money they moved out, relying on his mom's landlord to help them find a place of their own. Word of mouth was also the route to a social security card. Eduardo's was in his own name, and was hand delivered to his home by a guy a friend had told him about. "The only thing he say is to never carry with you, because if you got pulled over it could be a problem."

Eduardo's mom had a job making baskets for plants; his younger brother, who had also already been in the US for a couple of years, worked for a landscaping company. Elena found work in a local nursery right away, but it took Eduardo three months to find a permanent job: a position as a dishwasher at a Red Lobster seafood restaurant. He'd tried out landscaping with his brother but had hated the work. "They treat you like an animal, yelling, cursing," says Eduardo, who is tall, with broad shoulders, spiky black hair, a small patch of beard, and tattoos stretching from wrist to shoulder on both arms. He preferred the restaurant job.

A year later an uncle who was also working in Ohio told Eduardo about a better opportunity at a local factory that had contracts with big automakers. At the time, Eduardo spoke very little English. When he went to a restaurant, he just pointed at the menu and ate whatever they gave him. His first job at the factory was as a metal man on the night shift. The position didn't require much talking. But he had a supervisor, an older guy who told him, "If you want to earn money, learn English. You have to work smart, not hard."

Eduardo started listening to local radio, talking with people, trying to read books. He was constantly asking his supervisor and his landlord to explain the meaning of English words. After a year or so he was promoted from metal man to machine operator, and then later to assistant foreman, working under the same supervisor. A few years later, when that supervisor moved to the day shift, Eduardo was offered the night shift foreman position. They didn't have anyone else who could do the job, he was told. He'd be supervising close to forty workers, and he'd get a big pay bump as well as a promotion.

The same week Eduardo was offered the promotion he was called unexpectedly to the office. One of the workers on his shift—a Mexican guy, as it turned out — had snitched on him, gone to the boss, and told him that Eduardo was working under a fake social security number, that he was in the country illegally.

"Okay, Lopez, tell me what's going on," the boss said to him. There wasn't much choice but to come clean. "Okay, sir, maybe you're going to fire me after this, but I have to tell you, I didn't have a social," Eduardo recalls saying. "I'm illegal. But I do my job. It's up to you, you want to fire me, that's fine. I understand. If you don't, just let me work."

Eduardo's boss looked at him for a few seconds. "Go back to work," he said.

Substitutes or Complements?

Giovanni Peri of the University of California, Davis is among the most prominent immigration economists in the post-Card/Borjas generation. Peri argues that the most important thing to understand, whether one is looking at a narrow geographic area or at the nation as a whole, is to what degree immigrants are "substitutes" or "complements" for native workers. If immigrants are filling in the exact spot on an assembly line that would otherwise be filled by a native worker, they would be considered substitutes. But if immigrants take busboy jobs that allow native-born waiters to serve more tables, they are complements.

By examining immigration by Mexicans and Central Americans into California over time, Peri shows that immigrants are not perfect substitutes for native workers.[33] On the contrary, he finds that native wages actually *increase* by an average of 5 percent in response to immigration. The wage gains are smaller (less than 2 percent) for natives without a high school degree, but according to Peri's study, the only group to actually lose out economically from new waves of immigration are immigrants who arrived in earlier waves — precisely those who are most similar in their labor-market skills. As journalist Roger Lowenstein points out in his *New York Times* profile of Borjas, the number of immigrants in the US labor force far surpasses the total number of unemployed: "[T]he majority of immigrants can't literally have 'taken' jobs; they must be doing jobs that wouldn't have existed had the immigrants not been here."

The story of substitutes and complements also plays out in the historical study of the 1920s immigration restrictions described earlier. In cities most affected by the crackdown on immigrants from southern and eastern Europe, new workers from other cities came in to take the place of the immigrants who were no longer admitted to the US. These workers were closer labor substitutes for the existing US-born work-force — and pushed wages downward relative to the situation when immigrants were working in the city.

How could complementary immigrants raise native wages? As we discuss in more detail later, immigrants may improve the productivity of natives by allowing for specialization, or by contributing to production at a lower cost. They may allow firms that would otherwise produce offshore to invest in the United States, or they may slow the pace of automation in a way that also helps American-born workers. Immigrants use social networks, language skills, and the knowledge of their home countries' cultures to facilitate international trade. And they are also consumers, spurring demand by purchasing goods and services from the native born. These benefits are not equally shared — direct job competition faced by workers who are close substitutes for immigrant labor may be enough to more than offset the general beneficial impacts, leaving some workers worse off.

Many Americans are not convinced that the advantages of the complementary economy apply to them. Joined by economists Anna Maria Mayda of Georgetown University and Walter Steingress of the Bank of Canada, Peri finds evidence that US voting behavior is consistent with perceptions of labor complementarity or substitutability, even if voters don't use that jargon.[34] When less-educated immigrants move to a county with a lot of existing less-educated residents, those existing residents tend to vote more for Republican candidates, presumably because the Republican platform tends to favor more restrictionist immigration policies, the authors find in examining election data from between 1990 and 2010. These impacts are particularly pronounced in rural areas, which the authors posit is because local economies are less dynamic to begin with in those areas, so labor-market competition is viewed as more of a threat. The shift toward Republican voting doesn't happen when highly educated immigrants move into the same areas —

in those cases existing residents tend to vote more Democratic—or when immigrants of any education level move into highly educated areas. It appears that less-educated US natives vote for more immigration restrictions when they specifically view their own employment opportunities as threatened by immigration.

The Effects of Unauthorized Immigrants on the Labor Market

Most studies examine the wage impact of immigration in general, not the specific impact of undocumented immigration. Of course, it is the latter that has the most direct relevance for enforcement policy, and for this book, but it is hard to find data on undocumented workers precisely because of their status.

Julie L. Hotchkiss, Myriam Quispe-Agnoli, and Fernando Rosa-Avila[35] offer a creative way to study undocumented workers in on-the-books jobs. In a 2015 paper they examine administrative records from the state of Georgia, which between 2000 and 2010 experienced an unusually large increase—70 percent—in its number of undocumented residents. By looking for social security numbers (SSNs) in state administrative data that look "fishy" (in this case, number patterns that could not possibly be SSNs), the authors estimate how many payroll workers are using fake social security numbers in formal sector jobs. This turns out to be roughly 1 percent of workers. (The undocumented population in the state is estimated at 4 to 5 percent of total population, implying that perhaps three-quarters of undocumented workers are using valid SSNs that belong to someone else, or are off the books altogether.)

The Hotchkiss et al. analysis does show an association in the expected direction: Firms that employ more undocumented workers tend to pay lower wages to other workers (US natives and documented immigrants, who are indistinguishable in the data set). Might this fact simply reflect the reality that the types of firms that employ undocumented workers tend to be different from firms that don't? Perhaps these firms are the ones that would pay low wages even in the absence of immigration.

The authors address this challenge—that firms hiring undocumented workers might just be low-paying firms in general—by looking at changes within particular firms over time, comparing a firm without many undocumented immigrants to the same firm, later in time, when it has more undocumented immigrants. They examine wage *changes* within firms that experienced an influx of undocumented workers, and they compare those changes to general wage growth happening in other firms—a comparison that Georgia's rapid immigrant growth made possible. Taking this approach, the results are quite different: Wages of natives and documented immigrants actually *rise* within a firm as the share of undocumented workers goes up, leaving legal workers with more wage growth than their counterparts in other similar firms see. These results are most pronounced in the hospitality industry, retail services, and manufacturing. (In contrast, undocumented immigrants have essentially no impact on construction wages and a negative impact on agricultural wages.) The authors theorize that the wage benefits associated with the presence of undocumented immigrants are due to specialization within the firm: Cheap immigrant labor frees up US-native workers to do tasks that are more highly valued by the market, and the native workers get paid more as a result.

How Does Immigration Enforcement Affect the Labor Market?

Other studies that investigate the impact of undocumented immigrants on wages take a different tack—looking at how enforcement of immigration law influences wages. Mixed results come out of a study examining the 2007 Arizona adoption of E-Verify, a federal program that screens workers for immigration status before they are hired.[36] The researchers—Sarah Bohn at the Public Policy Institute of California, Magnus Lofstrom at a German labor economics research institute called IZA, and Steven Raphael of the University of California, Berkeley—did find that the wages of less-educated, non-Hispanic white men went up in Arizona compared to other states after E-Verify was adopted. Presumably, these higher wages are the result of reduced competition from undocumented workers. On the other hand, employment opportunities also fell for the same group of white men, which the authors attribute to companies facing higher production costs and lower demand for their products and services. In other words, with fewer unauthorized workers in Arizona, employment opportunities for authorized workers shrank, but those that were hired commanded a higher wage.

Peri and coauthor Annie Laurie Hines, then a graduate student at the University of California, Davis, use a broader set of changes in immigration enforcement to try to determine the impact on native wages. They look at arrests spanning from 2005 to 2015, a period when US immigration enforcement ramped up in the Bush years and early part of the Obama administration and then fell again toward the end of Obama's presidency. Importantly for the researchers, the ramp-up and decline of apprehensions varied a lot across places within the United States — arrests per capita increased almost ten times as much in Arizona as in Maryland in the 2007–2011 period, for example. The authors find no evidence that wages were improved for less-educated natives in places that pursued aggressive enforcement.[37]

A group of researchers from the University of Colorado Denver — Chloe East, Philip Luck, Hani Mansour, and Andrea Velasquez — similarly exploit differences in immigration law.[38] The federal Secure Communities program was rolled out county by county starting in 2008; it was responsible for hundreds of thousands of detentions by 2015 (we discuss Secure Communities in detail in part 2). Comparing wages in places that adopted Secure Communities early to those that did so later, the researchers find no statistically detectable effect on employment of less-skilled men, defining "less-skilled" as those working in occupations where fewer people have a college degree. The researchers do, however, find that "high-skilled" men in industries with a lot of undocumented workers lost employment opportunities when enforcement ratcheted up, which they attribute to complementarities between undocumented workers and those in more educated occupations. In other words, unauthorized labor is beneficial to those in higher-education occupations.

In sum, the limited literature on how unauthorized immigrants in particular affect the labor market for US natives comes to a conclusion similar to the findings for immigrants' effects on the labor market in general. Cracking down on unauthorized immigrants in the US does not appear to benefit American workers on average, and it may harm more highly educated Americans.

San Antonio, Texas, 1980s

Anabel Barron was born in Mexico in 1980, but spent most of her childhood in San Antonio, Texas. She was the sixth of eight kids, and for years her family rented a single, large room in the home of another Spanish-speaking family. Anabel's mother was allowed to use the couple's kitchen, but the family of ten ate their meals in the same room they slept in. The siblings attended the local public schools, where the student population was entirely made up of Hispanic and Black kids, Anabel recalls. Her dad worked as a landscaper, scraping together under-the-table work. Sometimes Anabel and her sisters would go with him on his jobs. They might be paid $20 to clean the house while their dad earned $40 for half a day's yard work.

All of Anabel's siblings were born in Mexico, too. In the 1970s and 80s the border was far more porous than it is today. Every time Anabel's mother was approaching her due date, she would return to Mexico to have her baby. If she had given birth near her home in Texas her children would have been US citizens: The Fourteenth Amendment to the Constitution guarantees birthright citizenship; any child born in the United States is born a citizen, regardless of the citizenship status of their parents. "I remember asking her once, 'Why are you doing this, Mom?,'" Anabel recalls. "She said, 'Because if I go to the hospital, they will take you away.' She didn't know how to read, she never went to school, she had some misunderstanding."

When Anabel's pregnant mother returned to Mexico, she'd take her older kids with her. After the birth, they'd cross back to Texas again with their mom, the newest baby carried snugly on her back. As a child, Anabel thought the desert treks were an adventure. "We used to walk and walk and walk and when the helicopters were on top my mom would say 'hide,'" Anabel says. "It was like a game for us. We didn't understand."

When she was sixteen, Anabel got pregnant and quickly married her baby's father, a US citizen whose parents were originally from the same city in central Mexico as Anabel's. The same year, Anabel's mother returned permanently to Mexico, taking Anabel's youngest sister and brother with her. The decision was a sudden one. "She was fearless in Mexico," Anabel says. "Not here. Here she was very shy, because she didn't know English, she didn't know how to communicate." Not long after, Anabel's young marriage fell apart, and she decided to move north to Ohio, where her older sister was making a life for herself.

Anabel soon had a new boyfriend—a man who was also Mexican, working without papers in the construction industry—and a second baby girl. She was just twenty-one years old in December 2001, when she got an unexpected—and heartbreaking—phone call: Her mother had died.

Though they'd talk on the phone, Anabel hadn't seen her mom since she was sixteen. Her own daughters were just one and three at the time. They'd never met their grandmother. Though her sister urged against it, Anabel felt she had no choice but to return to Mexico. "My mom, she was very close to me," Anabel says. "A lot of times I felt like I disappointed her. I needed to say goodbye. I needed to kiss her and say, 'I'm sorry.'"

Anabel spent two weeks in her mother's hometown of Dolores Hidalgo, a small city in the central Mexican state of Guanajuato. It took another two weeks to make it back across the border. On the first attempt, she was in a group led by a coyote. They were caught wading across the Rio Grande and fingerprinted by the US Border Patrol before being transported back to Mexico. After several more unsuccessful tries with coyotes, Anabel and another of her sisters decided to attempt the border on their own: "We were crossing the river but the water wasn't too high, just up to our knees," she says. "We saw the Border Patrol coming and we hid in the bushes."

They waited for about an hour and, with no officers in sight, simply walked into the nearest town. They rented a car and drove back to Ohio.

Distinguishing Immigration from Population Growth

In the 1960s, the US working-age population (defined as eighteen- to sixty-four-year-olds) grew by fifteen million people, or around 15 percent. There was limited immigration during this time; the change was simple population growth. Were Americans worried that there were a fixed number of jobs and that the new fifteen million workers would displace the existing workforce? Of course not. They presumably realized that the growing population would also eat, get haircuts, buy cars, go to the movies, and create economic demand even as they supplied labor. In the first decade of the 2000s, the working-age population grew by a comparable amount (12 percent, or twenty million people.)[39] But this time, most of the growth could be attributed to immigration. The circumstances were different but the result was the same: more people.

When economists think about the impact of a rising population on the labor market, they look at both supply and demand. More people looking for a job means an expanded labor supply, which tends to push wages downward when everything else is held constant. But more people also mean more demand for goods and services, which tends to push wages upward. If the new larger workforce is similar to the old workforce—just bigger—we don't expect to see much of an effect on wages. So, why treat immigrant-driven population growth differently? There are some good reasons, which may impact wages.

First, immigrants are, on average, poorer than the native born. Since their spending power is lower, they don't have as much of a stimulative impact on the demand side of the economy as would a comparable increase in middle-income Americans. They also may spend their money on lower-cost, lower-quality goods, thereby changing the product mix available to consumers.[40] For example, cities that have greater immigrant inflows have more growth in big-box stores per capita, according to one study of California by economists Francesca Mazzolari and David Neumark. The researchers also find that these immigrant-rich cities have more varied restaurants, including more options serving food that is not traditional American cuisine. (The researchers link this more to the expanded supply and diversity of restaurant employees than to any demand stemming from immigrants eating out themselves.)

Second, immigrants spend less of their earnings within the US than the native born do. World Bank data suggests that in 2018, immigrants in the US sent $68 billion back to their home countries, more than immigrants in any other country in the world (the number explains why so many immigrant neighborhoods are peppered with Western Unions and MoneyGram storefronts).[41] A survey of Mexicans returning to Mexico from the United States found that about 31 percent of the migrants' earnings had been remitted (sent home) while they were working in the US.[42] Obviously, immigrants remitting a substantial fraction of their earnings stimulate local economic demand less than natives who make the same income and spend most or all of it in the United States.

In a 2014 study, Will Olney of Williams College demonstrates the link between remittances and local economic activity directly, using an unusually rich German data set.[43] For each 1 percent increase in remittances, native wages in Germany fall by 0.06 percent, presumably because the increase in labor supply is not matched by a comparable increase in labor demand. The effect of remittances is more pronounced for the native born who work in local service industries (restaurants, for example, because immigrants send money home rather than going out to eat). Because of remittances, some of the economic benefits of immigrant-fueled population growth to the host country are muted, instead benefiting residents of immigrants' home countries.

Interestingly, legal status is associated with the degree to which immigrants send money home. San Diego State professor Catalina Amuedo-Dorantes and coauthor Francesca Mazzolari show that remittances to Mexico fell after the 1986 amnesty, for example (commonly known as Reagan's Amnesty, this federal law legalized about three million people then living in the US without authorization).[44] This finding suggests one way that legalization could indirectly benefit native US workers: Immigrants with deeper and more secure connections to the United States spend more of their money in the US.

A third reason why workforce growth fueled by immigrants is distinct is that immigrants have a different skill profile: migrants have fewer years of education, on average, and lower English-language skills. These skill differences mean that the effects of immigration on the labor market are different than they would be if immigrants were exactly like natives. Because immigrants typically have fewer nonwork options for support than natives (for example, immigrants have less access to public or family financial support), they are in a weaker bargaining position and are often willing to accept lower wages. That willingness, in turn, weakens the bargaining power of natives who are close substitutes in the labor force. At the same time, the differential skills of immigrants are precisely what make it possible for them to have positive overall benefits for the economy. Cheap labor leads to business profits and lower consumer prices for products and services that are dominated by immigrant labor: everything from strawberries to manicures to car washes to housekeeping to hamburgers. And for workers who have skills that are complementary to those of immigrants, productivity and wages go up.

Washington State, 2010

After four years, Jorge Ramirez felt like he knew the stucco business. He'd developed friendly relationships with a lot of clients over time, and some of them were calling him directly for small jobs. He'd also fallen in love.

It was dancing that brought Jorge and Yuuko together. There was a club that was a favorite of one of Yuuko's girlfriends, a restaurant that turned into a dance club at night. Jorge was new to the area and didn't go out much. But, like Yuuko, he also had a friend who loved salsa night at the suburban restaurant, and after he saw Yuuko there one night in 2009 he made a point to go back.

Jorge didn't really dance much salsa. But he liked salsa music and he couldn't stop thinking about Yuuko. Both describe it as almost like love at first sight. They started dating and things moved quickly. They'd been together for two or three months, seeing each other almost every day, before Jorge's immigration status came up in conversation. Yuuko had been dreaming about trips they might take together someday. *Obvi-*

ously, that's not going to be possible for me since I don't have a visa, Jorge
thought to himself. His immigration status wasn't something Jorge intended to hide from Yuuko, but it wasn't something he was used to
talking about, either. "It was a little hard, but I had to do it, we had to
talk about it," he says of the moment he told his new girlfriend he had
been in the US illegally for the past several years.

It wasn't something Yuuko had ever considered in the time they'd
been together.

"I was shocked," she says.

Yuuko is also an immigrant. Born in Japan, she came to the US
legally as a twenty-one-year-old college student in the early 1990s. She
graduated with a teaching degree and a specialization in music history.
But even though she was a dean's list student and had glowing recommendations from professors, she couldn't get the work status to teach
in the US. "I was lucky in a way that I met someone and I got married,"
she says. The marriage allowed her to get a green card, and by the time
the union ended in a divorce almost a decade later, Yuuko had become
a US citizen. Despite her relatively smooth path to citizenship, Yuuko
had had her own struggles with immigration. After 9/11, there was a
mix-up with her paperwork, which prevented her from leaving the
country for several years, she says. A lawyer she hired to try to resolve
the problem scammed her out of thousands of dollars. When Yuuko
learned of her new boyfriend's immigration status, she knew exactly
what it meant: "I have to say I was hesitant. I knew it's going to be difficult."

But the relationship kept progressing, and Yuuko was a positive influence in helping Jorge decide to go into business for himself. "I decide to get my own license," Jorge says. "Because people already know
me. I'm very responsible with my job. I like to do my job the best that
I can, and I try to do everything clean and make sure all the clients are
happy with the result."

One of the vagaries of living as an undocumented person in the
United States is that while you cannot work legally, there's generally
nothing preventing you from becoming an independent contractor or
business owner and employing other people. All you need is an ITIN,
an Individual Tax Identification Number. "The ITIN number is simi-

lar to a social security number but you can only use it to pay taxes," Jorge explains. "You can get it for free because obviously they want you to pay, and when you get that number you can get your own license and open your own business." Jorge attended a couple of orientation classes. He got a business license and purchased insurance and a bond for his new company. Yuuko had her own full-time job—but she helped Jorge with the letters he used to approach clients, as well as with estimates and invoicing. His license qualified him to do exterior and interior residential plastering, new construction, and smaller touch-up jobs.

As Jorge became more settled in—with work and with Yuuko—he focused more on saving for his own future. But he continued to send money back to his family in Mexico as well, now through a bank account at Wells Fargo. He talked to them regularly, and often sent gifts for his mom, clothes and special orthopedic shoes that were too expensive in his hometown. "The first year I send every single penny over there," Jorge says. "I only keep enough for gas and rent. Then when I came to Washington I started sending a little bit and saving a little bit here."

Greasing the Wheels of the Labor Market

Immigrants play another role in the American economy that is sometimes underappreciated: Because they are relatively mobile—both across borders and across regions of the United States—immigrants can help booming economies grow and provide a cushion in downturns. In this way, they make the labor market function more efficiently than it would with less mobile workers.

It is easy to see this effect at the macro level. When the Great Recession hit, the number of new migrants to the US slowed to a trickle. Immigrants come to the US mainly for jobs, and when jobs are scarce, they would rather stay home. To some degree, migration flows operate like a spigot that adjusts automatically when no more water is needed.

But inflows to the United States are only part of the story. In an important 2016 paper, Brian Cadena of the University of Colorado Boulder and Brian Kovak of Carnegie Mellon University found that out-migration of Mexican men in response to the Great Recession reduced the economic impact of local economic downturns by about half.[45] In places where the recession hit hardest, Mexican immigrants were much more likely than the native born to move to a different city or leave the US altogether.

To investigate the response to the Great Recession, the authors exploit the fact that some US cities were hit harder than others; they compare how native-born and foreign-born workers responded to the negative shock. It's well established that college-educated workers (in general) are quite mobile in response to labor market conditions.[46] Cadena and Kovak's findings echo the usual pattern: for a 10 percent negative employment shock, the population of college-educated US natives fell by 4 to 5 percent in a local area, while the population of college-educated immigrants fell by over 7 percent. Workers with a high school education or less, on the other hand, tend to be slower to move away when times are tough. In the Cadena and Kovak study, the response of non-college-educated native workers to the same 10 percent shock was closer to 1 percent — so small it could not be statistically distinguished from no response at all. In other words, US natives with only a high school degree tend to stay where they are despite a bad economy.

Less-educated immigrants, by contrast, do not follow this pattern. Their response to a 10 percent employment shock is in the 4 to 5 percent range, similar to that of natives with college degrees. The migration of immigrants within the US helps cushion local economic shocks so that the native born don't suffer the full consequences of a downturn. Essentially, immigrants leave when times are bad, reducing the supply of workers and as a result aiding the prospects of the native born. If the construction work underlying the mid-2000s housing boom had been carried out overwhelmingly by US-born workers, the labor adjustment to the housing bust would have been even more severe. Instead, many foreign-born workers in the South and West relocated or left the US, and they weren't replaced.

The evidence from the Great Recession builds on earlier work by George Borjas titled "Does Immigration Grease the Wheels of the Labor Market?"[47] In that study, Borjas shows that immigrants promote the economic convergence of regions of the United States—meaning they help struggling areas catch up to booming ones. Economic theory predicts that workers in general should migrate to places with better opportunities, lowering wages in receiving regions and raising wages in sending ones. And this does happen to an extent. But the mobility of US-born workers, especially less-educated workers, is not adequate to erase the differences in rich and poor areas.

In a classic 1992 study not specifically related to immigrants, economists Olivier Blanchard and Larry Katz looked at how quickly states responded to an economic shock.[48] A state that has a negative 1 percent employment shock in one year (say, because its employment happened to be concentrated in an industry that suddenly wasn't in demand, as when the Rust Belt faced a drop in demand for autos during the 1980 recession) returns to its normal unemployment rate within five to eight years. All of the adjustment happens because some workers leave the depressed area (or don't move into it) and instead move to an area with better opportunities. While the total population of the state never fully recovers, enough people leave that the labor market conditions for those who remain aren't too bad.

Immigrants help with this process. There are costs to moving, including financial costs and the significant psychological costs of leaving friends and family behind. But migrants who come to the United States looking for work have already moved—those costs are "sunk," in economist jargon. They tend to gravitate to places with more job opportunities and better wages. Of course, immigrant settlement patterns are also strongly determined by social networks, so the story is a bit more complicated. But overall, newly arrived migrants are more responsive to labor market conditions than natives. In a sense, immigrants migrate so that natives don't have to move. As a recent immigrant, Jorge Ramirez didn't have deep roots or employment obligations in an arrival city like Las Vegas. When he heard about a better opportunity in another state, he was quick to pick up and move—as were plenty of other immigrants in similar shoes.

Economist Brian Cadena examined this idea in the context of the comprehensive 1996 reform of the US welfare system.[49] This law promised to "end welfare as we know it"[50] and made it much harder for single mothers to receive cash assistance, especially if they weren't working. As a result of the legislation, there were substantial increases in the number of American women in the low-wage labor force.

Although welfare reform was national, there were local differences in how former welfare recipients responded. Cadena compared cities with bigger influxes of new American workers into the labor market to those with fewer. The result? Cities with bigger supply shocks attracted fewer immigrants. Cadena finds that for each two native-born women newly in the labor force as the result of welfare reform, one fewer female immigrant entered the labor force. Immigrants responded quickly to changing labor market conditions by migrating to places with more opportunity and avoiding places where there were a lot of native-born workers flooding the market.

Springfield, Massachusetts, 2004

Fatima Cabrera gave birth to her first child when she was just seventeen years old and still living in rural Guatemala. The baby's father didn't stick around and wasn't willing to help out, according to Fatima. She tried to make ends meet, helping her family grow coffee beans on the small plot of land they owned. But it wasn't long before she decided she couldn't adequately support her son there. When he was about a year and a half old, in 2004, she left the boy with her parents and made the trek with a coyote through Mexico to Arizona. She crossed the border without anyone stopping her.

Fatima had a cousin in Springfield, in central Massachusetts. She arrived there in the early fall. Her cousin had promised her there was ample work, and it was true. People helped each other out. You just had to ask around and you could find a job, she found. By October Fatima had a temporary position at a chocolate factory, taking candy off the belt and packing it into boxes. The owner seemed to have a lot of undocumented workers — "our people," as Fatima puts it — and never asked for papers. The pay was good, and Fatima saved most of it since she was living with her cousin. At first, her earnings went to paying back a relative in Guatemala who had financed her trip to the US. After a couple of months, and before the job ended, she had repaid the debt.

The next spring, her cousin brought her along to the flower farm where she worked. The owners gave Fatima a job, too, and she has worked there every spring since. She arrives at 7:00 a.m. and puts in nine or ten hours, five or six days a week. She cleans, plants seeds, fertilizes the flowers, and hangs the pots, all for $12 an hour.

In the early years, Fatima moved around, following seasonal work opportunities. One year when jobs dried up in Massachusetts someone Fatima's cousin knew arranged to take a group of workers north to Maine. Fatima worked in a factory that made tiny Christmas trees from pine branches, sweeping up the scraps of pine that her fellow workers discarded.

She'd quickly grown close with another worker on the Maine trip. He was also from Guatemala, the brother of the trip organizer. The brothers' father had died when they were young, and Fatima's new boyfriend Luis was put to work in the fields at a young age, where he suffered physical abuse, according to Fatima. At age fourteen, he'd come north with his brother looking for a new start.

Luis and Fatima soon became inseparable. There wasn't as much work in Maine as they had hoped, so the new couple joined a group going down to Florida to look for work. They lived in a house with lots of other workers to save up their money.

Soon, Fatima was pregnant with a baby girl, and the couple moved back to Springfield. It wasn't healthy to be moving around all the time with the coming baby, they agreed. A few years after their daughter was born in Massachusetts, they welcomed another child—a son. They rented a modest two-story wood-frame house in an older part of Springfield. Some of the other homes on the block showed wear and tear, but Fatima tried to keep theirs looking tidy, hanging delicate white curtains in the window.

Supporting a family in Massachusetts, even in what most Americans would consider a low-paying job, felt much more achievable to Fatima than in Guatemala. In two hours of work in Massachusetts Fatima makes what she would make in a full day in Guatemala, and the work is easier, she says. She sends much of the money home to support her older son, who is now a teenager. She hasn't seen him in fifteen years.

Fatima says she appreciates the generosity of her boss at the flower farm — he's hired her year after year and gives her paid sick days when she needs them. Most of her coworkers there are from Jamaica. Though she suspects the owner knows her situation, he's never asked about her immigration status. But Fatima has noticed that he's shied away from hiring undocumented immigrants lately. She thinks he became worried that something bad would happen, especially after the election of President Trump.

In June, work at the flower farm wraps up for the season. In recent years, Fatima has worked at a nearby potato farm starting in July, a job she originally found through Luis, who worked at the same farm taking the orders and operating the forklift. She cleans the potatoes and separates the good from the bad as they pass by on the belt, working eleven to twelve hours a day in the harvest season. The men at the farm do more taxing work, hauling potatoes in fifty-pound bags. During the season when both Fatima and Luis are working, they hire a babysitter to pick the kids up at school at the end of the day and stay with them until they can get home at night. In the winter, when the work at the potato farm ends, Fatima stops working for a few months and has more time to spend with her kids. February to November is a long time for the kids to barely see their parents, she says.

The Jobs That Americans Won't Do?

An often-heard refrain is that immigrants are willing to do work that Americans are simply unwilling to do. If so, it would imply that immigrants and natives are often not in direct competition for jobs, and therefore that the wage impact of immigrants on native workers should be minimal.

It's clear that the conditions and pay of many "immigrant jobs" are unattractive to the typical American worker. Figure 8 uses American Community Survey data to show the types of positions most commonly held by noncitizen immigrants without a high school degree — the group most likely to be undocumented. This group commonly works in construction, agriculture, and cleaning occupations.[51]

FIGURE 8. Share of workers in ten most common jobs held by noncitizens without a high school degree, 2017

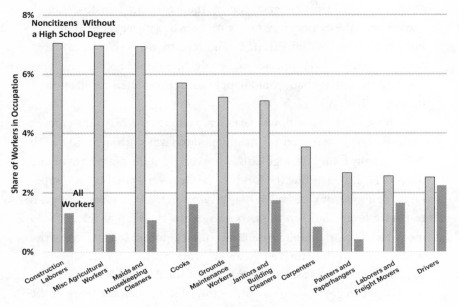

Source: Authors' calculations using American Community Survey data

Figure 9 illustrates the jobs that noncitizens without a high school degree do disproportionately, meaning jobs that they are much more likely to do than the average worker, even if the occupation isn't a particularly large one overall. Compared to a typical worker in the general workforce, a less-educated noncitizen is twelve times more likely to be an agricultural sorter or other agricultural worker, and nine to ten times more likely to be a plasterer or drywaller. In general, the jobs held by less-educated immigrants tend to pay relatively poorly, be physically demanding, and have an elevated risk of injury. Most Americans do have other options. In some cases that option is not working at all and relying on family or social assistance.

In an America without immigrants, would these less appealing jobs simply not get done? Or would wages rise and conditions improve to the point where Americans would be willing to do them? The answers are yes and yes.

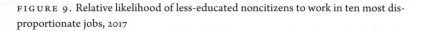

FIGURE 9. Relative likelihood of less-educated noncitizens to work in ten most disproportionate jobs, 2017

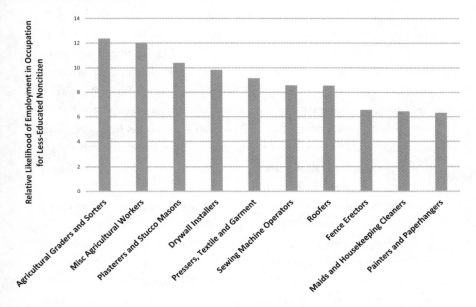

The key here is to think about how easily the work that an immigrant does could be done elsewhere or done without. Some jobs are in sectors that economists call nontraded; these jobs need to be done locally. The textbook example is haircutting services: It will never be cost-effective to leave the country for a haircut, full automation is a long way off, and people are unlikely to give up on getting haircuts entirely when they get more expensive.

On the other hand, some work is easily offshored. Why not process chicken in Mexico if the wages of US chicken processors get too high? In the absence of immigrant labor, some jobs would likely be performed outside of the United States.

Then there are some types of work that may just not happen in the absence of cheap immigrant labor, or that only happen because immigrant labor is plentiful. A prime example is the informal economy of Mexican gardeners—*jardinerías*—that exists in California and, increasingly, in other US regions as well.

It is worth considering the fact that different regions of the US are shaped and impacted by immigrant communities to vastly different degrees. Economists Ethan Lewis and Giovanni Peri point out in a 2014 paper titled "Immigration and the Economy of Cities and Regions" that California—the country's most populous state—is home to 25 percent of all the foreign-born residents of the US but to just 9 percent of native residents. Forty-three percent of the residents of Los Angeles and 62 percent of the residents of Miami are foreign born. New York City, the top immigration metropolitan area, hosts 14.5 percent of all foreign-born residents of the United States. In places like New York and California "the effects of those foreign born individuals, through their economic and labor market transactions, were felt, in some form, by natives," the economists write.

The personal economic advantages of immigrant labor may seem obvious to an upper-middle-class California family that employs a foreign-born nanny and gardener, gets their car washed for less than $10, and can quickly and easily hire day laborers to repair a fence or paint a room. On the other hand, in West Virginia there is just one immigrant for every ninety-nine native residents. Write Lewis and Peri: "It is much less likely that those few immigrants produced any noticeable economic or labor market impact on most native West Virginians."[52]

University of Southern California sociologist Pierrette Hondagneu-Sotelo and graduate student Hernan Ramirez, now at College of the Canyons, examined the codified structure of LA's local gardening economy—and the changing social norms that fed its growth—in a 2009 paper.[53] "Los Angeles is perhaps the mecca of the Latino immigrant informal economy, with vibrant sectors of day laborers, street vendors, garment assembly workers, nannies, domestic workers, and gardeners," they write. "Just as domesticas provide substitute paid labor for the work women once did for free, so too jardineros provide commodified labor that substitutes for the work of husbands and sons."[54]

In the 1950s and 1960s, proud homeowners and their teenage sons mowed the lawns of the postwar tract homes featured in magazines or television. "Green lawns still prevail, but it is rare to see middle class homeowners in Los Angeles mowing these. Mexican men are doing the work," the authors observe. "Residential maintenance gardening is not new, but in the early twentieth century, it was a service reserved for the rich. Today, those employing gardeners include a wider range of social classes."[55] In many regions of the United States, readily available immigrant labor contributes to a class stratification in which not just the very wealthy but much of the upper-middle class are able to out-source a large proportion of their domestic labor.

The increase in Mexican-born gardeners coincides with the over-all rise in immigrants to the US, and particularly with Mexican immi-grants to Los Angeles. As Ramirez and Hondagneu-Sotelo point out, "it is notoriously difficult to measure informal sector growth, as census data tends to undercount both informal economic activity and the em-ployment of unauthorized immigrant workers." The census data they rely upon reveal that there were eight thousand Mexican-born men working as gardeners in the Los Angeles/Long Beach metropolitan area in 1980. By 1990, they find, this number had more than doubled to 19,886. By the year 2000, there were thirty-one thousand foreign-born Mexican gardeners counted. "The numbers nearly quadrupled in twenty years."[56]

Weekly yard service in Southern California can cost as little as $60 a month, though gardeners typically make most of their profit on "ex-tras," like buying and planting annuals, delivering and spreading mulch, and pruning trees. While the typical new client will interview three or four gardeners and almost always select the one who provides the lowest bid, when it comes to the so-called extras, "they name a price, and most clients go for it," Ramirez and Hondagneu-Sotelo write. "In lieu of asking for raises or charging higher fees, they count on the ex-tras. When they charge for extras, gardeners position themselves as in-dependent contractors, such as professional painters, roofers, or appli-ance vendors."[57]

Ramirez and Hondagneu-Sotelo conducted in-depth interviews with forty-seven gardeners. Though thirty-six of the forty-seven were legal permanent residents or naturalized US citizens at the time of the interviews, many had once been undocumented immigrant workers, and all were born in Mexico. (Many of the once-undocumented inter-viewed gardeners benefited from Reagan's Amnesty in 1986, which gave them legal status.) Just thirteen of the forty-seven gardeners had attended school beyond ninth grade. While hired hands reported making $20,000 to $25,000 a year—for hard physical labor that often involved twelve-hour days, six- or even seven-day work weeks, and little to no vacation—the "route owners"—those men who were running their own businesses, with an established list of regular clients—claimed incomes of $60,000 to $100,000 a year.

"[The] occupational mobility is nothing short of stunning," the authors write. "Within several years, a newcomer rookie can gather his apprenticeship knowledge, a driver's license, and truck and modest savings, and use these to become an independent route-owner gardener. Acting as both worker and entrepreneur, he will need to strategically manage the route and to negotiate rising costs and stagnant fees, but if he does well, he might increase his earnings anywhere from between three to ten times greater than what the paid employees earn."[58] For the most successful of these men, the American dream is alive and well.

Of course, as discussed above, this landscaping economy is localized. In California, the majority of gardeners are foreign born and the cost of service is cheap. In states with few immigrants, there is not the same economy for gardening services, and use of such businesses is not as widespread. In short, when hiring a gardener is inexpensive, many more people choose to do so.

In some cases, the degree to which a market would survive without immigrants is hard to predict. Consider the agricultural industry. The Department of Agriculture Economic Research Service estimates that about 73 percent of the country's 1.2 million hired farmworkers are born outside the United States, and 48 percent are undocumented.[59]

How much would the agriculture industry contract if immigrant labor disappeared? Many farms would surely continue to operate, offering higher wages to attract native-born workers and charging higher prices. Others would rely more on technology. For example, it's hard for a machine to pick delicate raspberries when they are the perfect ripeness, but most of the work in planting and harvesting wheat can be done by machine. Labor-intensive crops facing stiff competition from abroad would largely cease to be grown in this country without immigrant labor. If less-skilled labor were scarce, some employers would offer a better package to recruit workers. Other firms would simply be priced out of the market.

The notion that Americans won't do those jobs can be misleading. Psychology comes into play. Perhaps a US-born worker will reject a job opportunity when public perception is that it's a job for immigrants. But when coworkers are more like her, pay is more in line with what others are making in the same region, and conditions are better, that sense of "I won't do that job" goes away. With fewer immigrants, some jobs would disappear, and others would transform into jobs that Americans would do.

In 2012, the US Department of Agriculture simulated the possible effects of a restrictionist policy, one that hypothetically reduced the unauthorized agricultural workforce by 34 percent over fifteen years.[60] Agricultural employment of US natives would increase 4 percent and wages would go up by 3 percent, they predicted. Legal permanent residents would experience similar gains. Those undocumented immigrants that remained would see wage increases of more than 13 percent. The higher labor costs would in turn translate into predicted declines in agricultural employment of 3 to 4 percent.

Not surprisingly, effects were shown to vary across agricultural sectors. Farms that depend heavily on human labor—especially unauthorized labor—rather than machines are most at risk. The study also took into account the consumer "demand elasticity" for different products—how much consumers will reduce their purchases as a product gets more expensive. Greenhouse and nursery products like flowers were much more severely affected in the simulation than soybeans and other oilseeds.

The importance of undocumented labor in the agricultural industry highlights a fundamental tension in immigration politics. Business interests, typically more aligned with the Republican Party, benefit from abundant immigrant labor. But to attract voters the modern Republican Party has relied on appeals to white identity politics and nationalism. To thread this needle, the party needs to appear to be tough on immigration without actually depriving businesses of the workers keeping the flower industry and so many others afloat. That may be why the Trump administration leaned into an Obama-era expansion of the H2A visa program for temporary agricultural workers, raising the number of visas from 134,000 in 2016 to 205,000 in 2019, even as the administration's rhetoric was focused on disparaging and discouraging immigrant workers.[61]

Lorain, Ohio, Early 2000s

Over the few years following her mother's death and her return visit to Mexico in 2001, Anabel Barron and her partner added two more children, a boy and a third girl, to their family. (Anabel's four kids, who were all born in the US, are United States citizens.) Until 2011, Anabel was focused on raising her kids. Her partner, who worked in construction, was the family's sole provider. When the couple separated in 2011, Anabel knew she'd have to find a job.

"I was a stay-at-home mom, volunteering at church. I wasn't making money," Anabel says. One of her friends gave her a lead. The job was helping to clean up after young hockey players, teenagers who came to Ohio for an elite training program. "I went to the interview and they didn't ask me for an ID," Anabel recalls. "I never lied. They asked me, you prefer cash or check? I preferred cash."

Anabel spent most of her days doing laundry, along with cleaning and cooking for the boys. She washed skates and helmets and mouthguards. Her employers were good to her, she says. They were understanding when she had to miss a day because of a sick child at home, and they gave her gas money when she had to drive to Texas to help care for her sick father.

She was paid $300 a week for four days' work, and she worked short days that coincided with her kids' school schedule, arriving at the hockey arena about 9:00 a.m., after she'd dropped her kids off, and leaving work in time to pick them up in the afternoon. The local public school offered a preschool program for kids as young as three — a "blessing" for her family, Anabel says — so all four kids had the same school day.

Anabel supplemented her income by cleaning on weekends, work that she found through the hockey community. She would make $100, sometimes up to $200, to clean a house; occasionally, she brought her oldest daughter along to help. "If I didn't have that extra, I wouldn't have money to feed my kids," says Anabel, who found that she sometimes showed up to clean an already spotless home. On her drive, she would seek out yard sales in the wealthier suburban neighborhoods on the shores of Lake Erie. "At that period of time, my kids were wearing only clothes from garage sales from that area," she says. "Believe me, every time that I saw a garage sale I would stop, and I would know that I would get name-brand clothes, only paying like twenty-five cents apiece or a dollar at the most."

Occasionally, Anabel was hired to organize closets, or help with meal prep for dinners her employers were holding at their home. The hockey players treated her affectionately. There was a big kitchen island the boys tended to gather around. "At least three of them would go and sit while I was cooking, and talk to me about girls, about their moms, about they miss home," Anabel says. The kids were high school age, and often from out of state, Canada, or even Australia. "I was like the mother figure, I would say."

Immigration and the Productivity of Natives

As we noted earlier, wages for US-born workers will tend to rise when immigrants arrive if those workers are complementary to the new labor. This wage increase typically arises because of increasing productivity: Immigrants can make the work of natives more productive by improving opportunities for specialization. A native-born woman who owns a small home-cleaning business might be able to spend more of her time on marketing and administrative tasks if she can hire two foreign-born cleaning assistants for the price of one native-born worker, for example. The demand for construction foremen might rise if more consumers are induced to build new homes because construction prices are low. In a 2016 paper described earlier, Mette Foged and Giovanni Peri show that the arrival of refugees in Denmark caused young native workers to enter more highly specialized and less-manual occupations, usually staying within their municipality.[62] The transition was gradual but resulted in long-lasting productivity improvements.

The Danish refugee example highlights one important answer to the question of how it is possible for the economy to absorb immigrants so quickly. Like the US, Denmark has a flexible labor market with low hiring and firing costs compared to many European economies. This makes it comparatively easy for workers to adjust to changes in conditions, increasing the likelihood that immigrants can make natives more productive. It is possible that the flexible, laissez-faire American economy is the best-case scenario for absorbing immigrant inflows, and that it's part of the reason US productivity benefits from immigration.[63]

Peri has also directly examined the effect of immigration on total productivity using comparisons across US states.[64] After carefully accounting for other factors, he shows that states with more immigrants are more productive, and that at least a third of the improvements in productivity stem from increased specialization of workers. When more immigrants are present, natives end up doing more communication-oriented tasks while immigrants do more manual tasks. It also appears that firms are able to adapt to the new worker skill mix and adjust their capital accordingly, using production techniques that rely on manual labor.

Importantly, it is precisely the fact that immigrants have skills that are different from those of natives that makes these productivity gains possible. If you took Economics 101, you may recall that when two countries are good at producing different things, there are big gains from specialization and trade. Suppose island A has a climate well suited for growing apples and island B can easily make bread, but residents of both islands prefer a mix of foods. In the absence of trade, residents of island A can choose between consuming ten apples per day or five apples and one slice of bread per day, and vice versa for residents of island B. With trade and specialization, residents of both islands might be able to consume five apples and five slices of bread daily. The same principle applies here: Immigration allows for more specialization — perhaps one worker focuses on designing the menu in a restaurant while others cook — which in turn raises productivity of the workforce.

Immigrants can also make US-born workers more productive by freeing up time taken up with tasks those workers would otherwise need to be doing at home. For example, a US-born doctor who outsources caring for her yard and cleaning her house and thus has time to see more patients each week will be able to produce more total value for the economy, even if she happens to be more efficient at mowing her lawn than the person she pays to do it. In a 2011 study, economists Patricia Cortes and Jose Tessada show that there is real-life evidence supporting this idea: High-wage women work more hours when they have an immigrant (i.e., low-wage) market for domestic work.[65] By reducing prices for childcare, house cleaning, and prepared meals, immigrants make it possible for high-earning women to invest more in their out-of-home work. Similar women in cities without the same immigrant labor pool work less out of the home and do more of this domestic work themselves. (By contrast, high-earning men do not typically do this type of domestic work, so are not expected to be similarly impacted by the number of immigrants in their local area, and studies on this topic typically do not examine men.)

This link between immigration and the care of children of well-educated native women was corroborated via time-use data in a 2014 study by San Diego State University professor Catalina Amuedo-Dorantes and University College London professor Almudena Sevilla.[66] They found that college-educated women in immigrant-dense cities spend the same number of hours on educational and recreational activities with their kids as women in cities where it is harder to hire immigrant domestic help—but with immigrant labor available, these highly educated women spend less time on basic childcare responsibilities.

Immigrants in the Healthcare Sector

Just as the immigrant gardener and cleaning workforce has expanded in recent decades, a significant increase of immigrant labor in the healthcare sector has impacted millions of Americans' everyday lives. According to a Migration Policy Institute report based on 2018 data, 2.6 million workers in the healthcare professions are foreign born, roughly 18 percent of all healthcare workers. As we've seen before, immigrants are disproportionately represented among both lower-paid occupations like home health aides (38 percent foreign born) and highly paid ones like doctors (28 percent foreign born).[67] These numbers vary across locations: 75 percent of home health aides in New York State are foreign born, compared with almost none in West Virginia. A separate study examining the unauthorized population in particular estimated that 11 percent of foreign-born healthcare workers and 2 percent of all healthcare workers are unauthorized.[68] Unauthorized healthcare workers are much more likely to be employed in long-term care facilities, home health agencies, and informal settings than other healthcare workers.

In ongoing research, Kristin Butcher of Wellesley College, MIT graduate student Kelsey Moran, and author Tara Watson investigate the impacts of the immigrant workforce in the healthcare field, exploiting the fact that the immigrant population varies across locations.[69] (The team uses a strategy similar to David Card's enclave approach to measuring labor-market impacts, which predicts the current immigrant population based on historical settlement patterns.)

Butcher, Moran, and Watson find that having more immigrants in a local area expands the supply of less-educated workers like home health aides and housekeepers. This expansion, in turn, affects care for the native-born elderly. The elderly are more likely to "age in place"— that is, avoid institutionalization in a nursing home or care facility— when there is a more expansive immigrant workforce, presumably because of increased ability to find affordable home supports. Similarly, economists Delia Furtado of the University of Connecticut and Francesc Ortega of the City University of New York find that immigrant inflows are associated with fewer falls among nursing home residents, a result they link to an increased supply of licensed practical nurses and nurses' aides.[70]

Painesville, Ohio, 2013

By 2013 Eduardo Lopez was making $19.50 an hour at the northern Ohio factory. He worked long hours. Most often it was 10:00 p.m. to 7:00 a.m., but when things picked up he would go in at 7:00 p.m. and work a twelve-hour shift. He was always on Monday through Friday, and sometimes weekends as well. There were a lot of seven-day weeks. But the job allowed him to support his family. By that time, he had three kids: His oldest, Ariel, was six; Kylie was three; and the baby, William, just one.

His wife, Elena, had worked full-time until she became pregnant with Ariel. After a few years at the plant nursery she had found a factory job. The facility made kitchen cabinets, windows, and lids for washers and dryers. She thought that job would be less physically taxing than the transplanting work that had her on her hands and knees all day. But early in the pregnancy, her doctor told her that the chemicals she was exposed to at the factory were too dangerous, that if she kept working there she would risk losing the baby. "You know what," Eduardo told her. "You don't have to work anymore. The money I'm making, it's enough."

The couple was living in a small single-family home in the picturesque town of Painesville, Ohio. The house was painted gray and had a tiny front porch and a small yard. There was a paved driveway with room for their two cars. With the long hours he worked, Eduardo brought in a paycheck that came close to $1,000 a week after taxes. Their rent was $650 a month plus utilities. When he got home in the morning Eduardo would give Ariel a ride to kindergarten and Kylie a ride to the Head Start program where all his children would eventually go. (Evidence indicates that Head Start boosts English-language learning for immigrant children, with the biggest effects for kids with less-educated parents.)[71] Eduardo played with William and then went to bed about 10:00 a.m. He woke up at 4:00 or 5:00 p.m. and talked with the kids about their days before his night shift began. On the weekends, the family would occasionally go to the Cleveland Zoo, or spend an afternoon out at a nearby Chuck E. Cheese restaurant.

Eduardo and Elena wanted to buy their house from their landlord. They'd saved some money for a down payment, but the problem was that they wouldn't be able to put the house in either of their names. No short-term solution was obvious, but the couple kept saving. Who knew when the government might come up with some legislative solution to their dilemma, they thought, some way for them to get legal status and move on with their lives.

Eduardo liked his work. He'd started at nothing—in the lowest level job, not even speaking English. Slowly, he'd worked his way up to

supervisor. Seeing his own progress was satisfying. And he liked knowing that his story could be an example for other workers. There were
plenty of other Mexicans at the factory. The daytime shift was about 40
percent Mexican, but the less popular night shift had close to 80 percent Mexican workers, Eduardo says. He knew many of them were undocumented and suspected management knew it as well.

"I was thinking I was living my dream," Eduardo says. He was supporting his growing family on a single income and had three happy,
healthy kids. "I got a good job. I making good money. I about to buy my
house. I got two cars. I didn't have to worry about nothing."

Capital and Technology

The indirect effects of immigration on the labor market go beyond immigrants' roles as consumers and facilitators of specialization. Though
many studies of immigration ignore the role of capital like factories
and machines, cheap immigrant labor could fundamentally affect capital and technological investment decisions.

For example, immigration may induce firms to build new factories within the United States, or to avoid relocating their production
abroad. Will Olney, a Williams College economist, finds in a 2013 paper
that immigration expands the number of establishments—especially
small ones—in an area.[72] (An establishment is a geographic place of
business; the US government collects many of its business statistics
at the establishment level. Large companies may have many establishments.) Evidence from Denmark shows that firms expand in size when
immigrants arrive.[73] This so-called capital deepening leads to economic
growth and ultimately improves the wages and employment opportunities of native workers. (As noted above, if firms relocate within the
US to take advantage of cheap immigrant labor, workers in immigrant-
dense cities will particularly benefit.) Olney and his coauthors also
find, using detailed European data, that firms in areas randomly as-
signed more refugees outsource less of their production.

Similarly, firms could alter their production methods to take advantage of immigrant labor. Ethan Lewis, a Dartmouth economist who has
become prominent in the field, shows in a 2011 paper that companies

do change how they produce goods.[74] Manufacturing plants in regions with heavy immigrant inflows in the 1980s and 1990s were slower to adopt automation machinery than similar plants in areas without an ample supply of immigrant labor. In the absence of immigrants, firms automate as technology becomes available to replace manual work. But it is not sensible for them to invest in this new machinery if there is abundant low-wage labor around.

A study of the post–World War II Bracero program also confirms this idea. This program was a massive temporary guest worker initiative that imported Mexican agricultural workers — known as *braceros*, literally "those who work with their arms" — between 1942 and 1964. At its peak, the Bracero program brought in over four hundred thousand workers.[75] Lewis and colleagues Michael Clemens and Hannah Postel look at what happened when the program abruptly ended. At first, the authors were puzzled to see minimal changes in wages or employment of the native born after so many immigrants left. They assumed that farms would need to offer high wages to US workers in order to continue to operate. But instead, farms turned to machines, adopting newer technologies that reduced the need for farm labor. For example, more-advanced tomato harvesters were introduced once low-cost workers were no longer available. Farms may have also shifted crop mix, focusing on varieties that were more amenable to machine harvesting. A similar effect was seen in rural areas following the 1920s restrictions on eastern and southern European migration: Farmers moved toward planting wheat rather than more labor-intensive cereals, and they moved toward tractors rather than horses and mules.[76]

It seems that immigrants sometimes substitute not for US natives, but for machines. This fact helps explain the small employment impacts of immigration: Immigrants essentially create their own jobs by offering an alternative to mechanized production.

Eagle Rock, California, 2012

Mia Park remembers a little about life in South Korea. She can imagine herself in the apartment where she lived with her parents and older brother, Michael. It was in Suwon, a city of 1.2 million people twenty miles outside of Seoul. She remembers her first-grade teacher and some of the many playgrounds in her neighborhood, where everyone lived in tall apartment complexes.

Mia and Michael's maternal grandmother and an aunt lived in California, where their aunt ran a successful textile business. Their aunt had been in the US for decades, had become a citizen, and had helped her mother — Mia and Michael's grandmother — immigrate and become a citizen as well. When Mia and Michael were very young they went to California for a visit. A year or two later, they were told they were moving to the United States — their dad had secured an F-1 student visa and the rest of the family would be on F-2 visas for dependent family members, though the kids understood nothing of these kinds of details at the time.

The family of four moved in with Mia and Michael's grandmother in Eagle Rock, a northeast Los Angeles neighborhood where single-story Craftsman-style homes are set back from palm-lined streets. Mia was eight, Michael ten when they started third and fifth grades at a local public elementary school. The only English words Mia knew how to say at the time were "yes" and "no." To Michael, some of the coursework was easy. He realized right away that the American kids were way behind the Korean classmates he'd left behind in math. But he also spoke virtually no English, and he struggled to understand anything that was going on in his English and history lessons. The other kids couldn't, or wouldn't, pronounce his given name, Jun-young, the only one he used at the time. Because he couldn't defend himself, he was always being blamed for mischief that wasn't actually his fault, he says.

Most of the students at the public Los Angeles elementary school were Caucasian or Latino. There were a number of kids from the Philippines. There were no other Korean kids, the siblings say, but there was one Korean American faculty member at the school. She was Mia's first teacher there and for the rest of their time in that school every time either Michael or Mia had a problem they'd be brought to that teacher, who'd call their mom. "I remember my mom would come to school crying," Michael says. "She thought I wasn't going to be a very good student, so I know she was very worried." Mia had a similar experience with teasing, and kids making fun of her name, Soo-jin.

The new name came from the credits on a movie poster at the Glendale Galleria, a local mall. "I thought, why not?" Michael says. Once her brother changed his name, Mia wanted to choose an M name, too, to match. Mia, she decided. "Short and sweet."

In Korea, Michael and Mia's mother had done human resources-type work at a big tech company. But she was ineligible to work in the United States with her F-2 visa, and once the family overstayed their visas, she, like her children, was in the country illegally. About one million Korean immigrants were living in the US in 2017, making up approximately 2.4 percent of the total immigrant population. Virtually all of those Korean immigrants are from South Korea and about 16 percent of them are undocumented.[77] The Los Angeles metropolitan area is home to 220,000 Korean immigrants, more than anywhere else in the United States, but Koreans still make up less than 2 percent of LA's population. Los Angeles's thriving Koreatown was only ten miles away from their home. But in their own school, in their own neighborhood, the Park kids felt out of place.

Michael was in middle school, Mia still in elementary school when their parents separated. The family didn't openly discuss difficult topics, and the kids didn't ask many questions. They had limited contact with their dad after that. Their mom was helping her sister out at the textile business. She never officially earned a salary, but her sister was paying their rent and helping with food and the kids' expenses. Mia and Michael's mom had her sister and her mother. But outside of family most of her community — her entire social life — centered around church. The family was Roman Catholic and had found a Catholic Korean church near their home in Los Angeles. Though Michael's mom had quickly transitioned to calling him and his sister by their new names, she did sometimes also call her son Elijah, his saint's name in the Catholic Church. It was through church that Michael made his only Korean friend in the US. The church community felt like home.

Before Michael Park started high school, the family moved from Eagle Rock to a larger suburb nearby. Both Michael and Mia had struggled socially in elementary school, but they each learned to speak English competently within a couple of years and were able to keep up, even excel, academically. Though their Los Angeles school was far more diverse than the typical American elementary school, as Korean immigrants struggling to learn English they always felt like they stood out. Even as she describes a number of her elementary-school classmates as having been born outside the United States, Mia identifies herself as the only immigrant in her class. The others had come as toddlers and spoke English fluently, she says. Their culture was all around them. She was in a different category.

Both Michael and Mia were attracted to the idea of going to a high school where more of their classmates looked like them. Their new school had a much larger Asian American population, as well as a reputation for excellent academics and athletic programs. "I saw people with my skin color speaking the language that I speak," Michael recalls of his high school years. "My mom was pressuring me to join something so I could make friends and have something for the college app." The Korean friend Michael knew from the church he'd been attending since the day he arrived in the US played on the high school football team. Michael joined in his sophomore year. He'd never played football before, but he devoted himself to it and learned quickly, making good friends on the team. By senior year, Michael was co-captain. Mia, meanwhile, had joined the cheerleading squad.

"I would cheer at the football games, my brother would play and he would make touchdowns and the whole school would go crazy," Mia recalls. A few years out of high school, both siblings say that that was the happiest they ever saw their mom — sitting in the bleachers on warm Southern California nights, hearing the crowd cheer for her son. "My brother used to get bullied, I used to get bullied, and to overcome that and for us to connect with these American students — she was just proud and she felt like it was worth it."

When the time came to apply for college, Michael knew football could help him. He was a solid student, but in his junior and senior years the team became his primary focus and his grades slipped. As a California resident, he could have paid in-state tuition at a public California university, about $12,000 a year not including room and board. State law AB-540, passed in 2001, allows all students who graduate from a California high school to pay in-state tuition, regardless of immigration status (twenty-seven thousand of the ninety-eight thousand undocumented students who graduate from American high schools each year live in California).[78] But given his grades, Michael thought he'd be looking at what his classmates considered middling schools.

He decided he'd rather go somewhere farther away. His high school had a decent football program, but it was far from nationally recognized, or even considered especially strong within the region. Nonetheless, Michael started contacting coaches. "I can accurately say that I've emailed at least two-thirds of the college football coaches in the US," he says. "I stayed up all night copy and pasting email templates, sending them my highlight tape and my grades. And a lot of them got back to me. That really fired me up even more." There were several good offers, but the one from a small private college in Kansas seemed like the best; the school flew him out for a visit and offered him a sports scholarship equivalent to $30,000 a year. "I love football. I didn't look twice; I just signed their letter and I went to Kansas."

Immigrant Assimilation and Language Ability

The economic and social impacts of immigration are determined in part by the degree to which immigrants do in fact assimilate into the so-called melting pot of American life. When economists talk about assimilation, they are usually referring to economic integration — specifically, whether the earnings of immigrants (or their children) reach levels that are typical of native-born workers. How immigrants fare in the workforce relative to US natives is an important component of how immigrants affect the economy more broadly. Immigrants who have higher earnings are more likely to fuel economic growth and less likely to rely on government support than poorer immigrants. As the economic status of immigrants approaches that of the US born, immigration becomes like any other form of population growth.

As noted earlier, a century ago most immigrants had little formal education, but most US natives did not have much schooling themselves. If immigrants could learn the language, they would be on roughly equal footing with a typical worker born in the US. Obviously, times have changed, and the American economic engine has shifted from "brawn to brains." The immigrants of recent decades have more education than immigrants of the early twentieth century, but less than midcentury immigrants and much less than today's native born. Since changes in immigration policy in 1965, immigrants are increasingly coming from poor countries with relatively weak educational systems. For example, twenty- to twenty-four-year-olds in Mexico had an average of 10.5 years of schooling in 2010, roughly the US level of 1950 and nearly three years less than contemporaneous US residents.[79] Researchers Robert Kaestner and Ofer Malamud have shown that Mexicans with somewhat lower-than-average education — those with seven to nine years of schooling — are the group most likely to migrate to the United States.[80]

There is no consensus on how much immigrant wages "catch up" to those of the US born. Early studies of economic assimilation such as those by Barry Chiswick in the 1970s found that immigrant wages converge to native levels in about fifteen years and eventually surpass them.[81] Harvard Kennedy School economist Borjas finds that earnings of immigrants arriving in the late 1990s grew more slowly than those of earlier arrival cohorts, and grew more slowly than US-born workers of the same age at the same time.[82] Recent evidence from Randall Akee and Maggie Jones shows that earnings of immigrants arriving in the first decade of the 2000s who worked in the formal sector do converge to native wage levels within five to seven years. Given the different data sources and periods of study, it's difficult to reconcile these conflicting findings. However, Borjas does note an important role for English-language acquisition, so perhaps some of the difference stems from differences in language in the formal and informal sectors.

In the context of the economics literature, English-language ability is typically viewed as a skill — a form of "human capital" in which immigrants can invest. Immigrants from non-English-speaking countries who report speaking "very well" earn more than otherwise-similar immigrants who speak no English. Within individual, localized economies, speaking English can result in a significant pay premium. In Los Angeles, where a large immigrant labor supply means employing a nanny can be more affordable than in other parts of the country, a Spanish-speaking caregiver who is also fluent in English may make $20 an hour or more for watching one child, while a woman who speaks very limited English may make closer to $10 an hour in the same job. Borjas notes that recent generations of immigrants are slower to learn English and that this delayed language acquisition may prevent the wage growth seen among earlier immigrant waves.

Dartmouth economist Ethan Lewis has used government survey data to examine to what extent English-language ability influences economic assimilation. Roughly half of immigrants say that they speak English "very well," while 98 percent of US-born Americans say the same. Lewis shows that immigrants who describe themselves as speaking English "very well" earn similar wages to US-born workers with the same education. There is also a strong gradient in English ability among less-educated workers — not speaking English very well is associated with 17 percent lower wages.[83] And when new immigrants arrive in a US city, it is the already-living-there immigrants with weaker English skills who face downward wage pressure.

Researchers have articulated the idea of a "critical period" for language acquisition — it gets much harder to learn a new language in adolescence or later. Lewis documents that immigrants who arrive by age ten tend to have better English skills. It's also the case that immigrants who arrive after age ten have lower wages, likely because English ability affects economic success.

Perhaps it's partially because of the language issue that upward mobility is high for the children of immigrants, who typically speak English well if they arrive as children or are born in the United States. Recent work by Ran Abramitzky of Stanford University, Leah Platt Boustan and Elisa Jacome of Princeton University, and Santiago Perez of the University of California, Davis uses historical data following millions of parent-son pairs over time to investigate upward mobility. They find that a cohort of children of immigrants, observed in the 1880–1910 timeframe, were much more upwardly mobile than children of US-born parents. Children of immigrants growing up in households at the twenty-fifth percentile of the income distribution ended up 3–6 percentage points higher in the income distribution than children of US-born parents at the same income level.

It turns out the same pattern holds true today: Children of immigrants observed in 1980 in the bottom half of the income distribution have earnings as adults that are substantially higher than those of nonimmigrants growing up in families with similar incomes. The researchers find broadly consistent results regardless of race, ethnicity, or parental country of origin. In other words, by the metric of upward economic mobility of the second generation, the dream of a better life in America often comes true.

Social Assimilation

Compared to economists, sociologists tend to be more focused on social and cultural integration. Do immigrants make social connections with native-born Americans, participate in American institutions, and ultimately become part of the dominant society? Not everyone agrees that full assimilation—represented by the traditional "melting pot" metaphor—is something to which the United States should aspire. Should immigrants have to abandon their home cultures, values, and languages to be considered successful? An alternative vision is an American "mosaic" or "salad bowl" whereby immigrants preserve a distinct identity but contribute to the greater whole. Even the melting pot—which literally refers to a crucible in which metals are mixed together—recognizes that "American" culture reflects a fusion of many backgrounds and traditions.

Clearly, economic and social integration are important determinants of public support for immigration. US natives tend to respond more favorably to immigrants who are similar to them—racially, culturally, linguistically, and economically. On the economic front there is considerably less objection to exceptionally rich migrants than to exceptionally poor migrants, though resentment is sometimes articulated about wealthy foreigners meddling with local economies. A 2014 article in the *Los Angeles Times*, for example, detailed how superrich Chinese home buyers were boosting suburban California housing prices.[84] Chinese buyers bought 12 percent of all US homes purchased by foreigners in 2013; half of those houses were in California and two-thirds of those were paid for in cash, according to the National Association of Realtors.

One change that has occurred since America's early twentieth-century immigration wave is the segregation of immigrant neighborhoods. In "Is the Melting Pot Still Hot?" economists David Cutler, Ed Glaeser, and Jacob Vigdor show that the residential segregation of immigrants declined in the early twentieth century but rebounded starting in the 1970s.[85] Interestingly, this rebound happened at the same time that racial segregation between Black and white households was waning in the US, and that residential segregation by race was being replaced by residential segregation by income. Low-income migrants now arrive at a time of widening income inequality and increased residential segregation by class. Segregated neighborhoods, in turn, usually mean worse schools, inferior housing, and less exposure to middle-class neighbors for newly arrived immigrants.

There are some benefits to immigrants living in communities dense with people from their own home countries, though. Immigrant enclaves can provide access to culturally appropriate goods and services, information, and social networks, making it easier for new arrivals to transition to life in America. Neighborhood networks can also provide access to jobs. A study of Cubans arriving in the 1980 Mariel boatlift, for example, found that by 1983 or 1984 about 30 percent were working for Cuban employers, compared with fewer than 10 percent of Haitian migrants who had arrived in Florida around the same time.[86]

Immigrants living outside immigrant neighborhoods may also be subject to harassment and discrimination. In one extreme case in 2014, a wealthy school district in the San Francisco suburbs hired a private detective to try to prove that a second grader was ineligible to attend school in the town where her mother lived and worked as a nanny.[87] (The girl and her mother had their own rooms in the employer's home and slept there during the week.) In California overall, 55 percent of all public-school students identify as Hispanic or Latino.[88] At the elementary school the nine-year-old attended, that number was less than 4 percent.

Immigrant residential isolation may also slow social adaptation to American culture and integration into the broader economy. Immigrants who live near other immigrants exhibit behaviors that are more similar to those of their own country-of-origin or language group than to those of the native born. For example, when immigrants from higher-than-average-welfare-using language groups live in cities with many members from their group, they are more likely to use welfare. By contrast, when immigrants from low-welfare-using groups live in cities with many members from their group, they are less likely to use welfare.[89]

Assimilation in a cultural and economic sense may have broader consequences. Economist Paul Collier, building on Robert Putnam's ideas about social capital (Putnam, a sociologist, is known for his books *Bowling Alone* and the more recent *Our Kids*), argues that immigration by people culturally removed from the host country promotes a climate of mistrust that reduces overall social cohesion and undermines the degree of cooperation among natives.[90] This social cohesion, according to Collier, is foundational to the institutions of finance, law, and government that make rich countries successful.

A 2019 survey from the Pew Research Center investigates attitudes toward immigrant assimilation by asking whether respondents agreed: "If America is too open to people from around the world, we risk losing our identity as a nation." Only one-third of Americans agreed with this sentiment. However, there were striking differences across groups. Whites were much more likely to espouse this view (38 percent) than Black (15 percent) or Hispanic (29 percent) respondents, with non-college-educated whites agreeing 44 percent of the time. Fully 42 percent of those aged sixty-five and up were concerned about losing "American identity," compared with only 18 percent of young adults under age thirty. And there were striking partisan differences, with 57 percent of Republicans agreeing versus 11 percent of Democrats. The survey highlights the divergent views among Americans about the desirability of a pluralistic society. For many young adults and Democrats, American identity is itself rooted in openness to immigration — the vast majority of both these groups agreed with the statement: "America's openness to people from all over the world is essential to who we are as a nation."[91]

San Francisco, California, 2009

Elizabeth Wood had just gotten out of the Marine Corps and was staying with her sister in the San Francisco suburb of Concord, California, when she went out alone one night in 2009. She wanted to see some music, and a Sublime cover band was playing at a local bar. A cute guy asked her to dance and offered to buy her a beer. Before she left, Elizabeth gave Marcos Perez her number. He called her the very next day. She fell fast. They saw each other almost every day from their first date on, and within a few months Elizabeth had moved in with Marcos in the apartment he shared with several roommates.

Elizabeth had joined the Army National Guard in 1999, when she was twenty years old, and the Marine Corps five years later. She was deployed to Afghanistan in 2003 and then spent three years stationed in Japan. She loved the Marine Corps—the purpose, the challenge, and the consistently high standards. But as she approached her thirtieth birthday Elizabeth started thinking about her future. She wanted to get married, to be a mom. The military lifestyle wasn't a good match with the future she envisioned for herself.

Elizabeth had grown up in small-town Ohio, and her own family was close. Though she'd introduced herself to Marcos as Elizabeth, growing up everyone called her Betty, and her family all still did. She was the third of four kids, three sisters and a brother. Her mom was a working mom; her dad had a law degree but didn't practice anymore. She saw the way military families spent long periods of time separated from each other. It worked fine for plenty of people, she knew, but it wasn't for her.

In Japan, Elizabeth had been an airframe mechanic on F-18s, leading teams in the paint shop and the toolroom. When she returned from Japan she was stationed for a year in Texas. But soon after she arrived in San Francisco she enrolled in a beauty-school program. "When I got out of the Marine Corps I wanted to do something super girly," she says. "I always liked nails and I had an attention to detail."

From the start, one of the things that Elizabeth found appealing about Marcos was that he was a hard worker. He seemed to never stay still. When he wasn't working, he was working out, and he played soccer in a men's league in the Bay Area. She couldn't even get him to sit down on the couch to watch a movie. Instead, he always wanted to be getting something done, making something or fixing something. When the couple first met, Marcos was working three jobs. He had a carpentry gig during the day. At night he was a busboy and barback at an upscale restaurant. And he knew a guy who called him for odd construction jobs on a regular basis. "He was working a lot; that's what attracted me to him: that he's not lazy, he's a worker," Elizabeth says. "I'm a worker, too, and I've had three jobs at times before, multiple times."

Marcos had been in the Bay Area for twelve years, and he knew the city well. His first date with Elizabeth was at the restaurant where he worked, called Chow. Everything was organic. Elizabeth was amused that the forks and spoons were made out of potatoes. Coincidentally, Elizabeth's sister, Rachel, worked at a different branch of the same restaurant, waiting tables and prepping food, including squeezing fresh juice every morning.

Some of Rachel's friends knew Marcos from work. "He doesn't have papers," Elizabeth's sister told her. "He's in the country illegally."

"No, he's not," Elizabeth protested. He had a driver's license he kept in his wallet. Elizabeth had seen it.

"Yeah. It's like that in California," Rachel said.

"He has ID," Elizabeth said.

"Everybody has ID," her sister told her.

Elizabeth brushed it off. She thought her sister was just being crabby. And what did it matter anyway? Marcos was always working. He obviously had no problem finding jobs. It didn't seem to Elizabeth that there was anything he couldn't do.

License to Drive

Though the ID that Marcos Perez kept in his wallet in 2009 would not have been a valid California driver's license, as of early 2021 sixteen states and the District of Columbia have laws on the books that allow undocumented immigrants to get a driver's license. These states — California, Colorado, Connecticut, Delaware, Hawaii, Illinois, Maryland, Nevada, New Jersey, New Mexico, New York, Oregon, Utah, Vermont, Virginia, and Washington State — are home to more than half of the country's unauthorized immigrant population.[92] Seven of those states, including California, Colorado, and Illinois, passed their current driver's-license laws in 2013; Delaware and Hawaii enacted their laws in 2015; New York, New Jersey, and Oregon all adopted legislation that would allow undocumented immigrants to get driver's licenses in 2019, in part in response to growing awareness that minor traffic violations were resulting in deportation for many immigrant community members. Virginia passed a license law in 2020.

Issuing driver's licenses is a state function under the Tenth Amendment to the Constitution, and over the past decade there's been a groundswell of state-level support for legalizing undocumented drivers. The federal REAL ID Act of 2005 explicitly gave states the authority to issue licenses to unauthorized immigrants, though the law requires those licenses be visually distinct from typical ones (REAL ID's primary purpose was to combat terrorism by creating national standards for state licenses because these licenses are frequently used for federal identification for things like air travel and entry into government buildings).[93]

State-level battles over licenses for unauthorized immigrants have been fought hard and repeatedly in many places. Oregon also enacted a driver's-license law in 2013; in 2014, 67 percent of voters in that state supported a ballot measure that rescinded it; in mid-2019 Oregon passed a new law that re-established immigrant licenses. Before the 2013 wave of new license laws, just two states issued driver's licenses to undocumented immigrants: New Mexico has had such a law on the books since 2003, Washington State since 1993. (Utah offered a more limited "driving privilege card.")[94]

There are several arguments in favor of expanding license privileges. The first is economic. The United States is one of the most car-dependent countries in the world and lack of transportation can be a significant impediment to job mobility and advancement. "People who drive are more likely to find jobs, work more hours, and earn higher wages," sociologist Sarah E. Hendricks writes in *Living in Car Culture without a License*,[95] a 2014 report from the Immigration Policy Center, the policy arm of the pro-immigrant American Immigration Council. An undocumented immigrant who works at a fast-food restaurant may have to decline a promotion if they rely on a coworker with a car to get to and from the job. A nanny or housekeeper may have to refuse a better-paying opportunity that is not near a public bus route. A young college graduate with a temporary work permit provided through DACA (Deferred Action for Childhood Arrivals), President Obama's 2012 executive action for young immigrants brought to the US as kids, may have to turn down a professional position that isn't accessible by bus or subway. (Whether DACA recipients should be eligible for driver's licenses was the subject of court cases in the aftermath of Obama's 2012 executive order that established the program; though Arizona and Nebraska initially denied driver's licenses to DACA recipients, all states allow DACA recipients to become licensed drivers as of mid-2020).[96]

"[W]orkers with cars tend to make more money than those who commute by other means," Hendricks writes, "and lack of access to transportation may constrain upward economic mobility and contribute to the perpetuation of poverty." Lack of car access has also been shown to prevent immigrants from attending community college classes, from participating in events at their children's schools, from enrolling preschool-age children in early childhood education programs, and from taking advantage of preventive healthcare services that can reduce costly emergency room visits.

Of course, undocumented immigrants in many states regularly risk steep fines and criminal penalty — even deportation — by driving without a license. Many treat driving as an essentials-only activity, commuting to work and school and driving to the grocery store and doctor when necessary but avoiding optional outings as much as possible. One of the strongest arguments, especially among nonimmigrants, in favor of expanding the pool of people eligible for driver's licenses is safety. To get a driver's license for the first time you generally must pass both written and road tests. Licensed drivers are also required to show proof of insurance in almost all states, though critics of new driver's-license laws have pointed out that immigrants could cancel their insurance policies once their license is in hand.[97] It's often possible for undocumented immigrants without a license to buy car insurance, though it's also possible that the insurance company will refuse to pay out when that insured-but-unlicensed driver is in an accident.

The reality is that the majority of unlicensed drivers are uninsured, and when an unlicensed driver is involved in a car crash, the cost burden falls solely on the insured, licensed driver. Most undocumented immigrants work in low-wage jobs; their cars are likely to be older and more accident-prone than the average. Several studies have documented unlicensed drivers' increased risk of fleeing the scene of an accident. The high rate of hit-and-runs in many immigrant-dense communities can be tied to the reality that even a fender-bender can lead to deportation for an undocumented immigrant.

A case in point is the experience of Jesus Leza Lopez, an undocumented Wisconsin dairy worker who brought his family to the US from Mexico more than twenty years ago. When he first moved to Wisconsin, Leza Lopez was able to get a driver's license. But then the state passed a law that required drivers to have a social security number. By 2012, when Leza Lopez was involved in a minor accident near his home in Green Bay, he was driving without a license — something he did every day to get to and from his job feeding and caring for veal calves. (Forty percent of the workers in Wisconsin's $43 billion dairy industry are immigrants, the vast majority of them Mexican, according to a 2008 University of Wisconsin study.) Leza Lopez feared that if he called the police to report the accident he would be deported. He panicked and drove away. And he officially became a criminal: the violator in a hit-and-run.[98]

Within an hour, though, Leza Lopez had a change of heart, called the local police, and turned himself in. No one was injured in the accident, and because the judge didn't consider Leza Lopez a public risk, he didn't serve jail time. He was charged with a felony and placed on probation. But because the local Green Bay police department cooperates closely with federal Immigration and Custom Enforcement (ICE), "they had him on the list," says his daughter Marisa, who was twenty-two at the time of her father's arrest, and just four years old when her family crossed the border illegally in 1997. "There's no driver's licenses here for undocumented people. There's no way to get identification. The first instinct he had was to run away."

Two years later, in March 2014, ICE unexpectedly showed up in the driveway of the Green Bay duplex where Leza Lopez's family had lived for seven years. "It was a raid. They blocked the whole street," Marisa says. "They could have taken my mom, too. But for some reason they didn't." Leza Lopez and one of Marisa's three brothers were arrested and put on a plane. Back in his hometown of Saltillo, Mexico, Leza Lopez soon found odd, part-time farm jobs. But they paid only a half to a third what he was making in Wisconsin, Marisa says, and the work was hard to find.

Public safety was the leading justification for California's driver's-license law, Assembly Bill 60 (AB 60), which was signed by then-governor Jerry Brown in October 2013 and which went into effect in January 2015. The bill's author argued that the law would allow undocumented immigrants already driving illegally to become properly trained and insured. A 2012 study conducted by the California Department of Motor Vehicles found that unlicensed drivers are three times more likely than licensed drivers to cause fatal car crashes — though that study was considering all unlicensed drivers, including people who have had their licenses suspended or revoked, not just undocumented immigrants.[99] As in other states, California's licenses for unauthorized immigrants are visually distinct from the state's regular licenses, and are intended to be used for state driving privileges only, not as an official form of identification. AB 60 had wide support in California, which during Brown's tenure became a poster child for immigrant-friendly state policies. The Los Angeles police chief at the time, Charlie Beck, stated that the number of hit-and-run accidents would decrease as a result of AB 60.

In terms of uptake, the California law was an immediate success. Close to four hundred thousand licenses were issued in the first six months after the bill went into effect on January 1, 2015. By the end of 2016, 806,000 new driver's licenses had been issued to undocumented Californians. "It's a completely different feeling because you no longer have to worry about seeing a police car," a 46-year-old San Jose driver, who asked to be identified only by his first name, Ramon, told the *Mercury News* in December 2016. "You're much more at peace when you drive. You can drive long distances with your family — to Disneyland or to the Monterey Bay Aquarium — with confidence. You don't live in fear."[100]

To immigrant advocates, the numbers speak to these laws' astounding success. In California alone, hundreds of thousands of people are better-trained and better-insured drivers. Hundreds of thousands more people have better job mobility, easier access to healthcare, more transportation options to get their kids to the doctor, to preschool, to open-house night at school, or to community college. They have better access to a wide range of resources, and as a result are more likely to engage and participate in the wider community.

To critics, that's exactly the problem. There's little doubt that driver's-license laws make living—and making a living—in the US easier for immigrants who entered the country illegally. They also make it easier for immigrants to compete with American citizens for jobs. They make it more likely that undocumented people will use health and educational resources that are legally available to them. And they do send a mixed message to immigrant families, as David Seminara, a fellow at the conservative Center for Immigration Studies, has pointed out. "If the state takes their photo and hands them an official-looking card, that gives them a feeling of legitimacy and no doubt confirms their impression that the United States isn't serious about enforcing immigration laws," he wrote in an op-ed on the Center's website in 2014.[101] That impression, in turn, may serve as a magnet drawing more immigrants into a country that they expect to allow them to function much as legal residents do.

San Francisco, California, 2009

Marcos and Elizabeth had been together less than six months when Elizabeth got pregnant. There was never any question in her mind that she and Marcos would raise their baby together. But California was so expensive. The couple had started looking for their own apartment. It was 2009, and the tiniest one-bedroom they could find was about $900 a month. As her pregnancy progressed Elizabeth quit her nail-salon job. The fumes were making her nausea worse. They were living off Marcos's salary, and even with him working three jobs it didn't seem like it'd be enough for them to get their own place and support a baby.

Plus, Elizabeth felt like she wanted to experience her first pregnancy with family close by. She knew they could rent an apartment in Cleveland equivalent to what they'd seen in San Francisco for half the price.

Marcos had a daughter from a previous relationship. She was twelve and lived nearby with her mom. Marcos had a problematic history with his ex. They'd fought when they were together, and at least once his ex had called the cops. Another time Marcos had been arrested following a bar fight. To Elizabeth, it seemed like fairly normal stuff, and, besides, it had happened years ago. She knew Marcos was on decent terms with his ex now, and she knew he was troubled by the idea of moving so far away from his daughter.

But he also wanted to make the right choice for his new family. They packed up Elizabeth's car and headed east. When they reached Ohio, the couple crashed with Elizabeth's brother for a few weeks until they found a place—a single-family house in the Cleveland suburb of Mayfield Heights, a town close to the one where Elizabeth had grown up, and where her parents still lived. The rent on the two-bedroom, single-story home was $650 a month. It was private, in a nice neighborhood, with a huge backyard. To Elizabeth, it seemed like a perfect place to start a family.

But from the start Marcos had a hard time finding work. He'd first come to the US almost seventeen years before, in 1993. He was encouraged by a brother who was living in San Diego at the time. The journey wasn't too difficult. Marcos put plastic bags over his boots and waded across a small river and toward the mountains on the US side of the border. "The mountains where we cross were totally free, no immigration, no people, nothing," he remembers. For several years Marcos lived in San Diego with his brother. He returned to Mexico a couple times, once crossing back near Imperial Beach, a surfing community that borders Tijuana. But when he decided to come back for what ended up being the final time, the crossing was much harder. It took several attempts—almost a month of waiting and trying. Then he was in a group of nearly sixty people, mostly men, with a handful of women, walking for almost three days across the desert. There was one young woman who had terrible shoes. She had to take them off and walk barefoot. Then she had blisters covering her feet, and she said she couldn't walk anymore.

"The people who we call coyotes, the people who take you to cross, they want to leave the girl right there in the desert," Marcos recalls. She was 300 yards behind when Marcos turned around. "I'm going to help you," he told her. "I carry her like a mile and a half. I feel like Superman, really strong." (Known deaths of migrants crossing the desert borderlands over the past two decades range from an annual low of 249 in 1999 to a high of 492 in 2005. Dehydration, heatstroke, and hypothermia are common contributors.)[102]

The group met a van, were packed in impossibly tightly — one body pressed against the next — and were dropped off a couple hours later in what Marcos thinks was Tucson, Arizona. For Marcos it was the last time, the last crossing. "We leave this girl and that was really powerful for me," he says. "You know what, we make it. We make it. But it was really hard, it was super hard the last time."

Over the years Marcos had worked in a wide variety of jobs in California: landscaping, roofing, restaurants, construction. He'd rarely had trouble finding work. But things were different in Ohio. He filled out an application at the Cheesecake Factory, listing his extensive restaurant experience. No call back. Day after day he went out looking for work, talking to managers and filling out applications. He felt like people who didn't even know him were treating him like they were angry with him. Police officers eyed him like they hated him. "There's a lot of discrimination, a lot of racism here," Marcos told Elizabeth. "God, you're so paranoid," Elizabeth scolded her boyfriend. "Chill out."

Elizabeth's dad made a living with carpentry work, and Marcos started helping him out when he needed it. Elizabeth's family liked Marcos right away. But the work with Elizabeth's dad wasn't steady, nothing that would reliably pay the rent and bills. Finally, Marcos got a job at a local Chipotle restaurant. Elizabeth never asked him what social security number he used to fill out his paperwork, or whether he put one down at all. She didn't even think about it, really. "I didn't want to know, I guess. I just wanted to pretend like we were normal." She hadn't told her family about Marcos's immigration status. She didn't see it as something she was intentionally hiding; it just didn't come up. It didn't seem that important to her. She figured that once they were settled they'd figure out the paperwork and get everything straightened out. "We're having a baby, we're together, this should be an easy fix," she says of her thinking at the time. "We give a lawyer money, it's not a big deal."

PART TWO

ARRESTS

Lorain, Ohio, 2013

Anabel Barron was running late. It was the morning of Friday, May 17, 2013, and the thirty-two-year-old mother of four had dropped her kids off at school before heading to work at the hockey camp in the Cleveland suburbs. She saw the waiting police car just as she crossed the line from her lakeside community of Lorain, Ohio, into a neighboring town. The posted speed limit decreased from thirty-five to twenty-five miles per hour, but Anabel had not slowed down. Her heart rose into her throat as she saw the lights begin to flash. She gripped the wheel and pulled to the shoulder. Anabel knew that being late for work — or paying a traffic ticket — was the least of her problems. She assumed that there was a computer record of her illegal reentry and removal order from when she'd returned to Mexico after her mother died in 2001.

Though Anabel had lived in Lorain for more than fifteen years, and in the US much longer, she didn't have a driver's license. (As mentioned earlier, a handful of states had started allowing undocumented immigrants to obtain driver's licenses by 2013; Ohio was not among them.) Her ten-year-old Ford Escape was registered in a friend's name. She was petrified about what would happen next. She knew people — local parents with young children, individuals who had been in the US for decades — who had been deported in recent years. Some of them had nothing on their records except for one minor traffic violation.

When Anabel couldn't produce a driver's license, the cop said she had no choice but to call her chief. "I've been here in Ohio for years,"

Anabel pleaded. "I have four kids who are US citizens." When the police chief arrived a half hour later, he offered Anabel two options: "We need to verify your legal status to be in this country," he said. "You can either go to your house and wait for Immigration or you can wait here for them."

Tears were streaming down Anabel's face. It was still morning; her kids were at school. But maybe ICE wouldn't arrive at her house until afternoon, and her children — the eldest was then fifteen, the youngest just five — would have to watch her being dragged away. She said she'd wait. "I was thinking they're going to send me to Mexico," Anabel recalls. "I started making phone calls to my friends, letting them know."

She called a woman she knew who volunteered for a local immigrant-rights group. Maybe they could help. She called her sister and asked her to meet the kids after school, and to take care of them if she didn't come home. Then Anabel erased all her messages; she didn't want to get any of her friends in trouble if the ICE agents examined her phone.

By noon, the white SUV pulled up. The agents treated her more kindly than she'd expected. She was never handcuffed, and after she told them about her children, the agents let her keep her phone, so that she could make arrangements. "I understand what I did. I know I'm not supposed to be here," she tried to explain to them. "But I'm in love with this country! And I'm worried about my kids." The two agents drove Anabel to a detention center over an hour away, where she was interrogated and fingerprinted. As she expected, the prints turned up a match in the computer system, a record of an arrest for illegally crossing the border more than a decade before.

A Brief History of Border Control

Attempts at controlling immigration date back as far as the first immigration laws in the late 1800s. Early immigration inspectors didn't aim to curb immigration of healthy European migrants, but rather to collect information about — and a small tax from — arriving passengers at Ellis Island and other major ports of entry. Enforcement was self-funded in the sense that the entry taxes collected supported all other enforcement efforts. Steamship companies were responsible for ferrying denied immigrants home, so they had incentive to conduct substantial screening for health issues before the beginning of the voyage. Other than Asians, who faced tighter restrictions, only a handful of immigrants were denied at the ports — namely those deemed to be criminals, contract laborers, paupers, or diseased.

The emerging enforcement regime at the ports in the 1880s did encourage some migrants to attempt surreptitious land border crossings. These included some European migrants who feared being turned away. For Chinese migrants excluded under the earliest immigration laws in the 1870s and 1880s, smuggling rings were particularly important. Smugglers helped individuals or small groups of immigrants cross the border from Canada to the United States, and shepherded them to existing northwest communities of Chinese Americans where they could blend in and pass as locals.[1] By the 1890s smuggling routes through Mexico had also been established. There were reported to be 150 trails through the hilly terrain near San Diego alone, and monitoring them was beyond the capacity of immigration inspectors.

As early as 1891, inspectors were testifying that they needed more manpower and equipment to address border "leak." By law, Chinese migrants caught at the border were to be returned to the Canadian or Mexican side rather than to China, providing an opportunity for attempted reentry. Much of the enforcement responsibility fell on customs officials who had little interest in controlling immigration. Though some smuggling operations were interrupted by the surveillance efforts of American officials, border enforcement played second fiddle to port inspections and was largely ineffective. During this time the border was more of a "social fiction," as historian Patrick Ettinger notes, than an actual demarcation of a state-controlled boundary.[2]

Like those arriving in the ports, Western Hemisphere migrants arriving by land were required to obtain an immigration visa. Doing so involved a perfunctory health screening, an eight-dollar entry tax, and a loosely enforced literacy test. Immigrants could be denied for "pauperism"; in practice, the use of this category varied based on labor needs in the American Southwest. In any case, the inspection process was often circumvented. Immigrants who could present themselves as temporary or local were waved past inspection points; others entered via smuggling routes. The lack of official status—in that era documented by a receipt for the entry tax—made Mexican immigrants vulnerable when attitudes later changed.

It wasn't until 1924 that the US Border Patrol was formed. In the lead-up to the formation of the new agency, officials acknowledged that fully eliminating illegal entry was impossible; the goal was simply to reduce the numbers. Increased border control during the 1920s and 1930s caused Mexicans living in California to shift from a pattern of cyclical migration across the porous border to permanent settlement, a pattern that has resurfaced with the twenty-first-century expansion of border security.[3]

With the onset of World War II and an increased need for workers, Mexican migration was facilitated by the Bracero program. The 1942 agreement between Mexico and the United States allowed Mexicans to work in the US on short contracts of up to eighteen months. It seemed like a win-win: The US could access cheap labor for agriculture and railroads, and Mexico could stem the permanent out-migration that it viewed as detrimental to its economic growth. Over the two decades of the Bracero program, 4.6 million contracts were signed, with nearly five hundred thousand Mexicans working in the United States at the program's height in the mid-1950s.[4] Of the total four or five million workers who came to the United States as *braceros*—literally, those who work with their arms—it's estimated that hundreds of thousands stayed permanently.[5]

The program didn't eliminate unauthorized border crossings. Though the US agreed to secure the border as part of the Bracero deal, in reality it did little to curtail migration during the early years of the program, and unauthorized migration was widespread. In fact, undocumented migration was likely facilitated by the institutional structure and social networks emerging from the Bracero program itself. (This concern is echoed in the more recent era; expanded legal migration in the 1970s may have paradoxically *increased* the undocumented population, though evidence on this point is mixed.) The Mexican government grew so frustrated with the lack of border control that it sent five thousand troops to secure the border in 1954.

The same year, in response to pressure from the Mexican government and public anti-Mexican sentiment, the US government launched Operation Wetback. (The term "wetback" is a highly pejorative slur for Mexicans in the United States; it refers to the stereotype that they arrived by wading across the Rio Grande.) Border Patrol mobilized 750 officers to arrest Mexicans in US cities and border areas, who were then turned over to Mexican officials. The Mexican government relocated the migrants to areas of high labor demand deep within Mexico. The operation involved at least three hundred thousand deportations (though the US claimed it was a much higher figure), a remarkable number considering there were fewer than seven hundred thousand Mexican-born US residents recorded in the 1950 census.[6] Operation Wetback set the stage for large-scale, military-style border operations in subsequent decades.

Despite enforcement efforts, significant immigration flows persisted across the southern border; these flows continued in the decades following the 1965 Hart-Cellar Act, which ended the old quota system for immigration. Though reliable estimates of the unauthorized population are hard to come by for this time period, the Immigration and Naturalization Service (INS)—the precursor to today's Customs and Border Protection (CBP)—reported a total of thirteen million official returns (turning people back at the border) and removals (deportations) between 1966 and 1985.[7] By the mid-1980s there were an estimated four million undocumented residents of the United States—and widespread calls to address the issue.

Painesville, Ohio, 2013

Eduardo Lopez was on his way to work on a Wednesday evening in September 2013 when he came to a construction roadblock. There was a sign that read "Local Traffic Only." The factory where he'd been working for the past dozen years was just a couple miles down the road, so Eduardo continued on. A minute later there was a cop behind him, lights flashing. Eduardo pulled to the shoulder and the officer came up to the open window of Eduardo's ten-year-old minivan.

"You know why I pulled you over, right?"

"I work right down here," Eduardo said.

"Okay. Driver's license," the cop said.

Eduardo didn't have one. He handed over a fifteen-year-old Mexican ID.

The officer was back in the patrol car for a just a few minutes before walking back and opening Eduardo's door. "You're under arrest," he said.

Eduardo was brought to the local police station, where a different officer took his picture and fingerprints. They ran his prints through the computer.

"Man, you look so familiar," the officer said to him. "Did you do something wrong before?"

"No, sir."

"Why do you still look familiar?" He kept repeating the question.

"Well, Officer, you want me to tell you why I look familiar to you?"

"Yeah."

"You know the store, the Circle K?"

"Yeah."

"Well, you stop there Mondays, Wednesdays, and Fridays and buy a French vanilla coffee."

"Yeah! The big guy!" the officer said with a smile.

Eduardo regularly stopped at the same convenience store at the same time to buy either an iced tea or a Monster energy drink on his way home from work. The officer was always either right in front of or behind him in line, and they'd often make small talk about the day. At that time, unlike now, Eduardo realized, he'd be in his work uniform, khaki-colored long pants and a long-sleeved shirt that hid his tattoos, which included inked portraits of his young kids.

Eduardo watched the local cop's expression change: "I'm sorry, man. I already called Immigration."

A History of Interior Enforcement

There are several policy tools used in an attempt to reduce the number of unauthorized immigrants in the United States: those that make it more difficult to cross the border, those that make it more likely that a migrant already living in the United States will be deported, and those that make it less appealing to live or work in the US. Reducing flows of unauthorized immigrants over the border has long dominated both public conversation and government resources. But in a country that has over a million (mostly lawful) land border crossings *per day*, the task of fully securing the border is virtually impossible.[8] And as border control has tightened, an increasing proportion of unauthorized immigrants arrive legally by air or sea and overstay their visas. Interior enforcement is therefore a growing part of the effort to reduce the number of undocumented immigrants.

Significant interior enforcement actions are far from new, however—and historical events have some striking similarities to current policies. Though some small-scale raids occurred earlier, the Depression era witnessed the first internal enforcement on a mass scale. Economic conditions were terrible, and there was widespread concern that Mexicans were taking American jobs and burdening relief agencies. At the time, about 4 percent of US residents were born in Mexico, according to census records, and many lacked documentation that they had paid the required border tax.

President Franklin Delano Roosevelt established the Immigration and Naturalization Service (INS) in 1933. The INS eventually undertook responsibility for the internment of Japanese Americans during World War II, removed hundreds of thousands of Mexicans under Operation Wetback in the 1950s, and remained the federal agency responsible for immigration enforcement until 2003. But in the 1930s the federal enforcement infrastructure was limited. Local governments and independent organizations took matters into their own hands.

The era known as Mexican Repatriation began around 1929. An estimated four hundred thousand to one million Mexicans and US-born Americans of Mexican descent left the United States in the subsequent decade.[9] Most of these departures were not formal deportations by the federal government, but instead voluntary and coerced exits at the local level. Los Angeles was known for particularly aggressive efforts and was the main site of federal cooperation. Foreshadowing modern-day calls for "self-deportation," Los Angeles District Immigration Director Walter Carr stated that "a large number of these aliens, actuated by guilty self-consciousness, would move south and over the line of their own accord, particularly if stimulated by a few arrests under the Deportation Act."[10]

A significant number of those people who relocated during this episode in the 1930s were in fact US citizens of Mexican descent. After all, the 1848 Treaty of Guadalupe Hidalgo had only been signed a few generations before; prior to that, most of the US Southwest had been part of Mexico. Estimates suggest that perhaps half of those who moved or were moved to Mexico in the 1930s were born in the United States.

The Depression-era scapegoating was more about ethnicity than about legal status. A 2006 USA Today interview with a survivor of one such exile gives an account:

> His father and oldest sister were farming sugar beets in the fields of Hamilton, Mont., and his mother was cooking tortillas when 6-year-old Ignacio Piña saw plainclothes authorities burst into his home. "They came in with guns and told us to get out," recalls Piña, 81, a retired railroad worker in Bakersfield, Calif., of the 1931 raid. "They didn't let us take anything," not even a trunk that held birth certificates proving that he and his five siblings were US-born citizens. The family was thrown into a jail for ten days before being sent by train to Mexico. Piña says he spent 16 years of "pure hell" there before acquiring papers of his Utah birth and returning to the USA.[11]

The 1986 Immigration Reform and Control Act

The modern enforcement era began in 1986, when Congress passed the Immigration Reform and Control Act (IRCA), the most impactful piece of immigration-related legislation since the 1960s. IRCA had three main components. First, it made it illegal to hire unauthorized workers, which had previously not been the case. Employers could now incur civil fines for violations or face criminal penalties if they showed a "pattern or practice" of knowingly hiring or recruiting the unauthorized. The goal was to reduce job opportunities in the United States, thereby making it a less appealing destination for would-be migrants.

Second, the 1986 act increased border control efforts, calling for a 50 percent increase in border personnel relative to 1986 levels.[12] Though border spending increased at a slower pace than envisaged by the bill, it had doubled within a decade of the law's passage. It was hoped that by reducing the chances of successful surreptitious entry into the country, immigrants might not make the effort.

Finally, IRCA granted amnesty to 2.7 million of the estimated 3 to 5 million undocumented immigrants living in the country in 1986 (the legislation would come to be known by the shorthand "Reagan's amnesty"). To receive temporary legal status under IRCA's primary legalization program, immigrants needed to have lived in the US continuously since before 1982, have no felony record and fewer than three prior misdemeanors, and apply for a status change within a year of the law's passage. (Researchers have found that the documents showing an immigrant had lived in the United States continuously since 1982 were not carefully scrutinized, and a significant number of those legalized under IRCA had migrated back and forth over the prior several years or were new arrivals.)[13] The temporary status could be converted to permanent-resident status after immigrants demonstrated basic citizenship skills. Framed as a one-time fix, the amnesty recognized the humanitarian cost of interior enforcement while provisions of the full IRCA bill attempted to signal that the government would be less lenient in the future.

IRCA offered hope of a clean slate for the problem of illegal immigration. It sought to integrate those with unlawful status into the mainstream, eliminate job opportunities for new undocumented migrants, and secure the border. The goal was to drastically reduce the level of unauthorized migration, and by that measure it has been judged a clear failure.

In theory, when hiring the undocumented became illegal, job opportunities would dry up, and fewer migrants would want to come to the United States. However, according to a 2014 report by the Migration Policy Institute, employer sanctions were not realistic given the state of technology at the time. Employers had no way to verify information submitted by workers and therefore had plausible deniability regarding the immigration status of those they hired.[14]

After IRCA was enacted, there were some efforts to audit employers.

In 1990 there were almost ten thousand audits and approximately a thousand fines levied.[15] But at this level there was only a tiny chance of one of the country's millions of employers facing a penalty, and the numbers of employers facing fines subsequently decreased throughout the 1990s. The dollar value of fines peaked in the mid-1990s at just over $3 million for all firms combined. A report by the US General Accounting Office found that just 2 percent of all INS enforcement hours were directed to worksite sanctions.[16]

Even if the risk to employers was low, a 1988 government survey found 65 percent of employers complying with basic identity verification requirements.[17] The same survey found 10 percent of employers reporting that IRCA caused them to engage in discriminatory illegal acts — avoiding hiring workers with a foreign appearance or accent, or conducting identity verification only for those workers whose physical appearance led the employer to guess they might be undocumented. The law did have some adverse impact on work opportunities for unauthorized workers in the short run, but it by no means eliminated them.

The second leg of IRCA's "three-legged stool," increased border enforcement, was also a disappointment. More aggressive border security couldn't be implemented overnight. Between 1985 and 1990, border spending increased from $700 million to $918 million annually, a more modest change than the immediate 50 percent increase that had been authorized in the law.[18]

While IRCA certainly had a positive effect on the lives of millions of immigrants who were previously living in the country illegally, for the broader public, the law did not satisfactorily address the issue of illegal immigration. By the mid-1990s, there was a renewed outcry, stemming in large part from the fact that undocumented immigrants kept arriving. By the mid-1990s, the number of unauthorized immigrants had returned to and then exceeded the level from before the 1986 amnesty had passed, with estimates suggesting over five million unauthorized immigrants in 1995. Newly legalized immigrants may in fact have facilitated the migration of undocumented friends and relatives, though recent research does not support this proposition.[19] Regardless of the root causes, there were twelve million undocumented residents living in the United States by the mid-2000s.

IRCA and the Earnings of Immigrants

For immigrants themselves, IRCA was a great step forward: Almost 1.6 million undocumented individuals were converted to legal status through IRCA's general provisions, and almost 1.1 million more were legalized under IRCA's special program for agricultural workers, according to Migration Policy Institute calculations. The status of a small number of Cuban and Haitian immigrants was also normalized.[20] About 90 percent of those who applied were granted permanent residence; in most cases prior to 1993.[21] Though estimates vary, it's believed that two-thirds or more of all undocumented immigrants living in the United States when the law passed in 1986 adjusted to legal status as the result of IRCA.

Multiple studies have shown that legal status can make a substantial difference to immigrant earning power, especially in high-enforcement regimes. Legal workers are more easily able to secure employment in the formal sector, which tends to have better pay, benefits, and working conditions. In addition, documented immigrants are better able to negotiate for pay increases and to complain about working conditions without fear that their employer will use their status as a bargaining chip against them.

It is difficult to precisely quantify the benefits of legal status because immigrants with status tend to be different in multiple ways from those without, so the two groups likely would have different wages regardless of status. But so-called natural experiments like IRCA can help facilitate such comparisons.

In a 2015 paper, Miao Chi, a professor at Drew University, came up with a creative way to measure the impact of legalization on employment.[22] Using the 1990 census, she examines recently arrived Mexican men married to US citizens; these men are likely to obtain legal status by virtue of their marriage. Chi finds that marrying a US citizen is associated with much higher earnings for these recent arrivals. But it's possible these marriages are more common among those who are more educated, have better English-language skills, or who were excelling in their careers. In other words, perhaps men who marry US citizens would have had higher earnings than the typical unauthorized immigrant even in the absence of legal status. So, Chi also examines similar men who arrived earlier and therefore were likely granted legal status through the 1986 amnesty—in other words, men for whom marrying a US citizen is unlikely to matter. For the group arriving prior to IRCA, men who marry US citizens do not fare any better in the labor market than men who do not. In the end, Chi concludes that legal status confers an earnings premium of 35 percent. Other estimates suggest more modest benefits. Ying Pan of Louisiana State University compares immigrants in California who arrived just before and after the cutoff for IRCA's amnesty; she finds a 4 percent boost in wages for men due to IRCA eligibility.[23]

Some researchers have also looked at the flip side of the coin: the effect of IRCA employer sanctions on earnings. Cynthia Bansak and Steven Raphael, economists at the Federal Reserve and the University of California, Berkeley, find that Latino workers experienced wage declines in the nonagricultural sectors that were immediately targeted by IRCA.[24] Using data collected in Mexico on migrant families, sociologists Julie Anne Phillips of Rutgers and Doug Massey of Princeton also find that things got worse in the labor market for unauthorized immigrants after IRCA.[25] Even if the risks to employers in hiring undocumented immigrants were small post-IRCA, many employers complied with identity verification requirements.[26] In the short run, IRCA made newly arriving unauthorized immigrants worse off.

One interesting study by Matthew Freedman and Emily Owens, researchers at the University of California, Irvine; and Sarah Bohn, a researcher at the Public Policy Institute of California, investigated the downstream effects of IRCA-related hardship for unauthorized immigrants.[27] The research focused on San Antonio, Texas, and showed increases in drug-related criminal charges among likely unauthorized, newly arrived immigrants after IRCA relative to before IRCA. The researchers argue that worsening job opportunities led this group to turn to illegal sources of income generation. Even though, as we discuss in part 3, immigrants have lower crime rates than the general population, the availability of work opportunities makes a difference.

Mayfield Heights, Ohio, 2010

Marcos Perez wanted to name the baby Pelé, after the Brazilian soccer superstar. He and his girlfriend Elizabeth had settled into their modest rental home in the Cleveland suburbs by the time the baby boy was born in January 2010. They were planning a July baptism, with a party afterward. Marcos thought he'd formally propose to Elizabeth then, where she'd be surrounded by family.

They'd gone to see a lawyer soon after they'd arrived in Ohio from San Francisco, where they had met. The lawyer told them that they'd need to use the Freedom of Information Act (FOIA) to request background government records on Marcos. He'd been apprehended crossing the border years before and also had a couple misdemeanors, he knew, though he was unsure what details would be in his files. The fee would be $2,500, they were told. Elizabeth assumed that $2,500 would take care of the whole case; they'd get Marcos's background, file some paperwork, and everything would be good. She later realized that the $2,500 was a fee the lawyer was charging just for the FOIA request, a request that is free to make as a private citizen or journalist.

When Pelé was born, Marcos and Elizabeth were waiting to hear back from the lawyer. The autumn before, Elizabeth had enrolled at a local college. She was working toward her BA, with a major in social work. The GI Bill covered her tuition and she had some student loans and grants that were helping with monthly expenses. Elizabeth didn't go back to school the winter that Pelé was born; she'd be consumed with caring for the newborn baby. Marcos, though, had left his job at Chipotle and started a new, better job at a cleaning company.

Again, he didn't discuss the details of his application with Elizabeth. And she didn't ask. "It's not like it bothers me, because he has to do what he has to do," she says. Though the workers at the cleaning company were mostly African American, the operation was owned by a Mexican guy. After just a couple months, there was already talk of Marcos getting a promotion. His boss had brought up the possibility of Marcos supervising his own crew and becoming a manager himself in short order.

Elizabeth was relieved that it seemed like Marcos finally had a stable

job, with growth potential and hope for a rising salary. But she was living in the fog of early motherhood, her mind consumed with the baby.
She was tired, of course. And then soon she started feeling sick as well.
Pelé was only four months old when she took another pregnancy test.
She was expecting a positive result, and she got it. She downplayed the
test result to Marcos. Yeah, she'd been feeling weird. But maybe it was
just the hormones from the baby, from breastfeeding. She was making
a doctor's appointment to check things out, she told him — just in case.

Marcos had already arrived home from a morning of carpentry work
with Elizabeth's dad when she got back from Planned Parenthood. The
clinic visit had confirmed what Elizabeth already knew: She was pregnant again. Maybe they should go back to California, Marcos suggested. Living — and working — in Ohio was harder than he'd expected.
In California, there would be enough work. Things would be easier.

But to Elizabeth, another baby was another reason to stay close to
family. They'd need the extra help even more. Marcos had to be at his
cleaning job at 5:00 p.m.; he left the house with the debate very much
unresolved. After he was gone, Elizabeth took baby Pelé in the bedroom with her and they both quickly fell asleep.

Marcos was driving Elizabeth's car, a 2002 Mitsubishi Gallant, when
he was pulled over just a couple blocks from their home. "This guy see
me, I'm Latino, right away he stops me for no reason and start telling
me I didn't stop on the red light," Marcos says. The ringing woke Elizabeth up.

"Who is Marcos Perez?" the officer said.

"What happened? Is he OK?" Elizabeth asked.

"What's his social security number?"

"I don't know," Elizabeth said. "I don't know."

The cop told Elizabeth that if he couldn't identify Marcos, he'd have
to call ICE.

"Sir, you don't need to do that," Elizabeth pleaded. She tried to stay
calm and remain respectful. She knew how to talk to people in authority from her time in the Marine Corps.

"Oh, yes I do," Elizabeth recalls his response. The officer sounded
angry. "ICE will be able to identify him for us," he told her.

Then Elizabeth's phone battery died. She felt her heart drop as the reality sunk in. *Shit. Oh, shit*, she thought to herself. *What the hell is going on?*

Pelé was still sleeping. Elizabeth bundled the baby up, put him in the stroller, and, with her car gone, started walking toward the local police station. Before she left the house, she grabbed a letter from a new lawyer she and Marcos were considering hiring, a replacement for the guy who'd hit them with the $2,500 bill for a FOIA request. "I thought I'd give them this letter like, yeah, we're working with an immigration lawyer right now—he has a lawyer!—and they would just let him go," she says several years later. "That's where my mind was."

Instead, when Elizabeth showed the local police officers the letter, they accepted it as proof that Marcos was in the country illegally. The officers made little attempt to hide the motivation behind the stop. When Elizabeth's dad showed up at the police station, one of the officers—not realizing that he was a relative—openly told him that Marcos had been stopped because he looked like he didn't have papers.

Elizabeth called the lawyer they had recently met with, who advised her not to pay bail. The longer Marcos stayed in the local jail the longer they would have to develop a strategy. Marcos begged Elizabeth to try to come up with the money; after just a couple of days, staying in the cell was driving him crazy.

For the next week and a half, Elizabeth and her dad each visited Marcos every day. It was just a couple of cells in the local station, but there was a little visiting area where Marcos and Elizabeth could sit across from each other and talk through the glass. Every morning and every night she wrote Marcos letters; in the morning, she drove to the jail to drop them off. It was a little thing she thought would help to keep his mind occupied.

On the twelfth day Elizabeth was sitting on a bench in the police station, waiting for permission to visit Marcos and trying to console a fussy baby, when one of the cops told her to stand up and look out the window. A white ICE van was pulling out of the parking lot.

"He's in that van," the officer told Elizabeth. She thought he sounded pleased with himself. "That's probably going to be the last time you see him."

Getting Tough on Immigration

By the mid-1990s, a surge of energy was evident in the conservative movement, leading to Republicans assuming control of Congress in 1994. Though immigration enforcement was not a primary focus, the 1994 Contract with America — a GOP congressional manifesto — spent several pages devoted to the issue of "criminal aliens" within its crime section, which became a 1995 bill dubbed "Taking Back Our Streets."[28] Along with providing $10 billion for new prison construction, the Republican crime bill suggested actions that would make prompt deportation of criminal aliens easier, including providing $14 million in funding for a "Criminal Alien Tracking Center." That part of the Contract with America wasn't immediately put into law, though public frustration about immigration and the political strength of conservatives at that moment in time helped shape several major pieces of legislation that became law in 1996.

Most notably, the 1996 Illegal Immigration Reform and Immigrant Responsibility Act (IIRIRA) made substantial changes to enforcement policy. The law dramatically increased funds for border enforcement and internal enforcement. The budget for the Immigration and Naturalization Service (INS) doubled in real terms between 1994 and 1998, reaching almost $4.3 billion by the year 2000.[29] The number of positions in the agency nearly doubled between 1994 and 2000. There were commensurate increases in the number of interior arrests — from sixty-three thousand in 1994 to 138,000 in 2000 — and border arrests — from a million in 1994 to almost 1.7 million in the year 2000.[30]

Importantly, IIRIRA also took steps to shift some immigration violations from the civil sphere to the criminal sphere. Until then, unlawful presence itself had been deemed a civil rather than a criminal violation, and the penalties for residing without status were civil in nature (deportation) rather than criminal (jail time). The term "illegal immigrant" is misleading for this reason. But IIRIRA made human smuggling and the use of fraudulent immigration-related documents violations of criminal law, raising the possibility of criminal punishment for those whose only misdeeds were related to immigration. This broader definition of what constitutes "criminal" offense would give leeway for later politicians to advocate on public safety grounds for deportation of a larger fraction of the undocumented population, and to conflate criminality with unauthorized status.

IIRIRA and an additional anti-terrorism law passed the same year also cracked down on immigrants with criminal histories. For example, IIRIRA expanded the set of crimes which would, for immigrants without green cards, be grounds for removal without a hearing; that set was enlarged to include certain crimes (called "aggravated felonies" in immigration law) that were in fact not felonies but fairly minor drug offenses. The 1996 laws also made it harder for lawful permanent residents (green card holders) with criminal histories to seek relief from deportation.[31]

This aggressive approach led to cases of immigration enforcement which seemed disproportionate to the criminal offense. One example was the story of Mario Fredas, profiled by the radio show *This American Life* in 2000. In 1980, when he was seventeen, Fredas had come to the US — legally — from Portugal. At age twenty-four he was convicted on a cocaine charge and served three years. Since his release in 1991, he had cleaned up his act and started a family. He lived in Massachusetts and had a job as a construction worker laying concrete for the massive Boston tunnel project known as the Big Dig. Without IIRIRA, that likely would have been the end of the story. But because the law included a number of retroactive provisions, Mario was arrested and awaited a deportation hearing at the time the show aired in the year 2000.[32] The law's provision limiting hardship waivers made it unlikely that he would be granted relief on account of the support he provided his wife and three young children. (In 2002, the Supreme Court overturned some of the harsher portions of the law, granting more judicial discretion and eliminating the retroactive nature of the rules.)

Though it substantially altered the approach to enforcement, IIRIRA did not provide a resolution to the issue of unauthorized immigration, which continued on a large scale in the years that followed. According to Pew estimates, the number of undocumented immigrants more than doubled over the subsequent twelve years, from 5.7 million in 1995 to a historic peak of 12.2 million in 2007, right before the economic downturn in the US.

Since 1933, enforcement efforts had been led by the Immigration and Naturalization Service (INS). The events of September 11, 2001, led to a significant change to the organizational infrastructure for immigration enforcement. In 2003, the INS was swallowed by the newly established Department of Homeland Security (DHS) and its three immigration arms: Immigrations and Custom Enforcement (ICE), Customs and Border Protection (CBP), and the US Citizenship and Immigration Services (USCIS). Even as the organizational structure implementing immigration policy was in flux in the first decade of the 2000s, there was widespread agreement that more should be done. While the question of how to holistically address the immigration issue was mired in political debate, the 1996 IIRIRA law ushered in a striking expansion in the machinery of border control.

Border Control Today

Controlling the borders has long been the primary focus of enforcement activity. In the 1970s and 1980s, for example, efforts to stop people at the border dwarfed the muscle put into internal enforcement. During those decades there were 825,000 "returns" a year on average (people being turned back at the border or shortly after crossing without penalty), compared to 24,000 removals (mostly deportations as the result of internal enforcement activity).[33]

And since 1996's IIRIRA law and 9/11, there has been significant expansion, modernization, and improvement in the efficacy of border enforcement operations, fueled for many years by bipartisan consensus on the need for stringent enforcement and increased resources. Today, more than twice as much is spent on securing the border as on internal enforcement, and, organizationally, border control is managed separately from internal enforcement. The budget for Customs and Border Patrol was $6.4 billion in 2005; it had doubled in real terms to over $17 billion by fiscal year 2020.[34]

Much of the increase has stemmed from boosting manpower along the border. There were more than twenty-one thousand border agents in 2016, nearly ten times the 1980 levels. The Trump administration aimed to further expand that number by five thousand, but recruiting and retaining even twenty thousand agents proved difficult given the remote and dangerous conditions of the work.[35] Many CBP officers left to work for ICE, which offers better pay and more career-growth opportunities.

Border control efforts have also changed tactically, shifting from a voluntary return approach (known disparagingly as "catch and re-lease") to one that imposes substantial costs for getting caught, known in DHS jargon as a "consequences delivery system." In addition to risking having their attempt at crossing recorded as a "removal," which makes it harder to get a visa and increases deportation risk in the future, would-be migrants now risk being repatriated to a location far from their attempted point of entry. In addition, Operation Streamline, in effect in certain southern border regions since 2005, has emphasized the criminal prosecution of attempted border crossers, filing dozens of people into courtrooms at once, sometimes in shackles, and sentencing them to jail time or expedited removal.[36]

In recent decades, physical and technological barriers—including increased fencing and surveillance in traditionally common border-crossing areas such as El Paso and San Diego—have also increased the difficulty of entry. There is now some sort of wall or fence along about 700 miles of the 1954-mile border between the US and Mexico. (These barriers were in place even before the political clash over funding a border wall led to the longest government shutdown in history in 2018–2019.) Migrant flows have responded to these efforts, with larger numbers choosing to attempt hazardous desert crossings in less-patrolled areas, particularly in Arizona. The cost of crossing has increased along with the risk. Most migrants pay coyotes to shuttle them across the border. Twenty or thirty years ago, this service might cost a few hundred or a thousand dollars—and many immigrants would choose to take their chances at figuring it out alone.

Today, with increased barriers, the intelligence on routes and enforcement avoidance is more necessary, and border crossing has become more dangerous. Coyote prices have risen in response. A crossing now typically costs a migrant several thousand dollars. Which doesn't guarantee success—not even close. In addition to the hundreds of thousands turned back at or near the border each year, several hundred would-be migrants die annually in their attempts. In FY 2019, three hundred migrants died at the southwestern border, most succumbing to heatstroke, dehydration, or exhaustion.[37] Many bodies are never identified.

In the new border control environment, undocumented immigrants living in the United States are less likely to migrate back and forth — the so-called circular migration of the past is no longer the norm. Like Anabel Barron returning to pay final respects to her mother, those who visit family risk being unable to return — or live at higher risk of future enforcement action once they have. One unintended consequence of amped-up border control is that undocumented migrants become more disconnected from their home countries, and more likely to settle permanently in the United States. An estimated two-thirds of undocumented immigrants living in the US as of 2017 have been in the country for ten years or longer, compared with only 38 percent in the year 2005.[38]

A second consequence is that as border security improves, a majority of the undocumented will have entered on a visa. A 2019 study by the New York–based think tank Center for Migration Studies found that over 60 percent of unauthorized immigration in recent years has stemmed from visa overstays rather than illicit border crossings. (Widely cited estimates by the Pew Research Center in 2006 put the number at 40 to 50 percent.)[39]

The DHS also recognizes the growing prevalence of visa overstays. A DHS report finds that of 55.9 million visitors to the US who arrived via an airport or seaport and were expected to leave in FY 2019, about 497,000 remained by December 2019 without adjusting or extending their visa. These findings reflect a "suspected in-country overstay" rate of 0.89 percent.[40]

These numbers don't include visas for land crossings. Land travel is not tracked in the same way, though CBP is piloting programs that collect biometric data as visitors exit the US over the southern border. Including land crossings, there are about 180 million entries into the United States each year. It's easy to see the scale of the issue: Even with an overstay rate of 1 percent, a million people or more could come to stay in the United States indefinitely each year. CBP is seeking needles in a very large haystack.

Many longtime unauthorized immigrants crossed the southern border illegally when they first arrived in the United States, including members of five of the six families profiled in this book. But the data suggest that more-recent cohorts are likely to arrive in the United States legally, as temporary visitors. It stands to reason that the pendulum may have shifted too far in the direction of border control. If the goal is to reduce overall unauthorized immigration, some resources currently deployed to the border might be better allocated to strengthening the visa process.

Painesville, Ohio, 2013

The ICE officer showed up for Eduardo Lopez at the local jail early the day after Eduardo was pulled over on his way to his Ohio factory job.

"As soon as he sees me, he's like, 'Whoa! We got a big fish in this morning,'" Eduardo recalls. "I just looked at him and smiled."

Eduardo was cuffed at the wrists and ankles and driven to an immigration office in Cleveland, about forty-five minutes away. Way back in 2000, soon after he and his wife Elena arrived in the United States, Eduardo had been stopped in Mentor, a nearby Ohio town well known in the local immigrant community for its aggressive stance toward Hispanic drivers. The light that illuminated his license plate was out, he was told. On that stop, too, ICE was called in. Eduardo ended up spending five nights in jail and paying a $1,700 bond. He never received any further paperwork from the court and six months after his arrest got a check in the mail refunding his bond money.

Eduardo consulted a couple of lawyers and concluded his case was closed. But now, as soon as he told the ICE officials in Cleveland his name, the record of that twelve-year-old arrest came up in the computer, along with a mugshot from when he was eighteen years old. Then the immigration officer was telling him that they'd been looking for him for the past twelve years.

"How you guys can tell me you've been looking for me when I've been living in the same town? I use my same name. I still working in the same company!" Eduardo said.

"Why didn't you ever come to the office?" the ICE officer answered.

"Officer, just put yourself in my shoes," Eduardo pleaded. "I'm illegal. I'm never going to just show up to your office because I don't know what's going to happen!"

Eduardo was informed he was being transferred to the Seneca County Jail, a prison–turned–ICE detention center in Tiffin, Ohio, about two hours from Painesville. He was told he would be deported to Mexico the next Tuesday. He knew he had just a couple days to get help.

Eduardo called his wife, Elena, who called a lawyer they'd met through a local immigrant-rights group, HOLA. The group held weekly meetings at a local park in Painesville. A few dozen undocumented immigrants would gather to strategize ways to help detained community members — meetings with politicians, public protests, letter-writing campaigns. After the weekly meeting, there was often a potluck meal. The gatherings were held in a picnic area in a quiet corner of the public park. There was a playground nearby where young children played on swings and climbing structures while their older brothers kicked a soccer ball around the bright-green field. Eduardo had been to a couple of the meetings, but he wasn't a regular. Of course, he was concerned about the traffic stops that were leading to the deportation of Mexicans in the area. But he had a good job that he wanted to keep. His strategy had been to keep his head down, and it had worked for him for over a decade.

"When they went to the Cleveland offices I never went. Because I don't want to be on TV; I don't want to be on the radio," Eduardo says. "I don't want people to see me and ask why I'm there." Within a couple days he was in the Seneca County Jail. His lawyer told him he might be in for three months, or six. After that he might be deported, or not. He never knew how long the jail time would last.

The Role of Local Government

One pronounced change emerging from immigration policy developments over the past quarter-century is the increasing importance of local and state governments in immigration enforcement. Historically, immigration has been the purview of the federal government. Local law enforcement could—and did—contact the Immigration and Naturalization Service (INS) when someone they arrested for another reason was suspected of being in the country illegally, but local police officers were not in the business of enforcing immigration law. Immigration law was exclusively in the federal domain.

Section 287(g) of the 1996 IIRIRA law changed that, explicitly allowing selected local law enforcement agencies to actively take part in the enforcement of federal immigration law. Through what came to be known as the 287(g) program, selected local agencies signed memoranda of agreement with the federal government to act as de facto immigration officers after receiving federal training. Early on, some agencies were given "task force enforcement" capability, which allowed local law enforcement to investigate people suspected of immigration violations. This street-level enforcement led to public concern about harassment of minorities and racial profiling. Other agreements, called "jail enforcement" agreements, allowed local agencies to investigate the immigration status of anyone arrested, with trained local cops filling the role of immigration officers in the jail setting.[41]

The 287(g) program agreements were first signed in the early years of the first decade of the 2000s; by 2010, there were over eighty agreements in effect with local and state law enforcement agencies nationwide. At the program's peak, in fiscal years 2010–2013, the federal government spent $68 million annually on it.[42] The "task force" part of the program was canceled by the Obama administration in 2012, but about forty of the jail enforcement 287(g) agreements were still in effect when Donald Trump took office in January 2017. The new administration vowed to expand 287(g), and they did so. Nationwide, 287(g) arrests doubled between fiscal year 2016 and fiscal year 2017. As of mid-2019 there were eighty jail enforcement agreements plus ten agreements for a new Trump-era 287(g) program called Warrant Service Officers; the new program allows trained local officers to support ICE efforts even when state or local law restricts cooperation.[43]

The 287(g) agreements significantly expand the reach of immigration enforcement by leveraging local personnel to enforce federal immigration law. Although less than 10 percent of ICE arrests come from 287(g) programs overall, the program constitutes a large share of interior enforcement efforts in some areas.[44] As an extreme example, in Maricopa County, Arizona, there were over thirty thousand 287(g) arrests over the three-year period from 2008 to 2010. This figure represents about 7 percent of the entire noncitizen population of the county.

More recently, data from fiscal year 2017 show Gwinnett County, Georgia, with the highest number of 287(g) arrests in the country. About a quarter of the residents in Gwinnett, a suburban Atlanta county with nearly a million residents, are foreign born, and an estimated 7 percent are undocumented.[45] In 2015 and 2016, ICE was arresting forty to fifty unauthorized immigrants per month through Gwinnet's 287(g) agreement; in early 2017 the number shot up to between 150 and 200 every month.[46] A case study by the Migration Policy Institute suggests that this shift emerged as many more traffic offenses led to immigration arrests. Traffic charges represented 70 percent of immigration detainers in the county in early 2017 compared with 36 percent in 2016, when guidelines discouraged ICE from pursuing deportation of those without criminal records.[47] (A detainer is a request from immigration authorities for a local jail or prison to hold a potentially deportable immigrant so that ICE can take custody.)

Not surprisingly, throughout its history 287(g) has contributed to increasing unevenness in enforcement across different regions of the US. "[T]he 287(g) program has been criticized for inconsistent and divergent implementation, often driven by local priorities and political imperatives," reads a 2013 report from the Migration Policy Institute. "Given leeway in interpreting program mandates, some jurisdictions have targeted serious and dangerous criminal offenders, while others have adopted a more universal model that draws in large numbers of unauthorized immigrants with misdemeanors and traffic offenses."[48] Universal models were most heavily used in the Southeast, the Migration Policy Institute report found, and the program's implementation was the most controversial in that part of the country. "The ten sites with the largest share of detainers placed on traffic violators are all in the Southeast."

Even in non-287(g) jurisdictions, differences in local policing lead to extreme disparities in immigration enforcement. An undocumented immigrant in Georgia or Arizona faces a very different risk of arrest and deportation than does a similar person living in San Francisco or Los Angeles. Among immigrants themselves, some cities and towns become known as more dangerous than similar cities and towns in the same state. In places like the suburbs of Cleveland, Ohio, undocumented immigrants would take a longer route on their morning commute to avoid passing through individual towns known for stopping anyone who appeared to be "driving while Mexican."

Lorain, Ohio, 2013

After about six hours Anabel Barron, the mother of four arrested after a traffic stop on her morning commute, was released from custody and told to report to an immigration office early the next week. She knew that undocumented immigrants in similar scenarios had often been held in detention centers for weeks or even months.

The Cleveland area has proven to have some police departments that are particularly harsh, said Veronica Dahlberg, executive director of the Ohio immigrant-rights group HOLA, in a 2015 interview. A traffic stop in one town might get an undocumented immigrant waved along, while the same violation in a neighboring municipality could result in deportation.

Hundreds of thousands of undocumented immigrants already settled in the US are arrested by ICE each year. To Dahlberg, it felt nearly constant in the Cleveland area, even years before Trump's election. "It's almost an everyday occurrence," she said. "Kids are losing their parents. Going five miles over the speed limit can get you ensnared in this deportation machine. It's just chewing up families and destroying them."

Decisions about whom to detain or deport and whom to release have often been largely arbitrary, made at the whim of individual jurisdictions and officers. Concern about the fate of Anabel's children may have been a factor in her quick release. Phone calls from members of her church could have made a difference. Even the timing might have played a role: Agents may simply not have wanted to deal with the paperwork on a Friday afternoon.

The morning after her arrest, Anabel went online and started searching for lawyers. She had to check in with ICE on Tuesday morning, so she had hardly any time. On Monday morning she contacted Cleveland immigration attorney Jennifer Peyton, who agreed to represent her pro bono. Anabel was lucky, Peyton says. "They could have held her without bond, they could have put her on the next plane to Mexico."

Unlike criminal defendants, undocumented immigrants have no guarantee of legal representation within the US court system. Many are left to represent themselves, often in a language that they barely understand. Within a couple weeks of the traffic stop, Peyton had won Anabel a "stay of removal," a legal status that delays—but often does not stop—a pending deportation order. An entourage of seventeen local friends, advocates, and supporters from Anabel's church showed up for the meeting.

"If I walk in with someone with a final order [of removal] who literally can be picked up and pulled away, I want my backup," says Peyton, who calls the chance of getting a stay in a case like Anabel's "a crapshoot." Once the stay was approved, Anabel was able to file for employment authorization and get a temporary social security number, which would also allow her to get a US driver's license for the first time in her life.

Her situation exemplifies an irony of the United States' jumble of immigration laws: Sometimes the worst thing that ever happens to an immigrant can turn out to be the best thing that ever happens to them. Anabel was in Peyton's Cleveland office when the lawyer told her that her work permit had been approved. "She began to cry and I began to cry," Peyton recalls. "I said, you know what? The thing you've been dreading for twelve years, the thing that's been keeping you awake at night, the thing your kids are scared about, it's giving you an empowerment and a liberty you didn't have for twelve years."

Secure Communities

In 2008, the Bush administration piloted a different form of partnership between federal immigration officials and local law enforcement, the Secure Communities program, and in subsequent years the Obama administration oversaw its dissemination across the United States. The goal was to use information-sharing and biometrics to identify criminal aliens and to focus deportation efforts on those with criminal histories. Secure Communities aimed to screen everyone booked into jail for any reason, investigating both their criminal history and immigration status by comparing their fingerprints against both FBI and DHS databases. Because it relied on federal databases, it did not require in-depth training of deputized local officers in immigration enforcement like 287(g) did. The program gradually expanded to all jurisdictions by early 2013.[49]

The fingerprint checks allow authorities to identify some undocumented immigrants—for example, if an individual was fingerprinted during an attempted border crossing or for a visa application. If an immigrant is identified and ICE has probable cause to believe the individual is removable, they issue a detainer (also known as an "immigration hold") requesting the local jail or prison hold the immigrant for up to forty-eight hours—excluding weekends and holidays—after they would otherwise have been released. Within that time frame, the immigrant can be turned over to ICE and will likely enter deportation proceedings.

Secure Communities can result in deportation of unauthorized immigrants who are never charged with a crime, and it also means that those awaiting criminal trial are likely to be denied bail, increasing time in pre-trial detention.[50] Diversion programs that might otherwise be offered to those who commit minor crimes are not available to those with an immigration detainer.[51] Because of increased time in local jails, the financial costs to local law enforcement agencies associated with detainers are nontrivial. A Florida advocacy group's 2018 analysis of detainers in Miami-Dade County estimated that the county spent over $1 million a month honoring detainer requests, for example.[52]

Legal immigrants also have biometric information on file, and they may be subject to an immigration hold and deportation through Secure Communities. Unlike undocumented immigrants, though, legal immigrants typically only face detainer requests if they have been convicted of a crime.

From the start, there was significant opposition to the Secure Communities program. Opponents claimed that it resulted in deportations for less-serious offenses such as traffic violations or minor drug charges. There were also accusations that local officers in some jurisdictions were engaged in racial profiling, arresting minorities for minor traffic offenses for the purpose of facilitating immigrant removal.

In addition, many people believed that Secure Communities discouraged cooperation with the local police in immigrant communities. "Law enforcement experts have stated that the trust that exists between police and immigrant communities can take years to develop and can remain tenuous despite the hard work of local law enforcement agencies," according to a task force appointed by the DHS to study the program in 2011.[53] "When communities perceive that police are enforcing federal immigration laws, especially if there is a perception that such enforcement is targeting minor offenders, that trust is broken in some communities, and victims, witnesses and other residents may become fearful of reporting crime or approaching the police to exchange information," the Task Force warned. "This may have a harmful impact on the ability of the police to build strong relationships with immigrant communities and engage in community policing, thereby negatively impacting public safety and possibly national security."

Evidence supporting this proposition comes from Elisa Jacome, who studied the issue while a graduate student at Princeton University. Using incident-level data from the Dallas and Austin, Texas police departments, Jacome investigated the effect of suspending Secure Communities in 2015.[54] The federal transition to a less-aggressive approach was vocally supported by the Dallas sheriff, and the number of ICE detainers for those with no criminal conviction dropped substantially. The effect on crime reporting was nearly immediate: By late 2015, crimes reported by complainants with Hispanic ethnicity had increased by 10 percent. (The data do not include information on immigration status. Estimates suggest that about a quarter of the Latino population in Dallas is unauthorized.)

Jacome found there was increased reporting of both more- and less-serious crimes, and that non-Latinos did not have a similar reporting pattern—suggesting it was not a change in underlying crime rates that drove the rise in reported crime. Instead, it appears the change in immigration enforcement policy increased the Latino community's trust in police, and it made members of that community more willing to call when a crime occurred. The move away from Secure Communities did not have the same impact in Austin, where it was not accompanied by a public commitment to change the immigration enforcement environment.

In part because of concerns about crime reporting, the Obama administration abandoned the Secure Communities program in 2015. It was replaced with a new program dubbed the Priority Enforcement Program (PEP), which further prioritized the removal of convicted criminals and repeat border crossers. Though more a rebranding than a true overhaul, PEP did narrow the use of detainers and gave local law enforcement agencies more discretion in which immigrants were detained.[55] In some local areas, that made a meaningful difference.

The softer approach didn't last long. Like many elements of immigration enforcement, Secure Communities and PEP were born out of administrative discretion rather than law. Congress does not oversee the programs nor dictate how they are run. As a result, enforcement practices can change almost overnight. On January 25, 2017, during his first week in office, Donald Trump issued an executive order reinstating Secure Communities. In FY 2019, ICE issued 165,000 detainer requests, about twice the FY 2016 numbers, with most requests going to county or local jails.[56]

But both before and after Trump's election, many state and local law enforcement agencies were adamant that they would not cooperate with federal immigration authorities. Although city governments cannot prevent federal enforcement action within their borders, they are not legally bound to honor ICE detainer requests. An analysis of New York Police Department data suggests that the agency honored zero of

2,916 detainer requests in the year ending June 30, 2019, and cooperated in other ways with immigration officials only seven times.[57] The Trump administration threatened to withdraw federal aid from uncooperative state and local governments, but their authority to do so was restricted by the legal process.[58] Traditionally the siren of the political right, calls for state and local government rights have taken new shape in the era of aggressive immigration enforcement.

Sanctuary Cities

On the evening of July 1, 2015, a thirty-two-year-old Californian named Kathryn Steinle was shot in the back and killed as she and her father were sightseeing on a popular San Francisco pier. The man who discharged the gun — originally referred to by the alias Juan Francisco Lopez Sanchez but later identified as Jose Ines Garcia Zarate — was an unauthorized Mexican immigrant who had been deported five times in the past and who had a history of drug charges. Three months before the killing, Garcia Zarate had been released from the San Francisco County jail, despite a standard request that he be held until ICE could detain him.

San Francisco is one of hundreds of cities, counties, and municipalities in the United States that have so-called sanctuary laws that limit the degree to which local law enforcement authorities can cooperate with ICE. The term itself is controversial and divisive. "Sanctuary," of course, implies safety. But for people concerned about criminal immigrants, so-called sanctuary cities are the opposite of safe: they're the places that are harboring bad guys.

From the perspective of immigrant-rights advocates, the term is problematic for a different reason: Though some places, like San Francisco, have a broad definition of "sanctuary" and protect arrested immigrants in all but the most extreme situations, other cities with relatively mild limits on ICE cooperation are also labeled "sanctuaries." Without an official definition of the term "sanctuary," undocumented individuals could be led to mistakenly believe they are safe from deportation. In actuality, the federal government can and does enforce immigration law even when there is little or no local cooperation.

Steinle's death coincided with the early days of the primaries for the 2016 presidential election, and the tragedy quickly became a rallying cry for Republican candidates convinced that immigrants were driving up crime rates — or, more cynically, calculating that saying so would be a winning argument with certain voters. (We will discuss the actual impact of immigrants on the national crime rate in part 3.) Donald Trump, then considered a wild-card candidate, had announced his presidential bid on June 16, 2015. "When Mexico sends its people, they're not sending their best," he told the crowd at Trump Tower in New York City. "They're sending people that have lots of problems, and they're bringing those problems with us. They're bringing drugs. They're bringing crime. They're rapists. And some, I assume, are good people."[59]

In the weeks after Steinle's killing, Trump repeatedly used her death as an argument in favor of his proposed border wall and mass deportations of undocumented Mexicans living in the United States. He didn't change his tune when Garcia Zarate was acquitted by a jury in 2017, tweeting "The Kate Steinle killer came back and back over the weakly protected Obama border, always committing crimes and being violent, and yet this info was not used in court. His exoneration is a complete travesty of justice. BUILD THE WALL!"[60]

As it turned out, the pistol used in Kathryn Steinle's killing had been stolen from the vehicle of a Bureau of Land Management ranger a few days before the shooting. There was no evidence that Garcia Zarate had anything to do with that theft; instead, Garcia Zarate, who had seemingly been homeless since his release from San Francisco jail, spending his days collecting bottles and cans for recycling, randomly found the gun wrapped in a T-shirt under a bench on a San Francisco pier. Though his defense argued that the gun discharged accidentally without Garcia Zarate even unwrapping it, even if Garcia Zarate had intentionally pulled the trigger, he shot at random; ballistic evidence determined that the gun was discharged from close to the ground; the bullet ricocheted off the concrete pier, traveling another seventy-eight feet before hitting Steinle. The jury found no evidence that Garcia Zarate, who had no history of violence in his criminal record, had any intent to kill anyone.[61]

"The aftermath of the shooting, which propelled illegal immigration to the forefront of the 2016 presidential campaign, has also served as a reminder of the fragility of the politics of immigration—that one single event can galvanize a national public response and shift the direction and momentum of the immigration debate," Muzaffar Chishti and Faye Hipsman of the Migration Policy Institute wrote in a policy statement in August 2015, less than two months after the tragic incident.[62]

In the months that followed the shooting, dozens of state and federal bills were introduced aimed at punishing so-called sanctuary cities that shield immigrant offenders from federal authorities or refuse to cooperate with federal enforcement efforts. Many towns and cities had sanctuary programs or policies that were just a few years old, implemented in reaction to the Secure Communities program. By 2016 Washington, DC; California; Connecticut; Rhode Island; and 350 other local jurisdictions nationwide had policies that limited local law enforcement's role in enforcing immigration law, according to Hipsman, the analyst with the Migration Policy Institute. (Los Angeles is widely considered the first sanctuary city, declaring itself in opposition to federal standards way back in 1979.) Individual municipalities vary widely in what measures they take to protect undocumented immigrants, but areas are often lumped into the "sanctuary" category when they have policies that are more friendly toward undocumented immigrants than those of existing federal law.

"Now the pendulum is starting to swing in the opposite direction," Hipsman told us in early 2016, almost a year before Trump's inauguration. After Steinle's death, "the momentum is toward cooperation with ICE." More than a dozen national bills were introduced in the wake of the shooting on the San Francisco pier. In 2015, North Carolina passed a law banning sanctuary cities. Wisconsin, Virginia, and Florida debated new laws. Meanwhile, Trump continued to drum up fear of hordes of criminal immigrants, and support for policies of bigger walls, mass deportation, and increased limitations on legal immigration.

After Trump's election in November 2016, there was a desperate push in more immigrant-friendly enclaves to self-designate cities, towns, campuses, and even individual churches and municipal buildings as "sanctuaries." In the face of the threat of mass deportation, the sanctuary movement seemed to return to its roots in churches that sheltered immigrants in the early 1980s. Practical arguments about maintaining trust between police and local communities took a back seat as ethical and humanitarian pleas moved to center stage.

In January 2017, when Trump took office, the new administration issued an executive order to withhold all federal grants from municipalities refusing to fully cooperate with ICE directives. The promise set up a battle between the federal government and immigrant-friendly states like Washington and California, and it led to the unusual case in which left-leaning states and localities were making arguments against federal overreach. In 2018, US District Court Judge Manuel Real rejected Trump administration efforts to make local cooperation with ICE a prerequisite for federal community-policing grant dollars, finding that denying grants in response to noncooperation "upset the constitutional balance between state and federal power by requiring state and local law enforcement to partner with federal authorities."[63] The Ninth Circuit Court of Appeals also struck down the administration's efforts to withhold funding from California sanctuary cities, leaving an uneasy tension between federal enforcement efforts and local governments that are unwilling to facilitate those efforts.

Immigration Enforcement and the States

Individual municipalities have not been the only governments below the federal level influencing on-the-ground immigration policy in recent decades — states have also entered the fray. Some have passed laws protecting immigrants from federal rules. Others have adopted their own pro-deportation strategies without federal approval or support. Most notably of those that fall into the pro-deportation camp, Arizona passed SB 1070 in 2010, giving itself wide-ranging authority over immigration enforcement.

Officially named the Support Our Law Enforcement and Safe Neighborhoods Act, SB 1070 is the strictest and most controversial state anti-immigration measure. It codified an extreme approach to immigration of the sort that was championed by Joe Arpaio, the controversial sheriff of Maricopa County, Arizona, who was in office from 1993 until 2017. The law gave state and local law enforcement officials the explicit right to check the immigration status of anyone suspected of being undocumented, and *required* an immigration status check for anyone stopped, detained, or arrested for another reason. In addition, it criminalized the failure of immigrants to carry identification documents, and it prohibited undocumented immigrants from working.

Arizona's embrace of aggressive immigration policy likely stems from its fairly rapid demographic shift and relatively high concentration of undocumented immigrants. In 2010, 30 percent of Arizona's population was Latino — up from 19 percent in 1990 — and Arizona had the fifth-largest number of Latinos in the United States.[64] An estimated 470,000 undocumented immigrants lived in Arizona in 2010, representing 7 percent of the total 6.7 million residents at the time.[65]

Opponents of Arizona SB 1070 argued that the proposition would encourage increased use of racial profiling and human-rights violations. In 2013, the American Civil Liberties Union challenged SB 1070, arguing that it was unconstitutional because it violated Fourth Amendment protections against unreasonable search and seizure and violated equal protection.[66] Despite the legal controversy, 59 percent of respondents to a national survey conducted in 2010 by the Pew Research Center for the People and the Press favored SB 1070.[67]

The Department of Justice filed a lawsuit before the Arizona law was scheduled to take effect, and in 2012 the Supreme Court ruled that the state law could not preempt federal law. The state statute could not require immigrants to carry papers or bar the unauthorized from applying for jobs. However, the court did allow some controversial parts of the law to stand, including the mandate requiring local officers to investigate the immigration status of someone stopped, detained, or arrested for another reason if they have suspicion that person is unauthorized — the so-called show-me-your-papers clause. (That provision has since been weakened as part of a legal settlement, making it optional for local officers to demand papers.)[68]

In the years after SB 1070 passed, several other states, including Utah, Georgia, and Alabama, introduced "copycat" SB1070 legislation, but most of these laws were never passed or were blocked by the courts. As of 2020, Arizona arguably continued to have the harshest enforcement environment of any state, and to be held up as an example by then-President Trump, who hired one of the bill's authors, Kris Kobach, to be part of his immigration transition team.

There is evidence that Arizona's harshest-in-the-nation approach to immigration enforcement reduced migration. The flow of undocumented immigrants from Mexico across the border into Arizona fell between 30 and 70 percent in the months immediately following the announcement of the 2010 law, according to a 2017 study by Texas A&M professor Mark Hoekstra and University of Mississippi professor Sandra Orozco-Aleman. The study relied on Mexican government surveys of would-be migrants to the United States in Mexican border towns. Those immigration flows rebounded by about half after a judge announced the injunction of the law.[69] The authors find no evidence that Mexican immigrants already residing in Arizona left the state as the result of the SB 1070 law, however. The same finding is echoed in other settings: Aggressive enforcement does little to encourage current unauthorized residents to leave the United States, but it may deter future in-migration.

Springfield, Massachusetts, 2017

Fatima Cabrera and her husband Luis left the western-Massachusetts potato farm where they'd worked for a number of seasons on a chilly evening in November 2017. It seemed like any other day. Luis often helped other workers out with a ride home, and on this evening there were nine of them in the van headed back to Springfield. Five or six minutes after they'd left the farm, a car pulled out behind the van, lights flashing. Probably just an emergency vehicle needing to pass, Fatima thought at first. Luis pulled the van over to the shoulder. An official-looking car pulled in front of them and stopped. Two other cars pulled up behind.

An officer came over and said he was from Immigration. He asked Luis for a driver's license. Luis didn't have one, and the officer asked him to step out of the van. He was led away to one of the ICE cars.

"Then we were there in shock," Fatima recalls. "They took him away.

And all their agents came and they opened every single door, and we were inside the car, they did not ask us to get out of the car. They were telling us if we didn't have any problem, any criminal record with the police, we should not be worried," she says. "But after that, they start taking our fingerprints, taking pictures of us." After the fingerprinting, the officers detained two other men in the van. Then they told Fatima to call someone with a license to drive them home, or ICE would have to confiscate the vehicle.

It took a while for Fatima and her coworkers to get picked up. It was cold while they waited. An officer saw they were shivering and let them turn on the van for heat. Eventually they were allowed to leave, without Luis or the other two coworkers from the farm.

When Fatima heard from Luis, he asked her to try to find a lawyer to help get him released. But he had an old deportation order that he had evaded, making him a high priority for removal. Luis was deported to Guatemala within the week.

Fatima was devastated. She didn't know how to tell her children. The priest from her church agreed to help her explain it to her kids. But before he was able, Fatima had another encounter with ICE.

A week after Luis was arrested, Fatima dropped her kids at school and went to the grocery store just before 9:00 a.m. A car pulled behind her when she parked, and a man got out. He called her by her name. She was confused—how would Immigration know her name? She'd never been in trouble with the law, and they hadn't asked her for a name that day in the van. The only way they could know her name was because she paid taxes, she thought, or maybe because of school forms for the kids. But here was ICE, following her into the grocery store parking lot.

The officer asked where she was coming from, and she told him she had just dropped off her kids. He asked her how many kids she had and when they would be getting out of school. Then he asked her to come talk to them at the ICE office in Hartford, Connecticut. He thought she'd be back in Springfield before the end of the school day at 3:30 p.m.

She knew it was better to stay quiet. "Know Your Rights" campaigns typically advise unauthorized immigrants to say they wish to remain silent when questioned by ICE, and to speak to a lawyer first.[70] Anything she said might be used against her in immigration court, Fatima thought. But she didn't have any criminal record; she figured it would be okay. She told them that she wanted to call her lawyer and her priest before she talked to them.

The officer didn't speak much Spanish, so he got another agent on the phone. Fatima repeated her request to call her lawyer and her priest. The agent on the phone told her she wasn't allowed to make the calls now; it would have to wait until she got to the office. Fatima got in the agent's car.

It was around 10:30 a.m. when they arrived at the ICE office in downtown Hartford. The officer sat her down and showed Fatima a piece of paper with pictures of the other people that had been in the van with her that day. He asked Fatima if she knew where they lived. Fatima said no. She was confused. The ICE officers hadn't asked for names in the van, yet somehow they had everyone's full name on the sheet with the photos.

The ICE officer rifled through Fatima's handbag, going through everything. He found a couple of lawyers' business cards that Fatima had been carrying around. Her house had been robbed back during her first years in the United States when she lived with her cousin, and she had called and cooperated with the police. She had heard that she might be able to apply for a special visa because of that cooperation.

Fatima explained that she had those business cards because she was trying to fix her status. The ICE officer called the lawyer on one of the cards to confirm her story. Then he said that it was fine, and not to worry because she was going to get parole.

After a couple of hours they took Fatima to a different office, fit her with a metal ankle monitor, and then let her go. Her car was still half an hour away in the grocery store parking lot in Springfield. She called her priest to come pick her up.

Looking back months after the arrest from her sparsely decorated dining room in Springfield, Fatima's voice cracks with a mixture of sadness and confusion: "I still wonder how they were able to get to us."

The Failure of Comprehensive Reform and the Introduction of DACA

By the time Barack Obama was running for president in 2007 and 2008, it was clear that renewed immigration reform was needed, and he promised a solution. Obama favored a comprehensive (and familiar) legislative fix: an immigration reform bill that would both further increase border enforcement and provide a path to citizenship for undocumented residents. By then, "amnesty" had become a politically charged word and you could tell which side of the issue a politician was likely to take by whether they talked about rejecting "amnesty for illegal aliens" or ensuring "a path to citizenship for undocumented Americans."

But as the political barriers to a comprehensive bill became clear in his first term, Obama and immigrant supporters rallied behind the so-called DREAM Act (Development, Relief, and Education for Alien Minors), a less-sweeping proposal. They argued the DREAM Act would be a significant first step, offering protection from deportation, work authorization, and a pathway to citizenship for certain undocumented immigrants who arrived in the US as children. The "Dreamers" were a particularly sympathetic group: students and young adults who had in most cases not themselves been the ones to decide to migrate to the United States, and who often had no other country to call home. (The term "Dreamers" is disliked by many of the very people to whom it refers, who point out that people excluded by the designation, including their own parents, had and have dreams that are equally worthy of empathy.) First introduced in Congress as early as 2001, the DREAM Act was passed in an updated form by the House under Obama in 2010, but it was threatened with filibuster in the Senate.

In 2012, the Obama administration took executive action to give so-called Dreamers work authorization and protection from deportation, in an effort to kick-start a stalled legislative progress. The program, known as Deferred Action for Childhood Arrivals, or DACA, was limited to undocumented immigrants who had arrived in the US before their sixteenth birthday, and had lived in the country continuously since 2007. To qualify for DACA, someone had to have either finished high school, still be in school, or be in the military at the time of application. Anyone with a significant criminal record was eliminated, as was anyone over the age of thirty as of June 2012. Each applicant was required to pay a $495 non-refundable application fee. If approved, as about 82 percent of applicants were, DACA grantees received a work permit and a temporary social security number that could be renewed every two years, for another $495 fee. (The fees were designed so that the program would pay for itself.)

Unlike the proposed DREAM Act, DACA does not provide a path to US citizenship or lawful permanent-resident status. And as an executive action, DACA's fate is in the hands of each presidential administration. But its impact has been significant for hundreds of thousands of young people and their families.

Obama signed the executive order in June 2012, and USCIS began accepting applications in August. That year, the Migration Policy Institute estimated that 1.76 million undocumented immigrants could potentially be eligible for DACA. As of September 2017, when USCIS cut off new applications, approximately 793,000 immigrants had been granted DACA status at some point between 2012 and 2017. There were 690,000 people with current DACA status in September 2017, a number exceeding the total population of Vermont.[71]

Not surprisingly, DACA recipients tend to be clustered geographically. About half of all people with DACA status live in California or Texas. Nearly 80 percent of the individuals who've received DACA were born in Mexico.[72] The uptake rate was much higher among Latinos than in the Asian community, likely as a result of more-robust local outreach efforts as well as cultural differences, according to a report by the Migration Policy Institute.[73]

What about the eligible immigrants not receiving DACA? The National UnDACAmented Research Project (NURP), a study run out of Harvard's Graduate School of Education, surveyed DACA-eligible immigrants in 2013. Of those who did not apply, 43 percent said it was because they couldn't afford the application fee; 22 percent were missing required paperwork; 17 percent were "legally concerned" — perhaps fearful that exposing themselves to authorities was too risky; and 10 percent said they did not know how to apply.[74] Though the DACA application process could be labor-intensive and long—an extensive paper trail of a life in the US was required and a three- to six-month wait for a final decision was typical—the program was implemented with the explicit promise that those rejected would not have their private information turned over to ICE.

Nevertheless, concern that the extensive personal data collected through the DACA application process could later be used against applicants was significant from the start, particularly as many applicants—young, typically low-income individuals—were living at home with their parents, who were, of course, highly likely to also be undocumented. These fears were renewed and intensified when Donald Trump took office in 2017.

As DACA was implemented at the end of Obama's first term and beginning of his second, efforts at comprehensive legislative reform continued. The administration had implemented a significant expansion of enforcement activity, no doubt part of an attempt to demonstrate their seriousness about reining in illegal immigration even as they implemented DACA. Removals—the official term for a deportation—rose from 360,000 in 2008 to a peak of 434,000 in 2013.[75] The emphasis was on criminal immigrants, and some of the increase in removal numbers stemmed from a different approach to processing and recording individuals caught crossing the border rather than from internal enforcement. Even so, the sheer number of removals soon earned Obama the derogatory moniker "Deporter-in-Chief."

Things finally looked promising for reform in 2013, when a bipartisan "Gang of Eight" senators crafted a comprehensive bill called the Border Security, Economic Opportunity, and Immigration Modernization Act. It would have granted a pathway to citizenship to many unauthorized immigrants then living in the US, significantly increased manpower along the border, and substantially altered the legal immigration system. The bill was passed by the Senate 68–32 in April 2013, and it likely would have passed the House—but Republican leadership declined to bring it for a vote. This refusal proved to be the fatal blow to the Obama administration's hopes of a legislative solution.

DACA, though, continued—and Obama took further executive action in 2014. The administration attempted to expand the DACA program to a larger group, namely people who were too old to qualify for the original DACA. They also introduced Deferred Action for Parents of Americans and Lawful Permanent Residents (DAPA), an added executive action which would have provided the same two-year work permits to millions more people living in the country illegally, many of them the parents of the original "Dreamers." The proposed expansion of DACA increased the estimated number of eligible undocumented immigrants by 330,000;[76] another 3.6 million might have been eligible for DAPA.[77] Together, the two programs would have provided relief for approximately half of all undocumented immigrants then living in the US.

When President Obama first promised expanded executive action on immigration in the early summer of 2014, it was about a year after Anabel Barron was pulled over for speeding in the Cleveland suburbs. When Anabel heard about Obama's DAPA proposal, she prayed that the relief would come soon and be generous. Her stay of removal was scheduled to expire in March 2015. She knew people who had had stays extended year after year. But that was no way to live, under the constant shadow of the threat that your family might be ripped apart. "No, Anabel didn't spend a lot of time in detention," Dahlberg, the local activist, says. "But when you have the federal government saying you're going to be deported you're in a kind of prison until you get that relief."

As the parent of US-citizen children, Anabel was among the estimated 3.6 million undocumented immigrants who would have been eligible to apply for a short-term deferral of deportation as the result of DAPA, which was finally announced in November 2014 after months of buildup. The presidential decree also reemphasized the two categories of illegal immigrants to be targeted for deportation — serious criminals and recent border crossers — a mandate that would be put into place in early 2015.

Though the original DACA grew to have fairly widespread support, the further executive actions were viewed much more harshly as an example of executive overreach. Twenty-six states sued on these grounds, and a Texas judge ordered an injunction against the actions until the case could be resolved. The Obama administration's request for the Supreme Court to overrule the injunction was stymied when the court—by then down a justice due to the sudden death of Antonin Scalia in February 2016—reached a 4–4 decision, thereby returning the case to work its way through the lower courts.[78] With a new administration hostile to undocumented immigrants set to take office, the expanded versions of DACA and DAPA were effectively over before they began.

President Obama intended DACA as a stopgap measure—temporary relief for a particularly empathetic group of young immigrants in the time before comprehensive immigration reform could be passed. As it turned out, the limited executive action would arguably be the most significant immigration-related policy change of Obama's presidency. There was no change in law. DACA was created through executive action, and so was much more vulnerable to administrative change than the DREAM Act, or any other law, would have been.

Kansas, 2014

By the time Michael Park left his home in Southern California for his first year of college in Kansas in the fall of 2014, he'd had DACA status for over a year. Michael hadn't been aware of pre-DACA DREAM Act political debates as they were going on, and actually was himself a DACA recipient before he even understood what the program was. His concern had been a driver's license. "It was that point in high school where everybody gets a license and starts driving around with their permit," Michael recalls several years later. "When I asked my mom or my aunt, they were really vague about it, and when the time came, they told me I would have to get my fingerprint scanned and sign some paperwork."

He remembers his aunt pulling him out of school one day and bringing him to a processing center in LA where he had his fingerprints taken—for the DACA biometrics requirement, which comes late in the application process. At the time, Michael thought the appointment was simply another step in the process of getting a driver's license: "I was just excited that I could get a work permit and a social number and all that so I could start working and drive a car." When Michael applied to college, he used the social security number that came with the resulting paperwork; he used the same number to get a part-time job in a local sushi restaurant.

Despite the national media attention President Obama's controversial executive action had attracted, Michael was ignorant of the implications of his DACA status through his time in high school and into his first year of college. And though immigrant-rights organizations that assist young immigrants and their families with applying for DACA were prevalent in Southern California, the Park siblings were unaware of those services, or even that such services might be useful to them. Their family's instinct was to seek out a private lawyer, one who came at the recommendation of someone from church, and to leave the kids themselves out of those consultations. An estimated fifty-two thousand Korean youth were originally eligible for DACA, according to a 2017 Migration Policy Institute study on Korean immigrants in the US. But as of September 2016, four years into the program, only 7,693 of those young people had applied, a much smaller proportion than in the Latino community.[79] Of those petitions, 7,069 were approved; Michael's was one of them. It wasn't until well over a year after he'd secured his status — when he went into a military recruitment office — that he actually heard the term "DACA" for the first time.

Even as a first-year college student, Michael knew that he was interested in security. He'd always imagined himself someday working for the government. As a kid, he loved to watch *The X-Files* and other crime shows. He had a strikingly specific plan: Enlist in the Air Force, train in cybersecurity, and eventually transition to civilian work with the FBI, CIA, or Department of Defense. But when he finally walked into that military recruitment office in California, sat down, and had a conversation with the recruiter, he was told that he couldn't enlist because they weren't taking people with DACA.

"I looked it up and it was something like deferred action child arrival, that was the acronym," Michael says. "It basically means I can be in the US for the next few years, two tops. For someone who lived in the US for seven, eight years at the time and to hear something like that, when you're in college your freshman year, I mean, that's very shocking."

When he first came to America, he was a Korean immigrant, Michael says. After living more than half of his life in the US, he now thinks of himself as a Korean American. "This is where I am, and this is what I call my country now." But, especially living in Kansas, Michael stood out in a way he never had in Los Angeles. In class, on the street, anywhere he went, he often felt conscious of being the only minority, he says. He didn't like the attention. One day he was riding a city bus when a guy tapped him on the shoulder. "How do you say my name in Asian?" he asked Michael, apparently earnestly. Shocked, Michael just observed as a female passenger corrected the guy's thinking. Another time, Michael was invited to a Thanksgiving meal at the home of a man who worked at the campus bookstore, a kind gesture toward a young kid from out of state who wouldn't be going home for the break. The man was a local pastor and a dad. Over the meal, the family was asking Michael about his life in Los Angeles. When they asked him what kind of food he liked, he said Korean barbecue. "Is that dog meat?" the pastor's son joked, and the entire table, including the pastor, started cracking up. "I just didn't know how to respond to that," Michael says. He laughed it off, but it numbed him. "Thanksgiving table, all these people. I'm the only minority there, I stick out and I'm a guest. Stuff like that just really bothered me a lot."

Michael heard plenty of racial jokes growing up in LA, too. "But it's so diverse that it doesn't really offend you," he says. "Racial jokes in LA and racial jokes in central Kansas are very different. It sounds different to you. It feels different to you. You feel alone, I think that's the best way to put it."

When the time came for Michael to renew his DACA status, there was no processing center anywhere close by. "I had to walk in the snow for two hours to go to the bus stop at three o'clock in the morning," Michael says. He took a Greyhound to Wichita for an appointment at a government office there.

It wasn't until college that Michael understood that his mom was without papers as well. Though he felt resentful when he realized the truth, he recognized that his family's secrecy was an attempt at protecting him and his sister. "They probably don't want us to think we're going to get deported or something like that and kind of lose our hopes and lose sight of our dreams as students," he says. The impulse to stay quiet about it all stayed with Michael; he thinks of it as a type of denial. "I still don't say anything about it to my friends or anything like that," he says. "When people ask me if I vote, I just tell them that I'm a permanent resident or even a citizen sometimes because I don't want them to ask questions."

Michael's younger sister Mia describes a similar experience. When a Latina classmate opened up to her, telling Mia that she was applying for DACA, Mia pled ignorance. "I told her I have no idea about it, I'm a citizen here," she admits. "She was sharing her story, and I was like, oh my God, I'm going through the same thing. I wanted to tell her, open up . . . But I can't." Her classmate was just one person, but Mia's observation was that Latino kids were honest about stuff like that. "In the Asian community we are very closed. We are afraid that if we expose ourselves too much it could get back to us, make things hard for us in a way."

Though Mia applied for DACA halfway through her junior year in high school, the process took much longer than her brother's and she still didn't have any paperwork when it was time to apply for college. She didn't know about AB-540, the California law that allows undocumented students who graduate from California high schools to pay in-state tuition at state colleges and universities. Though she'd originally dreamed of going to the University of California, Irvine, she ended up at Glendale Community College, an affordable school close to the two-bedroom apartment where she lived with her mom. As a freshman in college, Mia had never held a regular job. She didn't have a driver's license. She was largely dependent on her mother and her aunt for money, transportation, and decision-making about her status. Though Mia got a letter in the mail from USCIS in December of 2016 — right after Trump's election — that led her to believe her DACA application was approved, she never received the final paperwork. She went to her biometrics appointment — then, nothing.

She didn't normally follow the news closely, but she watched the 2016 election returns at home, alone in her bedroom. Before the election, "we all thought it was a joke, he was a joke," Mia says. "The things he was saying didn't make sense. To build a wall? That was nonsense for us." Mia knew some of her professors were distressed by Trump's candidacy, but it seemed as though they didn't think he would actually win. "Our teachers just used to laugh at it. I was laughing with them, but inside I was actually scared. What if he does win? And once he did, I was just devastated."

DACA in the Trump Era

Trump's anti-immigrant rhetoric and promises were a cornerstone of his campaign. In addition to pledging to "deport them all" and to "build the wall" along the 1,954-mile US-Mexico border, Trump also specifically promised, on his campaign website, to "immediately terminate" the DACA program, which he calls an "illegal executive amnesty."

After Trump's election, the DACA-related fear was twofold: First was the not-unlikely possibility that nearly seven hundred thousand people with DACA could have their status rescinded overnight. They would lose their ability to work legally, and they'd be back to under-the-table work, often in jobs that wouldn't make good use of their skills or education. In many states, they would lose their driver's licenses as well. Second was the less likely but not-irrational fear that the extensive personal data collected through DACA and now held in government databases could be used against recipients and their families. After all, "Believe me" and "Deportation force" were two of the president's go-to catchphrases during the campaign, and within a week of taking office he announced two new executive orders designed to make it easier to deport unauthorized immigrants from the country.

Despite the promises, Trump did not immediately terminate DACA. And when the administration finally did attempt to phase out the program starting in September 2017, the courts intervened. USCIS stopped accepting new applications, but DACA status continued to be renewed for prior recipients. There were about 650,000 young immigrants who were still "DACAmented" at the end of 2019.[80] In June 2020, the Supreme Court offered temporary relief for DACA recipients when it ruled that the Trump administration had neither adequately provided a reason for its decision to rescind the program nor addressed the hardship to DACA recipients that would ensue. The court did not weigh in on the merits of the policy itself, just the procedural aspects associated with rescinding it. The approach to DACA changed again in January 2021. On his first day in office, President Biden issued a memorandum directing the Department of Homeland Security to "preserve and fortify" the DACA program.[81]

The economic arguments against scrapping the DACA program are robust. A 2016 survey found that 87 percent of DACA recipients were employed and paying taxes (many of the rest were still students). Ending DACA would result in company turnover costs of $3.4 billion and reduce social security and Medicare contributions by $24.6 billion over the next decade, according to *Money on the Table*, a report released by the Immigrant Legal Resource Center (ILRC) in December 2016.[82] The progressive think tank Center for American Progress calculated that ending DACA would result in a $433-billion hit to the country's GDP over the next decade (both numbers assumed the DACA population remained at its 2016 size).[83]

"We've seen that DACA recipients really improved economic conditions for their families," says Lena Graber of the ILRC. "They got their first jobs, they got better wages, they were more civically engaged, more able to feel like they could participate in their communities." The social security number also adds to financial security. "With that number you can get credit cards, and bank accounts, and access to financial services that are really hard for the undocumented population to access and that really make a difference to people's general well-being — and to their families," Graber says.

The DACA roller coaster illustrates the discretion that a presidential administration has in enforcement actions, and more broadly the wide latitude for a change in enforcement priorities that accompanies the arrival of a new administration. Even without new executive or legislative actions, a new president can mean changes in enforcement priorities under existing laws. When Trump became president in early 2017, the shift in tone was palpable in many immigrant communities, with advocacy groups holding back-to-back "Know Your Rights" sessions for undocumented immigrants living in fear of increased ICE action and towns, campuses, and even individual American families making known their willingness to provide "sanctuary" to protect the undocumented from an increasingly hostile federal government.

Mayfield Heights, Ohio, 2010

The ICE van delivered Marcos Perez to a jail in a nearby suburb; then, less than a week later, he was transferred to an ICE detention facility about two hours away from where he and Elizabeth had been living in Mayfield Heights. He spent just four nights there before he was loaded onto a plane to south Texas and walked across a bridge into Mexico. There was no notice. Elizabeth wasn't able to visit him in either facility. Every day Marcos was in jail, neither he nor Elizabeth knew where he'd be the next night. He got off the plane in July wearing the same work clothes he'd had on when he left the house in Mayfield Heights in June. He still had the same $17 in his pocket.

"So I stay in jail for almost a month for no reason," Marcos says. "It surprised me how it happened. Because I always try to do everything in the right way. Sometimes as an immigrant there isn't a right way."

When he was stopped, when he was locked up, Marcos felt incredulous that after seventeen years in the US such a small event would be the thing to upend his life. He thought about Elizabeth, their baby, her new pregnancy. His mind raced: "What am I going to do at the border when they take me out? What am I going to say to my family when they take me back?"

The lawyer who advised Elizabeth not to pay bail told her he would handle her case—take care of everything—for an up-front fee of $5,000. She cashed in her Marine Corps retirement fund to come up with the money. The only time the lawyer called her after that was to ask when the money transfer was coming through. He never talked to Marcos. He never visited him—or even called him—in jail, Elizabeth says. At the time, Elizabeth tried to talk herself into being patient. Her dad had been a lawyer and she knew legal stuff could take a long time. Once Marcos was back in Mexico, the lawyer advised them to file a visa application so that Marcos could try to get back into the country.

He spent his first couple of nights back in Mexico sleeping in a bus station. He didn't have identification with him, so there was no easy way for Elizabeth to wire him the money he'd need to get back to Mexico City, where he'd grown up and where most of his family still lived. Finally, he found a guy who would act as a go-between and accept the money for him at a local Western Union. Elizabeth wired some cash, and Marcos bought a bus ticket south.

Elizabeth started relying on her retirement money to pay the rent on the house in Mayfield Heights. A month later, she used another chunk of it to fly down to Mexico City. After what she recalls as "a two-week whirlwind of paperwork," Elizabeth and Marcos were married in a civil ceremony attended by much of Marcos's family. Marcos wore a white Guayabera shirt for the occasion; Elizabeth wore jeans and a blue sweater. Through the ceremony she held Pelé strapped to her chest in a baby carrier.

Marcos's family threw a party to celebrate both the union and Pelé's baptism, which took place the next day. "They decorated their house, made all this food," Elizabeth recalls. "I had just met them, but they all went in a circle saying something nice about us being married. I didn't know what they were saying, and it had to be translated. It was a little uncomfortable for me, but he has a great family."

When Elizabeth and Pelé got home to Cleveland, she gave up the lease on the house in Mayfield Heights and moved back in with her mom and dad. By September, all the money in her retirement fund was gone.

The Rise and Fall (and Rise) of Arrests and Deportations

Deportations are one of the most visible statistics related to immigration enforcement policy, the raw total number of removals serving as a powerful signal to undocumented immigrants of the risk they live with every day. Despite some periods of increased enforcement activity, deportations were uncommon throughout most of the history of the United States. Between 1900 and 1990, there were between one and two removals annually per thousand foreign-born US residents, including those who were formally removed at the border and not necessarily living in the United States. That number jumped from less than two per thousand in 1990 to six per thousand over the 1990s, reaching ten per thousand in 2010.

Part of the explanation for rising removal numbers is growth in the number of unauthorized residents. The undocumented population

FIGURE 10. Number of removals, 1892–2018

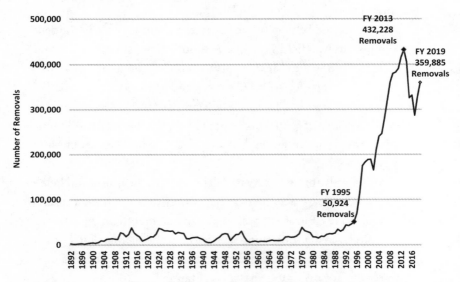

Source: Department of Homeland Security Yearbook of Immigration Statistics, 2018

more than tripled between 1990 and the 2007 peak, but growth in the number of removals far outstripped that, increasing tenfold over the same period. The annual number of removals *per thousand undocumented immigrants* grew from nine in 1990 to twenty-six in 2007, and kept climbing through 2013.

Between 2008 and 2013 deportations reached their highest rate in US history. Coupled with the fact that the total number of undocumented immigrants living in the United States was greater than it had ever been, the high numbers were largely a result of more aggressive enforcement ushered in by the 1996 IIRIRA law and changes to border policy. The highest year for ICE deportations — officially known as "removals" — was 2013, with over 430,000 immigrants ejected from the United States (see figure 10), about thirty-nine removals per thousand unauthorized immigrants. During these peak years, about ninety thousand of those deported each year claimed to have at least one child who was a US citizen.

When people imagine a deportation, they often think of the removal affecting those already settled within the US, people like Marcos. In fact, the total removal numbers reported by the DHS include

FIGURE 11. ICE removals stemming from border and interior arrests, 2008–2019

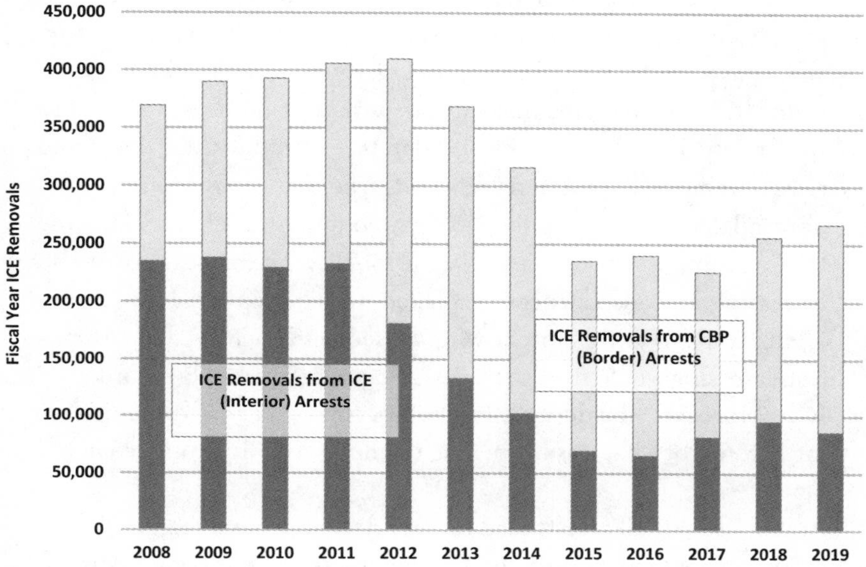

Source: ICE Enforcement and Removal Operations Annual Reports

both these interior removals, typically handled by Immigration and Customs Enforcement (ICE), and those that occur at or near the border, typically when immigrants are caught by the Border Patrol, a unit within Customs and Border Protection, or CBP.

For years many border crossers were given the option of a "voluntary return," sometimes disparagingly called "catch and release"; such returns were not recorded as official removals. But under Obama, recent border crossers increasingly were handled as deportations—in an effort to increase the adverse consequences for a failed border crossing.

The effect of this policy change can be seen in figure 11, which offers more detail about ICE-processed removals—those interior removals that started as ICE arrests and those that started as CBP border arrests but were later transferred to ICE. (Unlike figure 10, which shows total removal numbers, figure 11 does not show removals that are not processed through ICE; these are typically quick border removals handled entirely by CBP.) The figure 11 data present a somewhat different story: True interior removals peaked at almost 238,000 in FY 2009 (a year that partially reflected the Bush administration and partially the Obama administration), remained fairly stable for a few years, and sharply declined starting in 2012. At the same time, border-originated and, consequently, total ICE removals grew from 2008 to 2012.

In other words, Obama's high deportation numbers relative to Bush's largely reflect shifting border tactics rather than increased rates of removal of long-term residents. The change in accounting not only inflated removal numbers compared to past levels — making the Obama administration appear tougher on illegal immigration — it also increased the consequences of a failed border crossing. Now, immigrants stopped at the border who subsequently achieved a surreptitious crossing would have the failed attempt permanently recorded by ICE. Moreover, the deportation numbers give a somewhat misleading account of what was happening to immigrants living in the United States.

Because not all arrests lead to deportation, or may lead to deportation only several years later, it is helpful to look at data on apprehensions as well. ICE interior arrests were fairly stable — around three hundred thousand annually — during Obama's first term. Border apprehensions fell during the 2008 to 2012 period, presumably because fewer unauthorized immigrants were attempting to come to the US during the Great Recession, but many more of those border arrests resulted in removal. In the second term of Obama's presidency, interior arrests fell substantially as enforcement eased on those immigrants not prioritized for removal (see figure 12).

The upshot is a complicated legacy for Obama. In his first term, the administration presided over a record number of removals, but much of the increase was due to changed procedures at the border rather than interior enforcement. Those border tactics, though, mean that many long-term residents like Jorge Ramirez — the Mexican immigrant who runs a small stucco business — now have a much more serious immigration record than they would have in the pre-Obama era. Though unauthorized presence in the United States is not a crime on its own, entry without proper inspection is a misdemeanor, and unlawful presence after a previous order of removal — including one generated dur-

FIGURE 12. ICE and CBP apprehensions, 2008–2019

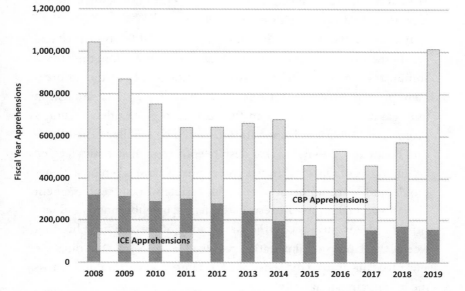

Source: Department of Homeland Security Yearbook of Immigration Statistics, various years

ing a failed border attempt—is a felony. The consequences of Obama's efforts to deter unauthorized border crossings are still being felt today in the removals of unauthorized "criminals" whose only crime was an attempt to surreptitiously enter the United States.

The numbers in figures 10, 11, and 12 also speak to enforcement in the Trump era. The first year of data fully reflecting the Trump administration is FY 2018, and it shows ICE interior removals of around ninety-five thousand, up 45 percent from where they were in FY 2016. In FY 2019, eighty-six thousand ICE interior removals were recorded. The data also show that interior arrests rose to 168,000 in FY 2018, compared to 114,000 in FY 2016, which was a low point in recent history. The 2019 data reflect a spike in border apprehensions, largely driven by Central American "surge" migrants surrendering themselves at the border to seek asylum. In sum, though Trump made good on his promise to ramp up enforcement relative to Obama's second term, the overall level of interior enforcement—as measured by both apprehensions and interior removals—remained well below the peak levels recorded in 2008–2013. Trump failed to deliver on the promise he made to his supporters to deport millions of immigrants.

In the end, the statistics describing enforcement levels just tell one part of the story. The anti-immigrant rhetoric coming from the Trump administration—and the increased unpredictability of the enforcement process—have an outsized effect in fueling anxiety and fear in immigrant communities. In an October 2020 piece titled "Trump's Promise of Millions of Deportations is Yet to be Fulfilled," the Migration Policy Institute noted that despite enforcement statistics lagging behind those of Obama, "arrests and removals have taken on a higher profile under Trump because of highly visible worksite enforcement operations and increased arrests in residential neighborhoods and sensitive locations such as courthouses, among other tactics."[84] In other words, the Trump administration removed fewer people but did so in a way that maximized the sense of uncertainty and vulnerability across the immigrant community.

It is possible the administration would have preferred to deport more immigrants but was stymied by bureaucratic and legal hurdles. Clearly, many immigrants arrested in the Trump era are still awaiting resolution of their cases. It is also plausible that the Trump administration sought to sow fear and confusion in immigrant communities primarily to reinforce a social hierarchy. An actual reduction in the number of unauthorized immigrants within the country is at odds with business interests and therefore may not have been a true goal at all. Regardless of motivation, the Trump administration pursued a "wide-net" approach to enforcement and engendered a great deal of fear in the process.

Prioritizing Criminals for Removal

Much of the rhetoric surrounding interior enforcement relates to removing dangerous criminals. Through a series of memos issued by then-ICE director John Morton starting in 2010, and in official 2014 guidance, the Obama administration prioritized removals of some types of unauthorized immigrants while discouraging actions against more sympathetic groups.

The "Priority 1" group included people engaged in terrorism or espionage, convicted gang members, and those with non-immigration-related felony convictions. This top tier also included "aggravated felonies"—a term developed as part of the Immigration and Nationality Act and expanded under the 1996 IIRIRA law. Aggravated felonies include a long list of crimes ranging from murder to low-level drug trafficking. Obama's top tier also included recent border crossers, presumably under the assumption that there are fewer adverse humanitarian consequences to removing new arrivals. Priority 2 included those convicted of three or more misdemeanors or one serious misdemeanor, such as domestic violence or driving under the influence (DUI). It also included those who crossed the border without authorization after January 1, 2014, or significantly abused visa programs. Priority 3 included those who failed to comply with a removal order issued in 2014 or later.[85] (As in the case of other immigration reforms, the priority system was more lenient toward long-standing immigrants and tougher on those who committed immigration violations after the policy was announced.)

The "Morton memos" and subsequent priority rankings encouraged officers on the ground to refrain from taking action against those without criminal histories, especially if the individuals in question had close family ties in the United States. But the priority system also highlights the often-misleading way individuals are described as "criminal" versus "noncriminal" in the immigration context. In many cases, the "crime" is an immigration violation, such as a felony for unauthorized presence after a prior order of removal.

A 2018 report by the Cato Institute, a libertarian think tank that generally supports immigration, analyzed ICE removals between October 2008 and February 2017.[86] About half of all removals (and a quarter of interior removals) were of individuals with no criminal convictions at all. Among the remaining half who did have a criminal record, only 12 percent had been convicted of a violent crime, most commonly simple assault. Another 27 percent had been convicted of a nonviolent crime that had a potential victim, such as theft or DUI. About 60 percent of "criminals" had committed a crime which Cato classified as victimless, including immigration offenses, drug offenses, and non-DUI traffic violations. In other words, even under Obama's priority system, the vast majority of deportations were not of violent criminals, but instead of those with much-less-serious criminal histories or whose only crimes were immigration-related.

Nevertheless, it is the case that the system does target those with criminal backgrounds to a significant degree relative to those without. According to estimates by the Migration Policy Institute, fewer than 8 percent of immigrants have any criminal record and fewer than 3 percent of immigrants have been convicted of a felony.[87] (Eight percent of the overall US population has a felony conviction, according to a recent University of Georgia study.)[88] Obama's administration made substantial strides in targeting those comparatively few immigrants with a criminal history. The fraction of ICE deportations (including both interior and ICE-processed border removals) that were of people with a criminal record rose from 31 percent in FY 2008 to 58 percent in FY 2016.

For its part, the Trump administration rejected the notion that there are priorities for removal, and specifically encouraged officers to pursue enforcement action regardless of criminal background. At the same time, it stayed true to its assertion that immigration enforcement's purpose is to protect Americans from danger, a paradox it rationalized by redefining every unauthorized immigrant as a threat. Trump's January 25, 2017, executive order stated that "[a]liens who illegally enter the United States without inspection or admission present a significant threat to national security and public safety."[89]

Trump's wide net has played out on the ground. In FY 2016, Obama's last year in office, 86 percent of those facing an ICE administrative arrest had a previous criminal conviction. That number fell to 64 percent by FY 2019.[90] There were more arrests made in the community (as opposed to in a jail setting), and more of the individuals arrested had no criminal history—the numbers in this "community arrests of noncriminals" category rose from 3,970 in FY 2016 to 10,245 in FY 2019. These types of arrests still did not dominate ICE activity, but they did send a strong signal to the undocumented community: Anyone might be at risk, at any time. The Trump administration also incarcerated those awaiting immigration proceedings more than ever before, adding to the sense of danger.

Despite substantial increases in arrests of noncriminals and in detention activity, actual deportations did not change as dramatically. Between 2016 and 2019, ICE removals increased about 11 percent, and the fraction of those with a criminal conviction remained nearly constant. At least 56 percent of ICE removals (and at least three-quarters of interior removals) in FY 2017, 2018, and 2019 fall into this category.[91]

It is perhaps surprising that increasingly sweeping street-level tactics have not translated to equally dramatic increases in removals. It is likely that those arrested with the wide-net approach have more compelling cases for relief, cases which often take years to work their way through the immigration courts. The Trump administration's policy choices have led to increased harassment, detention, and hardship for undocumented immigrants and their families, but in the end have not significantly changed the profile or increased the number of deported immigrants.

Deportation and the Latino Community

Data on ICE deportation proceedings initiated in fiscal year 2018 gives some indication of the groups most affected by deportation.[92] Over 90 percent of those removed were men. About 55 percent of those deported were originally from Mexico, and another 37 percent were individuals born in Guatemala, Honduras, or El Salvador. Over 95 percent of all deportations were of Mexicans, Central Americans, or South Americans, even though those groups make up only about three-quarters of all undocumented immigrants, according to estimates by the Migration Policy Institute.[93]

The disproportionate deportation of Latinos is explained in part by the fact that a large fraction of removals are of recent border crossers, and many recent border crossers are immigrants from Latin America. (Unauthorized immigrants from other parts of the world are more likely to have overstayed a visa.) Another factor is that many interior deportations arise as a result of traffic stops or other minor legal mishaps — and Latinos are more likely than other ethnic groups to be profiled as unauthorized immigrants. A finding of obvious racial profiling in the enforcement process is not enough to protect an unauthorized immigrant from deportation.[94] It's a safe bet that, in most parts of the country, a Latino man who has overstayed a visa is at greater risk of deportation than a Caucasian European man with the same violation.

Seneca Detention Center, Ohio, 2013

There were twenty men in Eduardo Lopez's cell block. Five others were Latino men in for immigration violations, the "noncriminals" as Eduardo, the undocumented factory foreman from Ohio, thought of them. The others were Black or white guys who seemed to be mostly drug offenders. "I grew up on the streets — I knew about the streets. But I don't know about the jail," he says. "So when they put me in that jail and they explain that these guys spent this many years in there because they sell drugs, I'm like, I'm with these people right next to me!?" Eduardo says. "It felt like something off of TV." The first night he called Elena. "I don't want to live like this," he told her. "I'm not a criminal."

There were a lot of fights in Seneca, Eduardo says, but most of them were about stupid stuff, like who got to control the TV, or who got the best pillow. Every day, Eduardo was grateful that he knew how to speak English. He noticed that the guards were especially hard on the inmates who couldn't communicate with them. "In that jail, if you didn't know English, they eat you, they killed you," Eduardo says. "They so racist." There were a couple of Mexicans from Chiapas, the southern Mexican state that borders Guatemala. They were in under the same sort of circumstances as Eduardo. Those men spoke a local language, but hardly any Spanish, Eduardo says. They couldn't communicate with anyone. A couple times Eduardo stuck his head out and attempted to reason with the guards. "I try to explain that not the way to treat people," he says. "That guy that he's yelling at and calling names, he's not here because he killed somebody. He's not here because he's smoking drugs. He's here because he was working and he got caught in the job."

After a little while, Eduardo felt like he had found a role for himself. "I can tell you, a lot of people got respect for me at the jail, a lot of people thinking I'm round the block," he says. "If I see somebody trying to bully you and you not doing nothing to him, I going to be there and tell the people that was wrong."

In the four months he was in Seneca, Eduardo's family never visited him. He didn't want them to; he was scared for them. All the adults that might bring his kids to the jail were also undocumented. "If they go in, they might not be coming out," he says. Plus, it had been terrible the one time his older daughter, Ariel, saw him at the local jail. At first, they'd told her he was just working. When Ariel, then just six years old, saw him in his prison uniform and handcuffs, she started crying.

"Why you lying?" she asked her dad.

"I'm not lying," Eduardo said.

"Yeah, you told me you were working and you're in jail. You're in jail. Why? Did you do something wrong? Did you kill someone?!"

Eduardo tried to explain why he crossed the border. That what he did was against the law, but that he wasn't a bad man. It seemed absurd to try to explain borders and immigration policy to a six-year-old. And after he did explain he could tell that it only made Ariel more fearful — of the police especially. "The kids, they living afraid, like they going to get deported," he says. "You can't have a lot of little kids thinking about immigration. Why you have to have these words in their mouths? They worry about his dad, about her mom."

For a couple weeks after Ariel saw Eduardo in jail, she wouldn't talk to him on the phone. She was mad at everyone and everything all the time. When she saw a cop car on the busy street outside their house she would run and hide in her bedroom. In the first weeks after Eduardo was taken away, William, then a two-year-old toddler, seemed to become deeply depressed. He wouldn't eat or speak or do anything. Elena eventually brought him to the emergency room. The problem seemed to be entirely psychological.

"I was always close to my kids," Eduardo says. "If I go wash my truck, they are right there next to me. Whenever I do anything, they are right next to me. So when this happened to me, they ask, 'Where he go? Where he go without us?'"

FIGURE 13. Average daily population in detention, 1994–2019

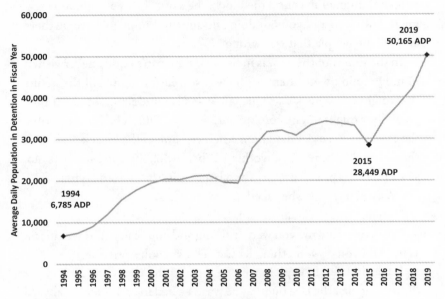

Source: Center for Migration Studies and ICE Enforcement and Operations Report, 2019

The Role of Detention

Immigrant detentions have massively expanded since the early 1990s, especially in the Trump era. Living in the US without authorization is a civil violation, not a criminal one, and violators are not subject to criminal incarceration. Nevertheless, the government routinely and increasingly holds immigrants in custody. There were 6,785 immigrants detained on an average day in 1994.[95] That number exceeded twenty-one thousand by 2001; it reached more than fifty thousand in FY 2019, with about twenty thousand of these originating from interior arrests.[96] As shown in figure 13, detention is one area of enforcement where the Trump-era statistics far exceed levels seen at any time in the past.

There are a few different ways an immigrant can be "booked in" to detention. Some individuals are arrested at the border by Customs and Border Protection. These can include surreptitious border crossers, who are often detained briefly and then put on a bus or plane home under "expedited removal"—that is, removal without legal process or judicial review.[97] Other border crossers, including asylum seekers, have the right to judicial review of their case, and often will be transferred to a longer-term ICE detention facility while they wait. Typically, first-time violators from Mexico or Canada have not been subject to expedited removal.[98] (In 2019, the Trump administration extended expedited removal to apply to interior removals of undocumented immigrants in their first two years of residence.)

Asylum seekers who present themselves at the border are also detained. They are given a so-called credible-fear interview about their asylum claim, and the officer on the ground makes a determination about which cases can go forward into the asylum determination process. The administration also has discretion as to which asylum seekers are allowed to live in the United States on parole while their case proceeds.

Recently, in a Trump administration push to reduce the possibility of migrants disappearing into society undetected while on parole — as well as to reduce asylum claims — many more asylum seekers have been held in detention.[99] Not surprisingly, this policy decision puts an additional burden on an already overcrowded detention system. In 2019, as immigrants seeking asylum continued to arrive at the border in large numbers, the Trump administration implemented the Migrant Protection Protocols (MPP, or "Remain in Mexico") which require many asylum seekers to wait in Mexican tent camps for immigration court dates that are months away.

Even with the adoption of MPP, border arrests by CBP led to nearly 373,000 bookings into ICE facilities over the course of FY 2019, nearly double the 2017 number.[100] Unaccompanied minors who arrive at the border are not included in these figures. Children are — at least in theory — supposed to be held in Border Patrol facilities for no more than seventy-two hours and then transferred to facilities under the purview of Health and Human Services (HHS) rather than ICE. With surging numbers of such children (defined as those under the age of eighteen) arriving from Central America in recent years, the system has been stretched past its limit. In the Trump era, fear has exacerbated the problem: Relatives, often undocumented themselves, may be hesitant to step forward to take children. The Trump policy of family separation placed more than 4,300 children,[101] the youngest-known just four months old,[102] in jail-like facilities or foster homes, sometimes thousands of miles away from their parents. The inhumane treatment of children and their parents led some states and nonprofits to refuse to help expand HHS facilities, generating lasting impacts on capacity even after the family separation policy officially ended. The result is a lack of infrastructure and horrific conditions for migrant children.[103]

Interior enforcement also generates a significant number of immigrants held in custody. In FY 2019, there were a total of 137,000 detentions stemming from ICE arrests, with an average duration of fifty-four days.[104] When someone is arrested for an immigration violation, ICE usually has discretion about whether to keep them in custody while awaiting immigration proceedings. Many individuals are allowed to stay at home with an ankle monitor or to post bond as they wait their turn in the queue, which may take years. (By mid-2020, there were over 1.1 million pending cases with an average wait time of 748 days.)[105]

Though most immigrants awaiting removal proceedings are not in custody, there are several circumstances which do lead to an individual being detained after an internal arrest. If an undocumented immigrant has a prior order of removal on their record, the deportation process can happen promptly based on a "reinstatement of removal order" with a brief detention period and no judicial review. Factors such as the individual's current family situation, how long the immigrant has been living in the United States, or flaws in the original removal proceedings are not likely to be considered.[106] This circumstance explains why someone like Marcos Perez, who had previously been apprehended crossing the border, could be summarily deported without seeing a judge. It also highlights how the Obama-era decision to classify failed border attempts as official removals had real impacts down the line.

Immigrants with a criminal conviction also end up in ICE detention. When an undocumented immigrant serves jail time for a serious crime and is then released to ICE, the law requires further detention during immigration proceedings. The exact parameters of who qualifies for such "mandatory detention" has been litigated, and in 2019 the Supreme Court ruled in favor of a broad interpretation of the statute, expanding the number of immigrants who are held without a bond hearing or parole.[107]

Part of the explanation for rising detention numbers is that as enforcement efforts have ramped up, the accompanying resources to process removals have not kept pace. In every year since 2008, for example, there have been more cases coming to the country's Department of Justice (DOJ) immigration judges than the judges are able to process. Though the number of judges increased from about 245 in 2010 to 442 in 2019, the backlog also steadily increased over that time. The DOJ's Executive Office of Immigration Review reported 1.1 million pending cases by April 2020, double the 516,000 in the queue at the end of FY 2016.[108] In FY 2019 the DOJ received nearly 538,000 new cases, significantly more than at any point in the Obama era. They processed just 276,000.[109]

The upshot is that there is often a significant delay between an immigrant's original arrest and the time of their court date — often years. Though most people are able to wait out the period at home, tens of thousands of individuals awaiting a court date remain in detention, at great personal cost to themselves and their families — as well as at taxpayers' expense. The detained population tends to move through the process more quickly because their cases are prioritized over the cases of those waiting while living in the community. But expediency is not necessarily desirable from the perspective of the immigrant, as a slow-moving process gives an unauthorized immigrant more time and ability to find a lawyer and develop their legal case.

Life in Detention

Immigrants held in ICE detention centers are there while they await the outcome of their immigration cases, not to serve time for crime. Yet the conditions in many detention centers are indistinguishable from — or, in some cases, worse than — those in prisons. A 2020 investigation by the American Civil Liberties Union (ACLU) of five newly built facilities revealed appalling conditions.[110] Immigrants often lacked access to adequate medical care and sanitation, were restricted from

talking to counsel, were subject to solitary confinement for minor in-
fractions, and were subject to verbal and physical abuse at the hands
of guards. In one extreme example, the Winn Correctional Facility in
Louisiana withheld a wheelchair from an immigrant with disabilities,
who then had to rely on fellow detainees to help him reach the toilet
and take a shower. When inspectors came to Winn for a visit in November 2019, the man — an asylum seeker from Honduras — was sedated
against his will and locked in a small room off the medical unit so that
he wouldn't be seen or interviewed.[111]

For the most part, ICE does not operate detention centers itself.
Only five of 211 facilities used to detain immigrants in ICE custody are
actually run by the agency, with the remainder contracted out to other
governmental authorities or to for-profit corporations. Though there
are explicit quality standards, a January 2019 report by DHS's own Inspector General concludes that "ICE does not adequately follow up
on identified deficiencies or consistently hold facilities accountable for
correcting them." Of the more than fourteen thousand documented
deficiencies at 106 facilities studied between 2015 and 2018 — including
failure to notify ICE about sexual assaults and failure to forward alle-
gations regarding staff misconduct — ICE had imposed financial penalties only twice.[112]

Despite criticism of for-profit immigrant detention centers, ICE
has nowhere near the capacity it would need to operate facilities itself
given the number of immigrants detained. Possible solutions include
devoting more resources to processing the backlog or expanding the
use of alternative ways of monitoring immigrants who are waiting for
their court dates. In the meantime, taxpayers spent $3.2 billion in FY
2019 housing immigrants awaiting a hearing, many of them in substandard for-profit facilities.

Alternatives to Detention

If an immigrant has family in the US, does not have a criminal history
or prior removal, and is not considered a threat to national security,
alternatives to detention are frequently used. In lieu of incarceration,

the individual awaiting an immigration court date might be outfitted with an ankle monitor, be required to check in with ICE regularly, receive a bond for release, or be subject to some combination of these options.

Like a bail bond in the case of criminal proceedings, the so-called delivery bond is paid by the immigrant to the government and later returned if the individual shows up to court as promised. Not all detained individuals have this option. In recent years, about half of those detained have received custody hearings, and bonds were granted at about half of those hearings.[113] The median bond amount in FY 2019 was $8,000, though amounts vary widely based on the individual and the immigration court.[114]

Of course, $8,000 is a huge sum for someone working a low-wage job, and it is not uncommon for an immigrant to remain in detention simply because they cannot afford the bond. In 2015, the ACLU filed a class-action lawsuit against the federal government, *Hernandez v. Sessions*,[115] arguing that the determining process for detained immigrants' bond amounts is unconstitutional, as it does not consider the immigrants' financial status. One of the plaintiffs was Cesar Matias, a gay man who had fled to the US from Honduras more than a decade before, and who worked in Los Angeles as a hairstylist and garment worker. Matias, who had no previous criminal record, was detained for more than four years while he waited for his asylum application to be processed, as he could not afford the $3,000 bond. In October 2017, the Ninth Circuit Court ruled that ICE must consider an immigrant's ability to pay when setting a bond; it must likewise limit the bond to a reasonable amount that will ensure a person shows up in court.

The courts have also weighed in on the right to a bond hearing. In the 2018 case *Jennings v. Rodriguez*, the Supreme Court overturned a circuit court requirement that immigrants be granted a bond hearing after six months of detention.[116] The case centered on Alejandro Rodriguez, a legal permanent resident who was brought to the US from Mexico as an infant and had been convicted of joyriding and drug possession as a young adult. Rodriguez appealed his subsequent order of removal, and he was detained for more than three years without any bond hearing while his case worked its way through the courts. He lost his job as a dental assistant and was separated from his two children. Though the Supreme Court, in denying the right to a guaranteed bond hearing, did not weigh in on the constitutionality of unlimited civil detention of noncitizens, the *Rodriguez* case highlights the weak due-process provisions applying to immigrants — provisions much weaker than many Americans expect and take for granted in the criminal sphere. (Rodriguez was eventually granted relief from deportation and remains in the US.)

Texas, 2010

By the summer of 2010, Jorge Ramirez's mom was getting sicker. She was having trouble walking, had debilitating back pain, and was spending weeks at a time in bed. Two of Jorge's brothers were working selling food in the local Mexican street markets; the other was largely unemployed.

Jorge and Yuuko were living together in a tiny studio apartment in Washington. "I know that she's my one so I know that I will be here [in the US] for her," Jorge says, referring to Yuuko. "But I need to see my mom because she was sick. I decided to go back to Mexico."

Yuuko tried repeatedly to talk him out of it. They both knew that Jorge would have no problem returning to Mexico. He only needed his Washington State driver's license to board the plane; when he got off in Mexico City, he would show his Mexican passport.

Getting back home, though, would require another illegal border crossing.

"I was against it," Yuuko says. "I thought that might be it, I'm never going to see him again." Jorge couldn't be swayed. He flew down and Yuuko followed for a visit a few weeks later. It was there, in his family home, over a dinner with his parents and brothers, that Jorge proposed.

"I don't think that she was suspecting me to," Jorge says, "but I know that I want to be with her. You know when you have met your person that you have to be with."

Yuuko said yes.

A couple of days later, she flew home to Washington while Jorge made his way to the Texas border, this time paying $2,000 to a coyote he found through contacts in his hometown. He was caught by ICE in early September 2010, soon after he reached the American side.

In his first week of detention, Jorge was transferred among three different jails. The ICE detention center closest to where he was apprehended was full, so he was initially sent to a regular prison instead, he says. "Every time I get transferred from one place to another, they have to tie me all the way, from my wrists to my ankles," he says. "You walk outside and people look at you like you must be a murderer or something."

The charge against him was "illegal entry," a misdemeanor. He was told he would soon see an immigration judge. There was a library in the detention center. Jorge remembered hearing something about how immigrants could ask for a bond that could release them from detention. He started looking up the policies in legal books in the library. After he had been in detention for close to a month, Yuuko flew down to Texas. In the past few weeks she'd been planning her wedding, though not the one she'd first imagined. Jorge had given her the phone number for the chapel in the detention center. She was able to talk to a nun who volunteered there. When Yuuko arrived in Texas, the nun was waiting for her. She had found a local judge who was available and willing to perform the marriage.

"The officers were saying that I'm crazy," Yuuko says. "Because I'm Asian they didn't think that I'm for someone from Mexico." In October 2010, Jorge and Yuuko were married inside the detention facility with the nun as their witness. "They did allow us one kiss," Yuuko says.

She had hoped she could be in the courtroom with Jorge. But as it turned out, neither of them would be there. The policy was for the judge to just review the detainee's file. When Jorge's record showed no criminal history beyond the border arrest, the judge approved a bond for $15,000 — far more money than Jorge and Yuuko had. When their lawyer brought their new marriage to his attention, he agreed to lower the bond to $8,000. Yuuko sold her car and the couple pooled their savings. They paid the bond and they both returned home to Washington.

Worksite-Based Enforcement

The 1986 IRCA law promised to address the employment of unauthorized immigrants by imposing penalties on employers. These efforts were weak throughout the 1990s. But a renewed commitment to internal enforcement was evident after September 11, 2001, with a focus on worksite enforcement. Worksite raids occurred regularly early in the first decade of the 2000s; agents from the Immigration and Naturalization Services (INS) — or, after the 2003 reorganization, Immigration and Customs Enforcement (ICE) — would arrest undocumented workers in well-publicized events. Between FY 2002 and FY 2006, the number of individuals arrested annually in worksite raids rose from 510 to 4,940.[117]

The largest raid took place in December 2006, when ICE arrested almost 1,300 workers in six states — Iowa, Minnesota, Nebraska, Texas, Colorado, and Utah — at meatpacking plants all owned by Swift and Company.[118] Roughly 10 percent of the firm's workforce was arrested, and hundreds of workers were deported. No actions were taken against the corporate officials, who had cooperated with ICE by failing to warn workers that the raids were coming.

High-profile events like the Swift raids have important chilling effects beyond the consequences for the individuals deported. Immigrant communities in the affected towns are severely disrupted as well, as families are separated and fear permeates daily life. A number of unaffected workers at the Swift plants never returned to their jobs for fear of further enforcement. A 2007 study by the Urban Institute estimates that one child is directly affected by worksite raids for every two adults that are arrested, and that a large majority of these children are US citizens.[119] Large-scale enforcement actions like the Swift raids have a negligible direct effect on the size of the unauthorized workforce; their purpose is to send a signal to undocumented workers and employers that they are at risk.

Priorities changed under the Obama administration. Although there were 5,184 immigrants arrested in worksite enforcement operations in FY 2008 for civil immigration violations, the number plunged to 1,644 the following year after Obama's inauguration, and in FY 2014 there were only 541 arrests resulting from worksite raids.[120] Instead, the Obama administration focused its efforts on employers who illegally hired unauthorized workers, relying on "paper audits" rather than high-profile raids. The number of audits and final orders and the size of fines increased under Obama; while $26,560 in fines were imposed in FY 2007, more than $16 million were imposed in FY 2014.[121] However, even with the shift of worksite enforcement to employers, the firms audited in 2013 represented only 0.0005 percent of the US's employers, and only 0.0001 percent received a fine.

Both employer– and high-visibility immigrant–focused actions ramped up after Trump was elected. In FY 2018, ICE opened over 6,000 investigations and arrested more than 2,000 people at worksites.[122] In August 2019, ICE launched the largest single-state worksite raid in history when they arrested 680 unauthorized immigrants working at agricultural-processing plants across Mississippi.[123] The primary target was the Illinois-based Koch Foods chicken-processing plant in Morton, Mississippi, which was under investigation for knowingly hiring unauthorized workers. No charges have been forthcoming against Koch as of mid-2020, and Koch is suing the government for illegal search of the plant.

E-Verify and Its Limitations

Though interior enforcement includes raids and deportations, less-visible policies can also have a substantial impact on the lives of immigrants. Immigrants come to the US for jobs, so reducing work opportunities for them could impact the decision of future would-be migrants to come to the United States in the first place. The 1986 IRCA law envisioned cutting off jobs as a key element of the overall enforcement package, but technology at the time was inadequate to support that goal. Developed starting in the late 1990s, E-Verify became the first systematic attempt to verify the status of people working at US firms.

Administered by USCIS, E-Verify is a voluntary online system that verifies work authorization status. Employers enter identifying information — like social security number, name, and birth date — about job applicants or employees; this information is then scanned against records from the Social Security Administration and the DHS. The employer receives a "tentative nonconfirmation" (TNC) if there is any discrepancy—meaning that the social security number or other information provided by the prospective employee does not match information in government databases. About 1.1 percent of submitted files result in a TNC.[124]

One concern with E-Verify is that occasionally workers who are legally in the country mistakenly receive a TNC. Such discrepancies can arise because of glitches in the federal database or because of confusion over a hyphenated name. As measured by successfully contested TNCs, the false-negative rate was only 0.15 percent by FY 2017, but the true rate could be somewhat higher because workers may not realize they can contest the TNC.[125]

From an enforcement perspective, the most important limitation of the E-Verify system is its weakness in detecting identity fraud. Unauthorized workers who submit documents consistent with those of an authorized worker are unlikely to be flagged. An early estimate suggested that half of the unauthorized workers who were screened with E-Verify were inaccurately found to be work authorized.[126]

E-Verify also has an important unintended consequence: It may drive unauthorized workers into the informal sector, or to states with less-widespread use of the E-Verify system. A 2011 Public Policy Institute of California study showed that Arizona's Legal Arizona Workers Act (LAWA), which mandated E-Verify use at firms across the state, drove many such workers into self-employment.[127]

Then there's the simple fact that, for some employers, E-Verify is unappealing. Adopting it may flag valued, longtime employees as undocumented—as well as limit the future pool of applicants. Third-generation Ohio nursery owner Mark Gilson considered adopting E-Verify a few years back but decided not to. "The argument has always been that immigrants are taking jobs from Americans," he says. "But that's really a red herring. The people who come into the country to do agriculture, that's the lowest rung. They really aren't displacing Americans." Without some sort of larger legalization or improvement in the existing worker-visa program, Gilson argues, E-Verify puts many employers in a bind. "I'm not a fan of it because it would be another regulation on the back of small businesses," he says.

Gilson is a former president of his local nursery-growers association. His own business would survive without unauthorized immigrant labor, he said in a 2014 interview. He only has about thirty-five employees, half of them immigrants, and most if not all of those are documented. But overall, his industry would be in trouble. When the issue was discussed at his local association "the consensus was it would put us out of business," Gilson says. "We would cease to be."

Despite its limitations, E-Verify is seen by many as an important tool in discouraging the hiring of unauthorized workers. Though the system is voluntary from the federal perspective, the Supreme Court deemed the mandated use of E-Verify in Arizona constitutional in 2011, and at least twenty-two states have mandated E-Verify use for some or all employers. Not all state laws support the use of the program, however. In California, employers are prohibited from using E-Verify for existing employees in most circumstances. Illinois similarly has protections for workers already on the books.

The program has steadily grown, and by March 2020 there were about 925,000 employers who were enrolled with E-Verify. Combined, these employers used the system for nineteen million cases in the first half of FY 2020.[128] A 2020 study by researchers Pia Orrenius, Madeline Zavodny, and Sarah Greer found that larger employers were more likely to participate in E-Verify, and that recent growth of the unauthorized population in an area also predicted use. But employers are less likely to use the program when the unemployment rate is low or when unauthorized workers are more prevalent in an industry. The authors conclude that E-Verify is costly to employers in situations where they rely on undocumented labor, making it difficult to mandate on a national scale.[129]

Employment-based immigration enforcement, whether through raids, audits, or E-Verify, highlights a key tension in immigration policy: Many employers rely on immigrants, including unauthorized immigrants, as a source of cheap labor. As discussed in part 1, certain industries would find it difficult to be profitable without the low wages that are afforded by undocumented workers. Business leaders are loath to see enforcement actions that would significantly affect their bottom lines. In many cases, both employees and employers were comfortable with the plausible deniability they had before E-Verify was introduced.

The Impact of Enforcement on Immigrant Earnings and Employment

Since jobs are a key magnet for unauthorized migration, it is not surprising that internal enforcement has often been focused on the workplace. As discussed earlier, it is illegal for firms to knowingly hire undocumented immigrants. Higher rates of enforcement may make undocumented workers less likely to try to find work in the formal sector and might make employers more cautious about who they hire. For example, in a 2015 paper, economists Pia Orrenius of the Federal Reserve Bank of Dallas and Madeline Zavodny (then of Agnes Scott College, now at the University of North Florida) examine the impact of E-Verify. They find reductions in male wages among the likely unauthorized after E-Verify goes into effect, suggesting that employers shy away from hiring the undocumented when stricter policies are enacted. Interestingly, likely unauthorized women increase their labor-force participation at the same time, perhaps because women are more likely to work in the informal sector and are able to compensate for the lower wages of their male family members.[130]

Other researchers — Sarah Bohn and Magnus Lofstrom at the Public Policy Institute of California, working with Steven Raphael at the University of California, Berkeley — find similar effects of LAWA, the 2007 Arizona law that required the use of E-Verify, and show that likely undocumented workers have worse employment prospects after its implementation.[131] Both studies lend credence to the idea that worksite enforcement pushes undocumented workers out of the formal workforce and toward the underground economy.

On the flip side of the coin, DACA offers temporary employment eligibility, and studies on the effects of DACA find a positive impact on labor-market outcomes for DACA-eligible individuals. The NURP study described earlier in this section reveals that approximately 60 percent of DACA recipients obtained a new job, and 45 percent increased their incomes after receiving the status. Not surprisingly, DACA increases labor-force participation while decreasing the unemployment rate for those eligible; an estimated fifty thousand to seventy-five thousand DACA recipients were moved into employment because of the program.[132] Another study finds that households headed by individuals who qualify for DACA were 38 percent less likely to be living in poverty after the program was implemented (the oldest DACA recipients are now in their late thirties).[133]

Enforcement and Migration

In part 1, we reviewed evidence that immigrants are unusually mobile when it comes to job opportunities. What about migration in response to enforcement? In a paper examining the 2007 Arizona law that mandated E-Verify, researchers Bohn, Lofstrom, and Raphael find that Latino noncitizens were indeed less likely to live in Arizona after the law was implemented.[134] The change might have been driven by out-migration or reduced in-migration. The situation in Arizona is an extreme case — enforcement on steroids. Starting in 2005, the controversial sheriff of Arizona's Maricopa County, Joe Arpaio, took up the cause of illegal immigration. Relying on 287(g) authority, Arpaio regularly conducted raids of Latino neighborhoods in and around Phoenix. Between 2010 and 2015, those sweeps rounded up about 1,500 county residents; about 57 percent of those residents were undocumented.[135]

Looking across the country, Pia Orrenius and Madeline Zavodny find a declining population of the likely unauthorized following state adoptions of E-Verify.[136] The authors find evidence that some newly arriving unauthorized immigrants are diverted to nearby states.

In another study, author Tara Watson examined implementation of 287(g) agreements around the United States through 2012.[137] As discussed earlier, at that time there were more than eighty agreements falling into two main categories. So-called task force agreements deputized local law officers to enforce immigration law on the street. Police could stop and question someone they suspected of being present unlawfully. The second type of 287(g) agreement is the "jail enforcement" agreement, which allows officers to check the status of anyone who is arrested.

To investigate how immigrants respond in their migration decisions, Watson looks at local areas before and after a 287(g) agreement goes into effect, comparing changes in the 287(g) localities to other similar areas that did not adopt 287(g).

It turns out the two types of agreements have different impacts on whether immigrants move away from their communities. Jail enforcement agreements did not have much of an effect on where immigrants chose to reside. Areas that adopted these agreements did not show different levels of in-migration of immigrants, out-migration to other parts of the United States, or changes in foreign-born population.

For task force enforcement, it's a different story. In broad terms, there is no evidence that 287(g) agreements caused immigrants to leave the United States, except perhaps for those residing in Arizona. There is evidence, however, that immigrants exposed to task force 287(g) agreements in other places moved internally, relocating within the US.

Surprisingly, though, those who moved were probably not unauthorized. The foreign-born movers were primarily highly educated, and some were naturalized citizens. Those who moved in response to aggressive enforcement were mostly nonwhite. In other words, the evidence is consistent with documented immigrants, rather than undocumented ones, relocating within the US when street harassment of minorities becomes prevalent in a local area. If the goal of the 287(g) task force agreements was encouraging "self-deportation" of undocumented immigrants, the programs appear to have missed their intended targets.

The single place where the data suggests that aggressive enforcement may have caused some undocumented immigrants to "self-deport"—leave the US altogether—was the extreme case of Arizona. The truth is, it takes a heavy-handed approach to enforcement to encourage people to leave the United States. The typical undocumented immigrant has been in the US for more than a decade and has US-citizen children. The alternative life is likely to be one with greater exposure to poverty and, in many cases, violence. In the US, most undocumented immigrants have a community, a routine, and the hope for a better future for themselves and their children.

Deterrent Effects of Enforcement

Overall, the evidence indicates that aggressive enforcement regimes do not do much to encourage self-deportation. Proponents of these programs often argue that a primary goal of these policies is to dissuade new migrants from coming to the United States. Unfortunately, there is limited evidence on the degree to which interior enforcement affects the initial decision to migrate.

A standard economic framework makes it easy to see why immigration enforcement would have a deterrent effect. Immigrants make a decision to undertake a costly investment to come to the United States. Anything that makes it more difficult to secure employment, to live comfortably, or to stay long-term would change the benefits side of the equation. For those who are weighing costs and benefits, aggressive enforcement might be enough to dissuade them from migrating.

Indeed, there is evidence that border control has impacted migration flows. In a 2010 DHS working paper, economists Bryan Roberts of the DHS, Gordon Hanson of the University of California, San Diego, and collaborators analyze smuggling costs across different sectors of the southern border. A 10 percent increase in linewatch hours devoted to enforcement in a sector translates into 2–3 percent higher coyote fees for that sector relative to others. The authors interpret the general increase in coyote fees over recent decades as evidence of the efficacy of border control efforts, noting that raising the financial costs associated with border crossing is likely to dissuade some would-be migrants.[138]

University of Southern California professor of Sociology and Law Emily Ryo cautions against blindly applying the rational-choice model to this context, however. Focusing on the deterrent effects of detention policy, Ryo interviews hundreds of migrants in custody, and concludes that "many detainees lacked even the most basic knowledge about procedural and substantive aspects of US immigration law." Because many of Ryo's interviewees viewed immigrating to the United States as the moral choice to support their family, they may have assumed US law would not be so unjust as to detain them in jail-like conditions for making that choice. Misinformation about the risk of detention was compounded by coyotes, who often misled immigrants about what awaited them at the border.[139]

In a contrasting finding, a group of political scientists from Vanderbilt University, the University of Kentucky, the University of New Hampshire, and the American Immigration Council studying the Honduran population in 2014 conclude that many potential Honduran migrants do have general knowledge about the situation at the US border.[140] Around 80 percent correctly identified increased risks associated with border crossing and deportations relative to the past. However, the perception that risks were higher did not have a statistically significant association with self-reported plans to migrate to the United States. Instead, crime victimization and perceptions of personal security in Honduras were far more salient factors. The authors conclude that enforcement is unlikely to be an effective deterrent for those among their study population coming to the United States, but acknowledge that economic migrants might have a different calculus than those fleeing an unsafe situation.

Edward Alden, a senior fellow at the Council on Foreign Relations, a foreign-policy think tank, notes that the proof is in the pudding. He cautions against looking at border apprehensions as a measure of deterrence—lower numbers could mean that many potential migrants are being deterred, but they could also mean that more migrants are successfully evading authorities. Instead, Alden draws on evidence about the number of successful unauthorized entries into the US, and such entries have fallen substantially over recent decades. Estimates suggest close to 1.8 million migrants successfully crossed the border illicitly in FY 2000 but fewer than two hundred thousand did so by FY 2015. Alden argues that much of the decline stems from the harsher consequences—including detention—associated with a failed crossing, leading to fewer attempts.[141] While many migrants surely entered into the pool of visa overstays instead, a substantial number decided to stay in their home countries rather than risk jail time.

A potential criticism of approaches like Alden's is that many factors have changed in recent decades, including the level of economic opportunity in Mexico and the political destabilization in other parts of Latin America.[142] An alternative way to understand deterrent effects is to study the short-term impact of large enforcement reforms. For example, one older study looks at migration choices before and after IRCA, the major 1986 reform that included amnesty for existing undocumented residents as well as heightened border protection.[143] Sociologists Katharine Donato from Louisiana State University, Jorge Durand of Universidad de Guadalajara, and Douglas Massey of the University of Chicago used data from the Mexican Migration Project, a survey which interviews residents of a series of communities in Mexico, as well as members of those same communities who had moved to the United States. They found no evidence in the survey data that IRCA deterred unauthorized migration. By contrast, Gordon Hanson and coauthor Antonio Spilimbergo of the International Monetary Fund did—after accounting for a number of other factors—find a reduction in unauthorized migration (as measured by border apprehensions) following IRCA. The deterrent effect was short-lived, however—it was no longer evident by 1990.[144]

A newer paper by sociologists Massey and Durand, along with coauthor Karen Pren, who manages the same cross-border Mexican Migration Project data at Princeton University, does show an unintended consequence of ramped-up enforcement at the border. Unauthorized migrants are much less likely to return home or to engage in the circular migration that was common in the past.[145] The results help explain why such a high fraction of today's undocumented population are long-term residents: Heightened border control paradoxically keeps undocumented residents *in* the country even as it is designed to keep people out.

Economists Brian Kovak and Rebecca Lessem of Carnegie Mellon University illustrate an additional reason that ramped-up enforcement may be an ineffective deterrent to unauthorized immigration. Right now, a person who is deported is prevented from legally entering the US for any reason for a period of time—ranging from five years if they faced expedited removal at the border to a lifetime entry ban for those who are deported twice. The risk of a legal-entry ban could deter some-one who thinks there is a possible path to legal entry on the horizon, but the deterrent effect is much reduced if no legal option exists.

Also using data from the Mexican Migration Project, Kovak and Lessem find that a high deportation rate does have a deterrent effect to some degree, because it makes the average benefits of migrating lower relative to the costs. However, according to the study, deporta-tions would have a much larger impact if there were a pathway to legal migration.[146]

In general, there is limited evidence on the deterrent effects of in-terior enforcement. But one lesson from the border deterrent literature almost certainly applies: Potential migrants with the strongest impetus to enter the United States are the least likely to be deterred by harsh policies. As Edward Alden puts it, "deterrence works best where the stakes for the individual migrants are the lowest." Individuals in dan-gerous or violent situations in their home countries are among those for whom stakes are high. (The thousands of Central American asylum seekers arriving at the border during Donald Trump's administration are a case in point.) Alden also notes that long-term residents and par-ents with children living in the United States are much less likely to be deterred by aggressive tactics than an economic migrant without close ties to the US.

Surely, with no border control there would be many more unau-thorized migrants making the journey. Though some individuals have found alternative ways of coming to the US, recent border control efforts have deterred substantial numbers of illicit crossings. But it remains unclear to what degree the decisions of potential new immi-grants are impacted by ramped-up *interior* enforcement efforts focused on long-term residents.

Effects of Enforcement on Civil Liberties

Some consequences of enforcement extend well beyond immigrant communities, including broad-reaching weakening of civil liberties. For example, there are widespread concerns that ICE activities include racial profiling. In a 2018 case, Michigan-born Jilmar Ramos-Gomez was arrested for trespassing on the roof of a Grand Rapids hospital. The Marine Corps veteran had been suffering from a psychotic break related to posttraumatic stress disorder. After Ramos-Gomez was booked into the local jail, ICE got involved — despite his being a US-born citizen with a valid driver's license. He ended up spending nearly a month in an ICE facility before a lawyer was able to intervene.[147]

Fourth Amendment protections against arbitrary stops and searches are also routinely ignored in the name of immigration enforcement. Federal regulations allow CBP to operate checkpoints not just at the border, but up to 100 miles inland from any border — an area which, in addition to the obvious land border regions, officially includes both coasts and a majority of the country's population. There are an estimated 170 checkpoints in operation. According to the ACLU, checkpoint agents routinely overstep constitutional rights and often conduct illegal searches without cause.[148] After an August 2017 checkpoint on I-93 in New Hampshire resulted in hundreds of dog-sniff searches without reasonable suspicion — some of which resulted in the discovery of drugs in the vehicles of citizens who otherwise never would have been stopped — the Supreme Court ruled that the searches violated the state constitution.[149] Checkpoints also contribute to a sense that the US interior is becoming militarized.

In addition, DHS increasingly monitors the movements of citizens as well as noncitizens using new technologies. The agency has recently started storing travel information for all US citizens who travel by air, rail, or sea.[150] In February 2020, the *Wall Street Journal* reported that the Trump administration had purchased cell-phone location data — from phones owned by citizens and noncitizens alike — for the purposes of pursuing immigration enforcement.[151]

ICE also purchases data on vehicle movements. A private company, Vigilant Solutions, maintains the license plate database for law enforcement agencies, and collects footage every time a car in a participating locality passes in front of a police-squad car or under a traffic camera. The five billion location records in the database allow ICE to track the movements of a given vehicle and to be notified anytime a given plate shows up in the system; the records are available with minimal oversight to thousands of ICE employees.[152]

As in many arenas, there are policy trade-offs between enforcement and freedom in the immigration realm. The increased government surveillance of citizens is an inevitable consequence of an enforcement system that aims to identify and remove noncitizens. Ultimately, Americans and their elected officials must decide to what degree they are willing to have their rights and privacy curtailed in order to increase detection and facilitate the removal of undocumented immigrants living in the United States.

Lorain, Ohio, 2015

Before her arrest, Anabel Barron would tell her kids to hide, to stay still, every time they passed a cop in their car. "I was making my kids scared of the police," she says. "When you're undocumented you try not to drive just to have fun. We don't have vacations. My kids never went to the zoo. You do what you need to do: Go to work, go grocery shopping, come back." Before she had her documents, Anabel was afraid to bring her children to the local pool, fearful she'd be asked for ID. Afterward, she was able to treat them to a visit to a popular local water park, and to occasionally go out dancing with her friends.

Soon after she got the temporary social security number that accompanied her stay of removal status, Anabel interviewed for a receptionist role at a local social services nonprofit, the type of position that she had always thought of as a dream job. She was shocked to be offered a higher-level caseworker position instead. The job came with her own desk and business cards. Her bilingual skills and warm, friendly demeanor were valuable to the organization, which worked mostly with Spanish-speakers — in addition to many Mexicans the area had a large Puerto Rican community — as well as with immigrants from Africa and other parts of the world. She soon had new friends, new skills, and a job that allowed her both to support her kids as a single mom and help people in her community. It was more than she ever expected for herself, Anabel says. "For the first time in my life my daughters say they're proud of me. That's the best feeling. Those words: I would never exchange them for anything."

Anabel started the job in March of 2014. Over the next few years, she was trained to serve as a medical interpreter at the local hospital, to provide crisis counseling, to answer an emergency phone line, and to assist immigrants with government paperwork. She eventually completed an online accreditation in immigration law, which allowed her to help clients submit petitions for relatives, or to walk people through the DACA-renewal process.

But even as Anabel's professional life was thriving, her personal life was in chaos. She worried constantly about her family's future. She had trouble sleeping and cried easily. She dwelled on the worst-case scenario. If she were deported, she'd take her youngest two back to Mexico with her, she decided, and leave her older daughters to finish school in the US.

Then, in August 2014, Anabel was at home in Lorain with her kids when her ex came to the door. Anabel knew that he'd been depressed. She didn't know that he had a gun until he had the barrel pressed against her head. The police stormed the house, and her ex was arrested. The situation was terrible for the kids, who were traumatized by the incident and who also soon suffered from no longer having a father in their lives. After serving time in jail, Anabel's former partner, the father of her children, was deported to Mexico.

Anabel was also traumatized by the attack, but once again inadvertently benefited from one of the worst moments of her life. Following the assault, she became a state witness in the case against her ex. The status meant she was potentially eligible for a U visa, which grants resident status to crime victims who cooperate with a state prosecution. Unlike the temporary social security number she was given while she waited out temporary stays of removal, a U visa might be a path to permanent residency in the United States and — eventually, if all went her way — to become a United States citizen like her children.

PART THREE

AFTERWARD

Mexico City, Mexico, 2011

Elizabeth and Marcos Perez had been living in separate countries for the better part of a year when Elizabeth packed up their two boys and moved from suburban Ohio to Mexico City. Pelé was fourteen months; baby Rocky just six weeks old. Rocky's given name was Marcos, after his dad, but Elizabeth joked that if Marcos got to name their older son after a soccer star, she should get to name their second after Rocky Balboa. It started as a joke, but the nickname stuck.

At first, Elizabeth had faith that Marcos would be back in the United States before their second son was born. They had a lawyer. They thought they were being led through a logical, if frustratingly slow, process. Though there is significant discretion involved in immigration law, in fact the chances that Marcos would be allowed to legally reenter the US so quickly were essentially zero. Anyone who has already been deported, as Marcos had, has to wait ten years before they can even apply for a visa. Even then, the wait to be admitted is likely to be long—years if not decades. That's a fairly firm standard of immigration law, though Elizabeth and Marcos's lawyer never informed them of it, Elizabeth says. Instead, he collected a $5,000 retainer fee, and had Marcos apply for a visa right away, even though he would not actually be eligible for any visa until 2020, ten years after his deportation.

Elizabeth's sister helped her make the first trip to Mexico with the two boys in April of 2011. Elizabeth packed four huge bags and a double stroller. She had about $400 in cash and the suitcases full of baby supplies.

Marcos had had trouble finding reliable work. He'd been in the US for almost seventeen years when he landed back in Mexico City. Half of his life — and the vast majority of his adult life — had been lived in the US. In addition to Elizabeth and the boys, his daughter and his closest friends were in California. His brother and his brother's family were still in San Diego. Years before, Marcos's brother had gotten his papers after being sponsored by his wife's parents. He was a US citizen now and had a professional job as a physical therapist.

Marcos was most skilled at carpentry work, but jobs were hard to find. For one, he wasn't used to working with the metric system after years of thinking in inches and feet. But he also sometimes just felt like an outsider, like it was harder to connect with employers than it had been in California, particularly. He found he often felt like more of an outsider in Mexico than he had in the United States. Still, he'd been able to rent an inexpensive house near where he grew up, on the outskirts of Mexico City.

The house was unfinished, made of concrete, and largely uninsulated. There were electrical wires hanging out of some of the sockets. When Elizabeth looked out the front window it was endless hills of closely spaced, mostly concrete homes. Out the back window, there was a big open field. She could see a garbage dump and then a towering green mountain beyond. To her, it felt like living on the edge of a strange world.

Elizabeth didn't think of herself as a picky person. She'd spent a decade in the military, after all, and was used to living without luxuries. She could cope with the chill, the damp that left clothes and towels mildewy, the muddy road, the lack of hot water. But the frequent brownouts were difficult. The fridge was the biggest problem. Elizabeth was used to pumping breast milk for Rocky so she could use a bottle or let Marcos feed the baby while she slept. But without a reliable power supply or refrigerator she couldn't easily pump or store her milk the way she was used to. There was nowhere to keep regular cow's milk for Pelé, who was an active one-year-old. There was no washer or dryer; Elizabeth was washing all the clothes at an outside sink.

Money was tight. First, Elizabeth stopped using diapers on Pelé during the daytime. She just kept him close and caught him when he had to go. Then, she stopped buying disposable baby wipes, instead using rags to wipe the boys clean. It cost about $30 to fill the gas tank for the stove. After a few months, Elizabeth and Marcos didn't have money to refill it. They'd walk down to Marcos's grandmother's house almost every day to eat. They never said that was the reason they came, they were just visiting, they wanted to visit. But without those visits, they'd be hungry. Elizabeth often felt hungry, and she worried about the impact that hunger might have on baby Rocky, who was getting all his nourishment from her milk.

She made it four months. The last thing she wanted was to be a single parent again, but it was just too hard to stay. The decision was — and still is — wrenching. "I question myself," Elizabeth says. "What's more important? A fridge or your family? It's your family. For a long time, I really had a lot of trouble with that. I mean, I still do." Marcos knew that Elizabeth was unhappy in Mexico City, and frustrated that he wasn't able to support the family at the level of comfort that they needed. Yes, it was hard to make a good wage, but Marcos liked how much there was to do in the sprawling city. "Cleveland is really small. Mexico City is really huge," Marcos says. "From the start, she don't like it. I don't think she want to live here most of the time."

The kids were too little to consciously understand what was happening. But as soon as Elizabeth and the boys were back in Cleveland, Pelé started having horrible nightmares. To Elizabeth, it seemed like what you see on TV when someone is possessed; he'd wake up in the middle of the night screaming, then alternately crunch down over his belly and arch his back violently. She'd try to hold him, and he'd scratch at her as he wailed. The episodes would usually last no more than ten minutes, and then Pelé would pass out asleep again like nothing had happened. The panic attacks would happen most nights of the week, sometimes four or five times per night.

Eventually, Elizabeth found a psychiatrist who would see a kid who wasn't yet even two years old. Pelé had had his regular doctor's visits; there was nothing physically wrong with him. But kids who have a lot of anxiety, the psychiatrist told Elizabeth, sometimes don't know how to let it out of their bodies. So their body lets it out while they're sleeping. It sounded a little crazy, but Elizabeth had no other way to explain it. Pelé suffered through the nighttime attacks for eight months, until Elizabeth flew with him and Rocky to Mexico again the next summer. They were there for a month without a single nightmare. When they returned to Cleveland again, he woke up screaming and writhing his first night home.

At first, Elizabeth told her kids that their dad was working, he was working in Mexico and that's why he couldn't live with them. As they got older, the boys understood that their dad was living in Mexico, and that he couldn't come back to Ohio. But Elizabeth never told them about the weeks in jail or used the word "deported" to them. The family talked on the phone every single day. When Pelé started school, they would typically call when they got in the car and talk on speakerphone until they arrived. Marcos would get the kids to practice a little Spanish with him. They asked the same questions every day: "Daddy, are you going to work?" Every night before bed, they'd have another call to say good night.

Immigrants and Crime

Like a majority of undocumented immigrants deported from the US interior during the Obama administration, Marcos had a criminal record. He'd had a handful of misdemeanors from around the time he and his daughter's mom had broken up, one related to a domestic violence incident with his ex, another a bar fight. He'd also had a prior deportation. All of the charges were more than a decade old by the time he was pulled over just a couple blocks from his suburban Cleveland home in 2010.

Marcos's history led him to be defined as a criminal under US immigration law — and the idea of immigrants, and particularly Mexican immigrants, having criminal tendencies has become central to contemporary anti-immigrant rhetoric. So, are immigrants — and, particularly, immigrants who enter the US illegally across the Mexican border — more likely than native-born Americans to commit crime? The overwhelming consensus among academics who have studied this question is no. Donald Trump's anti-immigrant rants[1] resonated with supporters who already believed immigrants were responsible for a lot of crime. Decades of public-opinion polls have consistently found that the majority of Americans think an increase in the immigrant population results in an increase in crime rates. A Pew public-opinion poll conducted in September of 2015, for example, found that 71 percent of Republicans believe immigrants in the US are making crime worse. Fifty percent of independents and 34 percent of Democrats agreed.[2]

That poll was conducted after Donald Trump was dominating headlines, and shortly after the high-profile fatal shooting of thirty-two-year-old Kathryn Steinle in San Francisco. But the 2015 Pew opinion numbers don't differ much from those of fifteen years earlier, when 25 percent of respondents to the National Opinion Research Center's 2000 General Social Survey said it was "very likely" and another 48 percent said it was "somewhat likely" that immigrants cause higher crime rates. Some surveys, including this one, suggest that Americans are more confident that immigrants raise crime rates than that they reduce job opportunities for Americans.[3] The assumption extends to the neighborhood and city scale, with the concentration of immigrants taken as a proxy for the level of disorder and crime. "This belief is so pervasive that the concentration of Latinos in a neighborhood strongly predicts perceptions of disorder, regardless of the neighborhood's actual amount of disorder or the rate of reported violence," Harvard social scientist Robert Sampson wrote in the *American Prospect* in 2015.[4]

Perhaps it is not surprising that many Americans believe there is a link between immigrants and crime. Many recent immigrants, after all, do have the demographic attributes of those who are more likely to commit crime: They are disproportionately male and disproportionately young. Immigrants are also more likely to have a low level of education, and to work in low-paying jobs that leave them living at or below the poverty line. In general, young men, and particularly low-income young men, are known to be responsible for a disproportionate share of crime. With so many young, male, minimally educated people entering the country, it may be a logical assumption that crime would increase.

But in fact, the data definitively undermine popular assumptions, repeatedly indicating that immigrants are actually significantly *less* criminally inclined than the native born. Some studies show that immigration has a modest negative effect on crime; others demonstrate a dramatic decrease stemming from immigration. A couple of unusual studies show small increases in property crimes, though not in violent crimes. There is simply no evidence to support the widely held belief that immigrants increase violent-crime rates.

It is perhaps necessary to explicitly state that there are certainly murderers, rapists, drug dealers, burglars, drunk drivers, and all manner of other criminals among the US immigrant population, which as we've discussed numbers nearly forty million, almost eleven million of them undocumented. That's a given. The relevant question is how immigrants' *rate* of criminal activity compares to the norm.

Evidence from Incarceration and Survey Data

One way to assess how likely immigrants are to commit crime compared to native-born Americans is to look at the demographics of the US prison population, often measured based on whether an individual is reported in the United States census to be living in an institution. (Among young adults and the middle aged, most of the institutionalized are in correctional facilities rather than in other types of institutions, like nursing homes.) Several scholars have examined census data over the past couple of decades and have concluded that despite lower educational attainment and high poverty levels on average, immigrants have much lower incarceration rates than the national norm. Analysis by the libertarian-leaning Cato Institute finds that unauthorized immigrants ages eighteen to fifty-four have a 0.76 percent institutionalization rate and legal immigrants have a 0.37 percent rate, both far lower than the 1.48 percent rate found in the US-born population. The gap in crime rates is probably even higher than implied by these numbers because the institutionalization statistics include immigrants held in civil detention for immigration violations.[5]

In a study using older 2000 census data, sociologist Rubén B. Rumbaut of the University of California, Irvine similarly found that institutionalization rates were much lower among the foreign born. The study focuses on men ages eighteen to thirty-nine. Among Latin American young men, the lowest incarceration rates were found among Salvadorans, Guatemalans, and Mexicans — the least-educated groups. "These are precisely the groups most stigmatized as 'illegals' in the public perception and outcry about immigration," Rumbaut writes in a policy paper titled "Debunking the Myth of Immigrant Criminality."[6]

Discussions of incarceration rates of the foreign vs. US born take place within the context of stark racial disparities in the incarceration rates of US-born men. Non-Hispanic Black American men have more than six times the institutionalization rate of non-Hispanic white American men in the 2000 census data, a deeply troubling fact that obviously impacts the overall numbers. But even focusing exclusively on US-born non-Hispanic white men Rumbaut finds that the same pattern holds: 0.86 percent of all foreign-born young men are incarcerated compared to 1.71 percent of US-born non-Hispanic white young men. (Since the year 2000 US incarceration rates have dropped significantly,[7] though the US continues to have the highest incarceration rate in the world.)

Of course, the incarceration rate is not a perfect reflection of actual crime committed. Some argue that crime that occurs within the immigrant community — immigrant-on-immigrant crime, if you will — is underreported. Undocumented immigrants who are the victims of crime may experience a chilling effect that leaves them reluctant to turn to the police, especially if, as discussed in part 2, they live in a region where local law enforcement doesn't hesitate to share data with federal immigration authorities. A researcher for the website fivethirtyeight.com, Rob Arthur, looked at data from Dallas, Denver, and Philadelphia, and found evidence that crime reporting by Latinos fell in those three cities following the inauguration of President Trump, for example.[8]

There's also the significant issue of inequity in sentencing. Racial disparities in the criminal justice system have been widely reported on and called out by policymakers in recent years. The census data counts men in prison, and if Black men tend to spend a longer time in jail for a given crime, the institutionalization numbers would give a misleading sense of rates of criminal behavior. That being said, it would be surprising if sentence lengths were shorter for the foreign born relative to white US-born counterparts committing the same crime, so this explanation is unlikely to explain the lower incarceration rates for immigrants.

More than a decade ago, Harvard sociologist Robert Sampson and some colleagues studied violence in 180 Chicago neighborhoods.[9] They analyzed the violent acts of almost three thousand young people, as well as census data, police records, and a survey of eight thousand Chicago residents who were asked about their neighborhoods.

They found a significantly lower rate of violence among Mexican Americans than among whites or Blacks. A quarter of the Mexican Americans studied were born in Mexico and half lived in neighborhoods that were predominantly Mexican. Those first-generation immigrants, Sampson found, were 45 percent less likely to commit violent acts than third-plus-generation Americans (those whose parents were born in the United States). His group also found that living in an immigrant neighborhood is strongly correlated with lower rates of violence.

While the data is clear that immigrants are far less likely than equivalent native-born Americans to be convicted of crime, the pattern doesn't hold for subsequent generations. As Rumbaut writes, "For every group without exception, the longer immigrants had resided in the U.S., the higher were their incarceration rates."[10] This so-called downward assimilation is also observed in some other social contexts, such as health.

Evidence from Comparisons across Places

An alternative approach to looking at incarceration rates or surveying individuals is to measure the impact that immigrants have on crime rates by examining the change in city-by-city or even neighborhood-by-neighborhood demographics against the crime rate over time.

Economists Kristin F. Butcher and Anne Morrison Piehl have studied the relationship between immigration and crime by examining information on metropolitan-area crime rates against immigrant density in big cities. They looked at the twenty largest metropolitan areas in the US between the years of 1990 and 2000 — and again between 2000 and 2005 — and found an inverse relationship between immigration and crime. "Areas with the largest increases in their fraction immigrant had the largest decreases in their crime rates," they report in a 2007 working paper published by the National Bureau of Economic Research.[11] Butcher and Piehl observe that this correlation is relevant for violent crime, but that there is not a statistically meaningful observation to be made about immigration and property crime. That violent-crime finding is consistent with several other studies; a 2002 review by criminologist David Mears of the published academic literature on the criminal activity of foreign-born immigrants in the United States did not find any rigorous studies that reach the opposite conclusion.[12]

The distinction between property crime and violent crime is noted in more-recent work by Jorg L. Spenkuch of Northwestern University.[13] He looks at how changes in county rates of violent and property crime relate to changes in a county's immigrant population; he finds a small positive association of immigration with property crime, but no such association with violent crime. Why does Spenkuch find a positive relationship between immigration and property crime, while at the same time so few immigrants are incarcerated? One way to reconcile this conflicting evidence is suggested by George Borjas, along with coauthors Jeffrey Grogger and Gordon Hanson. In a study aimed at understanding the employment challenges faced by Black men, the authors make the case that immigration could cause unemployment and a decline in wages specifically among US-born Black men—and that some of those men turn to crime as an alternative income source.[14]

The debate about whether immigration increases crime rates parallels the debate about the labor-market impacts of immigration. The cross-county approach taken by Spenkuch is fairly typical—the basic idea is to compare places with rapidly growing immigrant populations to those with little or no growth in immigration, and to see what happens to crime or labor markets. But, as discussed in part 1, Borjas and his colleagues prefer to use a national approach; they compare outcomes for those who more directly compete for jobs with immigrants based on their age and education (for example, a twenty-five-year-old without a college degree) to those less likely to compete (for example, a sixty-year-old with an advanced degree). They note that, despite overall drops in crime, crime rates have fallen less for groups most directly competing with immigrants for work. The national approach is controversial as a research method because it can't rule out other important explanations for declining fortunes of these groups, like technological change or trade. Still, it's important to recognize that immigration could affect the crime rates of other groups, even as the literature overwhelmingly suggests that immigrants themselves are less likely to commit crimes than the US born.

Explaining Immigrants' Low Crime Rate

Why do immigrants have such a low rate of crime compared to native-born Americans? Wellesley College economist Kristin Butcher has returned to this question repeatedly. Like Rumbaut, Butcher has studied census data and reached the conclusion that immigrants' rate of institutionalization (as of the 2000 census) was about one-fifth that of natives when comparing men of the same age. If you also account for education and income level, immigrant men are incarcerated at just one-tenth the predicted rate based on the experience of native-born men, according to Butcher's findings.[15]

There is a broad understanding among social scientists that so-called selection bias exists in who chooses to immigrate to the US. "Although there are exceptions, it is widely recognized that most immigrants, Mexicans in particular, selectively migrate to the United States based on characteristics that predispose them to low crime, such as motivation to work and ambition," Sampson writes in a 2015 article titled "Immigration and America's Urban Renewal," in which he argues that immigrants are partly responsible for lower crime rates, as well as for much of the revitalization witnessed in America's big cities in recent years.[16]

Others have noted that Latin American immigrants disproportionately have other attributes that are associated with lower crime rates, including regular church attendance and a propensity to live in two-parent households.[17] "Latinos tend to do better on various indicators of well-being than do other socioeconomically disadvantaged groups," Sampson writes, an observation commonly known as the "Latino paradox."

More generally, saving the substantial amount of money required to undertake the journey to the US, making arrangements for parents or children left behind in the home country, and starting from nothing in the United States — all these endeavors take motivation and perseverance. Is it any surprise that after making significant financial and emotional investments in establishing a new life in a new country, immigrants would be motivated to remain out of trouble?

Perception and Reality

It's interesting to note that misperceptions about the inclination of immigrants — and particularly undocumented immigrants — toward crime bump up against a widespread ignorance among the American populace about crime rates in general. Each year the FBI releases its Uniform Crime Reports, which provide what is probably the best data available on nationwide rates of both reported property crimes and re-ported violent crimes. US crime rates peaked in the early 1990s, declined dramatically through the early years of the first decade of the 2000s, and seem to have stabilized since then, with minor fluctuations from year to year. The violent-crime rate was nearly cut in half between 1993 and 2019, and the property crime rate showed even larger declines.[18] When many of today's parents lament that the world is different now than when they were children, they are right: The country is markedly less violent than it was in the 1970s, 1980s, and early 1990s. But to a large extent public perception does not reflect that reality, with both Gallup polls and Pew Research Center surveys finding that the majority of Americans report that the country has become more dangerous even as the opposite is empirically true.

The plunge in crime rates witnessed in the past few decades coincides with a rapid increase in the immigrant population during the same time period. "New York is a magnet for immigration, yet it has for a decade ranked as one of America's safest cities. Border cities like El Paso and San Diego have made similar gains against crime," Sampson wrote in a 2006 op-ed in the *New York Times*. "Perhaps the lesson is that if we want to continue to crack down on crime, closing the nation's doors is not the answer."[19]

It's difficult to say, though, if higher levels of immigration are partly responsible for decreasing crime rates, or if the timing is merely coincidence. Researchers have attributed the national crime decreases witnessed in recent decades to factors including the waning of the crack epidemic; a larger prison population (more criminals are locked up); improved policing techniques (criminals are deterred and crimes prevented); and, even, higher abortion rates in the 1970s (*Freakonomics* economist Steven Levitt posited, controversially, that the criminals of the late 1990s were simply never born). The debate over the relationship between immigration and crime has largely been separate from the debate over the cause of the widespread crime decrease witnessed since the mid-1990s, and the plunge in crime rates remains somewhat of a puzzle. Nevertheless, political rhetoric suggesting rising immigration has caused higher crime rates is woefully divorced from both evidence and facts.

Today's immigrants come from different parts of the world, but the gap between perception and reality is much the same as it was a century ago. Between 1900 and 1931—an earlier era of mass migration—three government commissions reached similar conclusions as the modern economists and social scientists currently seeking to understand the connection between immigration and crime. The Industrial Commission of 1901, the Dillingham Immigration Commission of 1911, and the Wickersham National Commission on Law Observance and Enforcement of 1931 were each charged with measuring how immigration pushed up crime rates. "Instead," Rumbaut writes, "each [commission] found lower levels of criminal involvement among the foreign-born and higher levels among their native-born counterparts."[20] Rumbaut recounts how a century ago the Immigration Commission concluded that "no satisfactory evidence has yet been produced to show that immigration has resulted in an increase in crime disproportionate to the increase in adult population. Such comparable statistics of crime and population as it has been possible to obtain indicate that immigrants are less prone to commit crime than are native Americans." The same conclusion holds true today.

Mexico City, Mexico, 2016

Soon after Marcos Perez was deported and returned to Mexico City, he enrolled in a course to become certified to teach English. He landed a couple gigs teaching community classes, but the pay was so low he decided that the work didn't make sense. Instead, he picked up more and more hours as a soccer referee. He was paid between $10 and $20 a game, which worked out to a better hourly rate than he got from his English-teaching jobs. Most of the referee work came on the weekends. Marcos would sometimes referee four games on a Saturday or Sunday. During the week, he had more free time. He spent much of it building things he hoped to sell, like dollhouses and nativity scenes made of scrap wood. He would cut and melt plastic soda bottles into abstract flowerlike shapes, then color them and attach them to wooden tables. The house was filled with his creations, as well as with furniture and cabinets he built himself.

Marcos and Elizabeth argued about the path forward. To Marcos, crossing the border illegally again seemed like the most rational option. Emotionally, there were moments when Elizabeth wanted him to do it. She needed him back. But she always talked him out of it. If he did that and got caught, she knew, any hope of his returning legally would be gone. All the work—and time—they'd already put in would be for nothing. An even bigger worry for Elizabeth was that if Marcos tried to cross, something awful would happen to him. Things were different than they had been during the early years when Marcos crossed back and forth to visit family. Elizabeth and Marcos both understood well that there were more physical barriers, more Border Patrol officers. Hired coyotes were leading groups of migrants through even more remote and dangerous stretches of desert. Elizabeth thought of Marcos as incredibly street smart; still, she'd heard so many horror stories about other people's crossings. "I would feel safe with him anywhere, but I don't feel safe with him crossing the border," she says. "He may be able to read a situation but that doesn't mean he can control it."

Elizabeth and Marcos fired their lawyer, the one who'd advised them not to pay bail and had demanded $5,000 up front. Elizabeth had kept a careful paper trail, and after pointing out the many legal mistruths he'd told them and errors he had made in their case, she was able to get her money refunded. Meanwhile, she kept talking to other lawyers. Their consensus: The chance of Marcos being allowed back in the country legally was, as Elizabeth says, "slim to none."

Every summer, Elizabeth took the boys to Mexico. In between, she was writing letters, calling Congress members, joining protests to stop other immigrants from being deported. She also finished her BA, graduating with a degree in social work, and passed the test for her social worker's license. In 2016, Elizabeth was advised by another lawyer that individual border-crossing agents had discretion to award "humanitarian parole" and allow deported immigrants back into the country. (This kind of parole has been used occasionally to allow short-term emergency visits, permitting recipients to — for example — attend a funeral or receive critical medical treatment.)[21] Together with her parents and a local activist friend, Elizabeth flew to McAllen, Texas. Marcos came to the border on the other side.

Going in, Elizabeth knew the approach was unlikely to be success-ful, but they were thrown a curveball no one expected. When Eliza-beth went to talk to the border agent, she was told that, yes, they could apply — but that if Marcos were rejected, it would be like another de-portation order on his immigration record. That possibility had never been raised before Elizabeth spent a couple thousand dollars on the trip. She'd looked at the instructions for humanitarian parole on a gov-ernment website. She'd talked to lawyers. She'd never seen or heard anything about any negative consequence to getting denied — that the rejection of a paper application could have the same consequence as being caught crossing over the nearby Rio Grande in the middle of the night.

It seemed outrageous, but on the other hand, it was no surprise. The only thing that was consistent when it came to immigration policy was its inconsistency. Elizabeth had come to expect it. In the past couple of years, she'd gotten more involved with advocacy, and she'd become familiar with the details of plenty of other deportation cases. "Some people get deported for a DUI that was like seventeen years ago. They can never come back, and they have like seven kids," Elizabeth says.

"Other people can stay and they've got felony drug convictions. So it's like, which one is it?"

When Elizabeth arrived in McAllen, Marcos was already on the other side of the border, waiting. Together, they decided it wasn't worth the risk. The border agent's warning was inconsistent with what they'd seen of written policy, but there was nothing they could do about it. There was one silver lining to the trip, though: Marcos was able to meet his baby daughter for the first time.

The previous year, the family had met for a vacation in Cancun. Elizabeth hadn't been intending to get pregnant. But she wasn't trying not to, either. They named the baby Georgia. Marcos spent a couple of hours with Elizabeth and his baby daughter in a room provided by the Mexican consulate. The next month, Elizabeth and the kids traveled again to Mexico.

The boys didn't remember their first trips out of the country. But by 2016 they were five and six years old, and devoted worshippers of their dad. Elizabeth and the kids spent a month or more of each summer in Mexico City. Every single day, Marcos brought the boys to the park. He was focused on teaching Pelé soccer moves, and the older boy couldn't get enough of it. Rocky wasn't as good at focusing on the ball, but he loved running laps as his dad directed. "I don't even exist when we're down there," Elizabeth says. The kids would hang on their dad's every word, looking for his affirmation constantly. Elizabeth noticed a change in Pelé over just a few weeks. "He feels so powerful around his dad," she says. "I could see him sticking his chest out more — literally — when he's walking. And talking with a deeper voice."

It was hard for her to see. And when they got home to Ohio, right before the start of school, the loss was obvious. "Other kids at school live with their dads; why can't we?" the boys asked Elizabeth. One or the other of them would start crying out of the blue. Not whining, really crying. Just saying they were sad, that they missed their daddy. Elizabeth and Marcos were both raised in Catholic families. Before bed, and before dinner, the boys were taught to say their prayers. "I want my daddy back home," Pelé would recite.

Back in Mexico City, Marcos was incredibly lonely. The apartment was filled with family, filled with life, and then everyone was gone again. Elizabeth worried about him, that he was alone, that he was depressed. "All my life stay behind me in the United States and I have my new life here without my family," Marcos says. "So it's kind of weird that that's how it is."

The strain had taken a significant toll on Elizabeth's health as well. For the first couple years, she'd kept her spirits up and focused on pursuing every possible avenue for getting Marcos home. She'd managed to finish her four-year degree with two little kids at home. But as time passed and options seemed to narrow, the situation began to impact her physical health. By 2015, the anxiety became so debilitating that she started collecting disability benefits from the Veterans Affairs department. She'd had some history of anxiety from back when she was on active duty, but the situation with Marcos intensified it, and stomped down on her coping mechanisms. She felt embarrassed to be collecting disability, yet there were times when she found it nearly impossible to even leave the house. She'd been alone, and a single mom, for more than six years. Marcos's deportation had become the event that defined her. "I just feel like this has consumed our life; it's become our life," she says. Friends, relatives, parents at her kids' school—the first thing they asked was: How's your husband? How's the case? "We're the family with the dad in Mexico."

Impacts on Children

One of the complexities of immigration policy is that targeting undocumented immigrants often has significant impacts on the lives of US-citizen children. A 2019 estimate based on 2009–2013 census data suggests there are 4.1 million citizen children living with an undocumented parent.[22] This number is one reason that an "us versus them" worldview is misguided when it comes to immigration policy: any policy that aims to make life harder for unauthorized immigrants living in the US inevitably affects the well-being of American-born children. There is simply no neat separation between immigrant families and citizen families.

Though immigration enforcement can affect many aspects of children's lives, the most devastating impacts often occur when a parent is deported. ICE reported that 27,080 deportees identified themselves as parents of US-citizen minor children in 2017; this data is the most recent available and reflects a number lower than in prior years.[23] If anything, this number may be understated, as immigrants may fear that by disclosing too much information, they may be putting other family members at risk. (Of course, deportees may also leave behind noncitizen children if they migrated to the US with their kids.)

What happens to children when a parent is detained or deported? Research has documented psychological trauma, residential instability, and material hardship resulting from enforcement actions. One study found that family income fell 70 percent on average during the six months following the arrest of a parent.[24] This finding is not surprising given that fathers are much more likely to be deported than mothers, and fathers are more likely to be their family's primary breadwinner. That financial stress is exacerbated by legal fees and other costs associated with navigating the system.

It is atypical for enforcement action to lead to a citizen child living without any parent in the United States. Parents may apply for a "cancellation of removal" if they can document that deportation from the US would cause "exceptional and extremely unusual hardship" to a qualifying relative or relatives who are US citizens or lawful permanent residents.[25] As a result, while children are frequently separated from one parent, being separated from both is a rare event.

When both parents are deported, or when a parent without a partner is deported, children — even US-citizen children — sometimes leave the country as well. An estimated 430,000 to 600,000 US-born children are currently living in Mexico, according to a 2016 study by Mexico's Ministry of the Interior, for example — though some of their families are certainly living in Mexico voluntarily.[26] When these kids grow up, some of them may return to the United States.

In other deportation cases, parents don't feel their home country is safe, or aren't willing to deprive their children of the opportunities that they believe living in the United States provides. In a survey of parents deported to Mexico in 2015, only 15 percent said they intended to bring their children to Mexico. (The survey included respondents with coparents still living in the United States.) Forty-two percent said they would leave their children in the United States, and another 23 percent planned to attempt reunification in the US, with the remainder undecided about the plans for the family.[27]

To facilitate the transition in the event of deportation, immigrant parents sometimes designate a caregiver in advance. One extreme example of such a caregiver is an activist in Miami, Nora Sandigo, who is a naturalized citizen born in Nicaragua. Sandigo started taking on the role of guardian for local children of immigrants in 2006, and since then her reputation as a trusted resource for undocumented families has grown. As of 2018, she had promised parents of 1,200 kids that she would look after them in the event of deportation. Most of these kids will never have to live with her, of course, but over the years she has adopted and fostered a number of children.[28] Responding to concerns about parental removal in the Trump era, Maryland and New York began to allow unauthorized immigrants to designate a guardian for their children in the event it becomes necessary, without fully abdicating their parental rights.[29] Such designation helps kids avoid foster care while guardianship is sorted out following a deportation.

It's been reported that there are five thousand children in the foster care system whose parents have been deported, but most of those kids were in the system because of child maltreatment that preceded the deportation.[30] (In general, immigrant families have lower rates of reported child maltreatment than native-born families.)[31] Obviously, the goals of the child-welfare system—particularly the goal of family reunification—are often at odds with the goals of immigration enforcement.

In one widely reported case, an immigrant father named Felipe Montes was deported from North Carolina to Mexico in 2010 despite his claim that he was the primary caretaker for his young sons.[32] The kids were left in the care of their American-born mother, who suffered from mental-health and addiction issues. Within two weeks the children were moved to foster care.[33] The resulting legal battle raised the question whether the courts could deny parental rights to Montes on the basis of his immigration status, with the court arguing that the children were better off living in the United States with an adoptive family than living in Mexico with their father. Eventually the courts reinstated Montes's parental rights, and he was able to return briefly to the United States for the purpose of retrieving his sons, bringing them back to live with him in a small town in the Mexican state of Tamaulipas.

Reliance on the foster care system is less widespread than one might assume, in part because judges tend to be reluctant to deport mothers. However, it's certainly true that when a primary earner is removed from the household, the remaining family members can become more likely to rely on safety net programs. Though ICE has kept track of overall parental deportations since 2010, the relationship between those deportations and the use of social services is not documented at the national level. Existing studies rely on local data from regions impacted by large-scale workplace raids; these studies find increases in safety net participation. In many of the cases studied, state or local groups actively worked to enroll impacted families and children in available benefit programs. It seems like common sense to conclude that, as a 2015 paper from the Migration Policy Institute and the Urban Institute points out, "[e]conomic hardship ensues when breadwinners are arrested and detained or deported, leading to the family's increased dependence on charity care and public benefits, even though eligibility for most benefits is limited to the US-citizen children in these families."[34]

Immigrants and the Safety Net

One of the most common frustrations voiced about the growing immigrant population in the United States is related to the belief that recent immigrants are the recipients of too many expensive government handouts — that US-born taxpayers are footing the bill for safety net programs for noncitizens. Included in this list of welfare programs are cash payments to low-income families through the Temporary Assistance to Needy Families (TANF) program; disability payments for the low-income population (Supplemental Security Income, or SSI); nutrition assistance (including the Supplemental Nutrition Assistance Program, SNAP, also known as food stamps); and free or subsidized healthcare services. The children of undocumented immigrants may receive other benefits beyond those traditionally considered to be part of "welfare": they typically go to public school and sometimes participate in the Head Start preschool program. Tax credit programs are also part of the safety net. (We discuss education, health, and taxes in later parts of this section.)

Rules surrounding immigrants' use of social service programs are nearly as complex as the individual programs themselves, and the rules have changed significantly over time as federal and state laws have evolved. Some of the debate about whether immigrants are heavy users of the safety net depends on how one thinks about benefits used by citizen children in mixed-citizenship-status households. Table 1 offers a broad-brush view of eligibility for different programs—and makes it clear that households with undocumented parents are often in a position to receive support for citizen children.

Undocumented immigrants are typically ineligible for—and therefore don't participate in—many of the programs that they're often vilified for overusing. Most federal safety net programs are restricted to "qualified" immigrants, which excludes undocumented immigrants in most cases (unauthorized immigrants deemed to be victims of trafficking or abuse are exceptions). Since a major overhaul of the welfare system in 1996, qualified (legal) immigrants are also restricted from using federal safety net programs for the first five years of residence in the United States, though states sometimes use their own funds to fill in the gaps for newly arrived legal immigrants. States that already had large immigrant communities, like New York and California, were among the first to offer benefits to new legal immigrants after the 1996 law.

Table 2 uses 2017–2019 data from the Current Population Survey, a national survey implemented by the Bureau of Labor Statistics, to characterize participation rates in programs. The survey doesn't ask about legal status, so respondents are grouped by citizenship, where noncitizens include both legal permanent residents and undocumented immigrants. Noncitizens have higher rates of participation in some public programs, but only when they live in households with citizens. This higher participation is generally because noncitizens tend to have lower incomes; if we focus exclusively on households below the

TABLE 1. Social benefit program eligibility

Program name	Description	Eligibility of undocumented immigrants
Cash and tax credit programs		
Temporary Assistance for Needy Families (TANF)	Cash support for low-income families	A reduced amount may be available on behalf of a citizen/legal permanent resident child
Supplemental Security Income (SSI)	Cash support for individuals with disabilities	No
Earned Income Tax Credit (EITC)	Refundable tax credit for low-income workers	No
CTC	Refundable tax credit for filers with children	Undocumented filers can claim citizen/legal permanent resident children
Health programs		
Medicaid: adult	Health insurance for low-income adults	No
Children's Health Insurance Program (CHIP)/Medicaid: child	Health insurance for low-income children	Varies by state
Emergency Medicaid	Coverage for emergency care, including childbirth	Yes
CHIP: unborn child	Prenatal care	Varies by state
Affordable Care Act (ACA) insurance exchanges	Subsidized private health insurance	No
Nutrition programs		
SNAP	Household food assistance (food stamps)	A reduced amount may be available on behalf of a citizen/legal pernament resident child
WIC	Food assistance for pregnant women and young children	Yes
NSLP	School lunch	Yes
Education programs		
Public school	K–12 public education	Yes
Head Start	Preschool	Yes
Public higher education	Reduced tuition for in-state schools	Varies by state
Federal student grants/loans	Loans and grants for higher education	No

TABLE 2. Program participation among citizens and noncitizens

	All incomes				Below poverty line			
	Citizens	Noncitizens	Noncitizens in mixed-citizenship households	Noncitizens in noncitizen households	Citizens	Noncitizens	Noncitizens in mixed-citizenship households	Noncitizens in noncitizen households
Proportion of households in population subgroup receiving any TANF benefit	0.03	0.02	0.03	0.02	0.10	0.06	0.06	0.07
Average dollar amount if TANF benefit > $0	$4,247	$4,353	$4,366	$4,280	$4,256	$4,119	$4,354	$3,215
Proportion of households in population subgroup receiving any SSI benefit	0.04	0.02	0.02	0.02	0.10	0.03	0.03	0.03
Average dollar amount if SSI benefit > $0	$9,491	$9,102	$9,049	$9,217	$8,498	$8,524	$8,934	$7,746

Proportion of households in population subgroup receiving any SNAP benefit	0.11	0.13	0.16	0.09	0.45	0.33	0.39	0.23
Average dollar amount if SNAP benefit > $0	$3,105	$3,219	$3,332	$2,862	$3,809	$3,795	$3,974	$3,275
Proportion of population subgroup receiving Medicaid for children under 18	0.37	0.41	0.44	0.37	0.79	0.58	0.66	0.55
Proportion of population subgroup receiving Medicaid for adults ages 18–64	0.15	0.19	0.21	0.14	0.45	0.31	0.35	0.24
Proportion of population subgroup below poverty line	0.12	0.19	0.18	0.19	1.00	1.00	1.00	1.00

Source: Authors' calculations using 2017–2019 Current Population Surveys

poverty line, we see that noncitizens are consistently less likely to participate in programs than citizens are.

Many people don't realize that the traditional cash welfare program, a monthly check provided indefinitely to a nonworking single parent, is a thing of the past even for the US born. The TANF program (Temporary Assistance to Needy Families) imposes work requirements; parents are expected to be working or doing a "work-related activity," such as a job training program, to qualify. Cash assistance through TANF is time-limited to five years over a person's lifetime. Ongoing cash assistance accounts for a minority of the TANF program's budget. Instead, about three-quarters of TANF resources are used for job training, childcare, and one-time "diversion" payments to help families with an unlucky break meet their rent payment or fix their car.[35] Even among those living in poor households with children (where "poor households" are defined as having an annual income under $26,200 for a family of four), just 11 percent of citizens receive income from the program. For noncitizens, the figure is 6 percent. Those who do participate receive about $4,000 in cash support annually on average. The traditional cash welfare system now serves a very small fraction of households and an even smaller fraction of noncitizen households.

What happens when a citizen child qualifies for TANF but their parent is ineligible? Parents may be unable to receive TANF because they are newly arrived legal immigrants in a state that doesn't allocate a budget to assist that group, or because they are unauthorized immigrants. In either of these situations, citizen children may qualify for the "child-only" TANF program, which supports children in nontraditional living arrangements, children whose parents aren't eligible because they receive disability support, and children of nonqualified immigrants. A study by the Urban Institute estimated that about 12 percent of all TANF cases as of 2009 were Ineligible Immigrant Parent (IIP) child-only cases, those in which the parent lacked legal status to receive TANF because they were undocumented or a newly arrived legal immigrant.[36]

According to a 2012 paper by Jane Mauldon of the University of California, Berkeley, et al., there are important differences across states in both TANF policy and the degree to which undocumented parents feel comfortable accessing the child-only TANF program on behalf of their kids.[37] Three states — New York, California, and Washington — accounted for less than one-third of the nation's unauthorized population but two-thirds of IIP child-only TANF cases in 2010. There were 116,000 cases in California alone. States vary in their policies as to whether unauthorized parents can access noncash forms of TANF assistance; these differences may help explain differing take-up of child-only TANF. Ultimately, the authors conclude that the accessibility of child-only TANF depends less on explicit policy differences and more on the general environment toward immigrants in the state. In other words, chilling effects impact the ability of low-income citizen children to get the aid they need.

At the same time that cash welfare has diminished, the use of the disability program SSI (Supplemental Security Income) has increased, and the program now serves about 2.5 percent of the population.[38] This change emerged in part due to expansions in what types of illnesses were eligible to qualify for SSI, and in part to a 1990 court ruling that expanded program access for disabled children. Even as general expansions were occurring, however, access to the SSI program was curtailed for legal immigrants as part of the 1996 welfare reform. Today, only 2 percent of noncitizens live in households in which any SSI income is received. For the tiny fraction who do participate in the program, household benefits average around $9,000 annually.[39]

SSI expansions notwithstanding, over the past few decades the safety net for immigrants and nonimmigrants alike has been increasingly dominated by in-kind benefits such as food and medical care. For example, the federal food-stamp program — now known as the Supplemental Nutrition Assistance Program, or SNAP — provides food resources to about 11 percent of the population.[40] Benefits are provided on an electronic benefit transfer (EBT) card, which operates much like a debit card, except that the funds can only be used to purchase nonprepared food. Adults with legal residence have to wait five years before applying for SNAP, but children with legal status are exempt from the five-year waiting period. Though SNAP operates at the household level, it's possible to obtain a partial SNAP benefit on behalf of the citizens and qualified immigrants in a household, even if the household includes some undocumented immigrants. As a result, noncitizens in mixed-citizenship households have a comparatively high rate of SNAP participation at 16 percent, compared to 9 percent of those living in noncitizen-only households (fully noncitizen households must include a legal permanent resident or other qualified immigrant to receive any benefits at all).[41] SNAP benefits average around $3,000 annually.

Though undocumented immigrants do not receive SNAP directly, there are some smaller food assistance programs that are offered regardless of legal status. The National School Lunch Program (NSLP) is available to all low-income students. Similarly, the Women, Infants and Children (WIC) program — which provides staple food packages to pregnant women, new mothers, and children under five — doesn't discriminate based on legal status.

Overall, noncitizens do have slightly higher rates of program participation than the native born because they tend to have lower incomes. However, poorer immigrants use social service programs at a substantially lower rate than native-born Americans with similar financial resources.

Painesville, Ohio, 2014

Eduardo Lopez was released from the Seneca County Jail on January 17, 2014, exactly four months after his arrest. While he was in detention, a boss from his company kept calling his lawyer for updates and so Eduardo was under the impression the factory wanted him back. But when he showed up at the office, he was told he couldn't be hired back without a social security number.

Eduardo had started working at the factory in 2001. Around 2013, the company had begun using E-Verify, the federal system that allows a company to electronically check a person's identity against government databases. (The free system is optional to employers in most states and is described in detail in part 2 of this book). Eduardo hoped he'd get a social security card eventually, and that he'd be able to go back to managerial work.

Many immigrants who have been released from detention pending a court hearing are granted a stay of removal, and some are issued a temporary Employment Authorization Document (or EAD) that entitles them to a social security number. Ironically, an arrest for being undocumented often leads to the issuance of the very documents that allow an unauthorized immigrant to work legally in the United States for the first time. But Eduardo was released from custody under prosecutorial discretion. He didn't know why he hadn't been given a social and he didn't know when—or if—he'd get one. Now his company was saying they wanted to hire him back—but that without a valid social security number, they couldn't.

Eduardo was optimistic that somehow, sometime soon, he'd get a social, but in the meantime he got a job at a Mexican grocery store close to his home. The store made tortillas and had a butcher shop. It was owned by another Mexican, a friend of Eduardo's who offered him $11 an hour—about half what he was making in his factory job. He knew it wouldn't be enough to support his wife and three kids like before, but Eduardo didn't have much choice. He owed money to his lawyer. The months in jail had eaten through the family's savings, the money they had been hoping to use someday for a down payment on their home. They were behind on their rent. In addition to paying all the normal household expenses, Elena had had to contribute to Eduardo's commissary when he was locked up. The prison meals left him hungry. At the commissary he could buy more food, along with the phone cards that allowed him to talk to Elena and the kids for ten or fifteen minutes each night.

At the grocery store, Eduardo worked butchering and packaging pork and chicken. He helped with receiving and at the cash register. He was used to logging sixty-hour weeks at the factory, but he was lucky to get forty hours at the grocery store. It wouldn't make much sense for Elena to try to go back to work, they concluded. With three kids, daycare would cost much more than her salary would bring in. Even after Eduardo was released, the kids had a constant fear of abandonment. Each time he left the house, they cried.

It was his landlord's wife who told them about the possibility of getting food stamps (the program officially called SNAP). As undocumented immigrants, Eduardo and Elena weren't eligible themselves. Eduardo had never even heard of SNAP before his arrest. But their kids, all American citizens, were eligible. "They ask you about how much you make, if you own a house, how much you pay for rent," Eduardo recalls. He brought in a record of his monthly housing costs and a handful of pay stubs. With three kids, Eduardo qualified for $200 a month in food stamps. "It help a lot," he says. "For some people that nothing, but for us, in that situation, it was a lot." Eduardo accepted the benefits because his family needed them, but he hated doing it. "I don't want to live under this government," Eduardo says. "I want to live with the government. It's two different things. Are you a child of this government or living with it?"

Eduardo and Elena did most of their shopping at the local Walmart, saving the EBT card for late in the month when cash was running low. When Eduardo was at the factory, he'd had health insurance for the whole family. Now, his kids qualified for Medicaid, and he and Elena went without insurance. Eduardo was bringing in about $450 a week from his grocery store job. Rent was still a moderate $650 a month. Then they had the water and electric bills, the gas, the car insurance. Eduardo's car was registered in a friend's name and he reimbursed him $90 for insurance each month. It was tight, but with the food stamps, they were able to make the budget work and pay their rent and bills on time.

Eduardo had been at the grocery store job for a year when he got a call from his old boss. "You got your paperwork yet?" he asked. Eduardo explained that he still didn't have a social—his situation was unchanged from the year before. His case had been temporarily resolved through prosecutorial discretion. Eduardo had a piece of paper, a letter from a judge, that he carried around with him at all times—basically a permission slip to remain in the country. At that time, mid-2015, he was hoping that President Obama's expanded executive action, known as Deferred Action for Parents of Americans and Lawful Permanent Residents, or DAPA, would be implemented. As a parent of US-citizen children, and someone who had been in the country illegally since before 2010, he thought he would qualify. But the action was held up in the courts (and ultimately rescinded by the Trump administration in 2017). Eduardo still didn't have a social security number; he couldn't work legally.

Eduardo's old boss told him he'd think about it and get back to him.

"Not even a week passed when they call me back," Eduardo says. "They like, you want to start Monday?"

Eduardo was back to his old job at his old salary. "As soon as I got my first paycheck, I just called the social worker and said, I don't want the food stamps no more," he says. His case worker told him he could collect another payment, but Eduardo said he didn't need it. A year later, in August 2016, Eduardo had no problem coming up with $300 to buy back-to-school clothes and supplies for his three kids when his youngest, William, started kindergarten.

At work, Eduardo used the same social security number as before. He paid taxes every month, benefits he'd likely never see the other side of. They told him in the office not to talk about his situation too much, and he didn't. He never had. A couple friends knew he still didn't have a social security number; he assumed the guys working under him assumed he had one now, and he also assumed there were still other workers at the factory who didn't have status. No one talked about any of it openly.

Do Immigrants Move to High-Welfare States?

If the widespread belief that immigrants are eager to take advantage of generous social services were true, it would be logical to expect that immigrants would disproportionately head to states with more-generous social services. Indeed, much of the foreign-born population live in traditional hubs of immigration like California and New York—states that also have a relatively generous safety net.

However, states that have seen the largest increases in their immigrant population in recent decades tend to be ones that have relatively low spending on social service programs. In a 2012 paper titled "Immigration and the Welfare State," Cato Institute economist Daniel Griswold compares changes in immigrant population by state in the first decade of the twenty-first century to state spending on welfare. He finds that the ten states with the largest percentage increase in foreign-born population between 2000 and 2009—states like Kentucky, Tennessee, North Carolina, South Carolina, and Georgia—spent far less on public assistance per capita in 2009 compared to the ten states with the slowest-growing foreign-born populations (states like Michigan, Rhode Island, and Vermont). The spending gap was wide: The average for the low-spending states was $35 per capita vs. $166 for the high-spending states. "The largest gains have generally been in states that are relatively stingy in offering public assistance," Griswold concludes.[42]

These results are perhaps not surprising in light of the evidence reviewed in part 1 of this book that establishes that most immigrants are motivated to move to the US by work. The least-generous states may not have had much to offer in the way of social support, but they did have good job opportunities. Most of these states have historically had few immigrants, but they collectively saw their immigrant population grow 31 percent between 2000 and 2009.

Griswold also looks specifically at unauthorized immigrants and finds that the undocumented population has in recent years been more likely than the broader immigrant population to move to states with low social spending. He attributes that trend to the fact that nearly all unauthorized men of working age are in the workforce and reliance on public assistance is negligible. "This almost universal propensity to work among undocumented men partly reflects the fact of US law that becoming a ward of the state is simply not an option," Griswold writes. "But it primarily reflects the fact that the low-skilled, predominantly Hispanic immigrants who enter the United States illegally do so for one overriding purpose—to earn money in the private economy."

Beyond Griswold, there is a larger literature examining the "welfare magnet" hypothesis by looking at migration to different US states, and most studies find that the safety net is not a significant driver of location decisions.[43] Older work by George Borjas does show an association between safety net generosity and immigrant location; specifically, though the direction of causality is unclear, he documents that those immigrants receiving public assistance are concentrated in more generous states.[44] But almost all other US-focused studies reach the opposite conclusion. For example, Neeraj Kaushal, an economist at Columbia University's School of International and Public Affairs, looks at newly arrived immigrants after the welfare reform of 1996; she finds no evidence that unmarried immigrant women sought out states with more generous benefits.[45]

One recent study examines a unique "natural experiment" in Denmark. Over the past two decades, the country drastically reduced, then raised, then again reduced welfare benefits available to non-European migrants. Three researchers then at Princeton University—Ole Agersnap, Amalie Sofie Jensen, and Henrik Kleven—find that migration to Denmark did respond to these changes. Migration from non-EU countries was lower when the safety net to support those migrants was less generous, consistent with a "welfare magnet" story. They also note that migration to Europe probably wasn't affected overall by these changes. Instead, individuals first decided to migrate, and then sought asylum or pursued family-based migration in other European countries that offered more support.

Overall, the evidence suggests that migration within the US is not primarily driven by welfare benefits. This finding holds particularly true for the migration decisions of undocumented immigrants (who cannot access most welfare programs). Still, the Denmark study does show that it is possible for welfare policies to affect location decisions of authorized immigrants. In the US context, it may be the case that the choice of which state to live in is affected by benefit generosity to a small degree, but factors such as employment opportunities and social networks dominate.

Immigrants and Healthcare

Health insurance coverage stands out as one of the largest components of government spending: The federal, state, and local governments combined spent about $604 billion on the Medicaid program, which is public health insurance for those with low incomes, in FY 2019.[46] This total includes Medicaid's sister program, the Children's Health Insurance Program (CHIP), at a cost of $18 billion. Affordable Care Act (ACA) private-insurance subsidies added another $55 billion.[47] Medicare, which provides insurance to almost all Americans over sixty-five, as well as to disabled Americans with an adequate work history, ex-

ceeds $700 billion in spending.[48] Because health expenditures are so
enormous in general, decisions about immigrants' access to public-
insurance coverage have huge financial implications.

Recent legal immigrants and undocumented immigrants face severe
restrictions in accessing health insurance. Legal noncitizens are not eligible for Medicare or non-emergency Medicaid during their first five
years of lawful US residency—though about half of the states have ex-
ercised the option to use their own funds to provide health insurance
to low-income legal immigrants who are subject to the federal five-year
waiting period. Legal immigrants can also receive ACA subsidies to
buy private insurance on the exchanges, regardless of how long they
have been living in the United States.

Undocumented immigrants, however, are excluded from the federal
Medicare and Medicaid programs, and are prohibited from purchasing private insurance through the ACA insurance exchanges. Six states
and the District of Columbia use their own funds to provide coverage
for unauthorized children.[49] Some undocumented immigrants do have
employer-sponsored insurance, through either their own workplace or
that of a relative. However, because the undocumented population is
more likely to work in low-wage sectors without benefits, this route to
insurance is often not feasible. In theory, immigrants can also purchase
private insurance on their own without using the ACA exchange, but
these options tend to be unaffordable. The upshot is that 45 percent of
undocumented immigrants are uninsured, compared with 23 percent
of legal permanent residents and 8 percent of citizens, according to
analysis by the Kaiser Family Foundation, a health policy think tank.[50]

Despite the many restrictions, though, it would be erroneous to say
that unauthorized immigrants receive no publicly supported healthcare. Federal law requires hospitals to stabilize patients who show up
with an urgent medical situation, regardless of insurance status or
ability to pay. If patients don't qualify for regular Medicaid because
they are newly arrived immigrants or undocumented, a program
known as Emergency Medicaid reimburses hospitals for their acute
care. The federal government spends about $2 billion a year on this pro-
gram, representing less than 1 percent of overall Medicaid spending.[51]

One might think unauthorized immigrants would be more likely to visit the emergency room than the general population because they are more often uninsured. But immigrants tend to be relatively young and healthy, and some of them may fear legal or financial consequences if they check into the hospital. Using 2002–2011 data, health researchers from the University of Nebraska and Harvard Medical School estimate that 6.7 percent of unauthorized immigrants and 7.7 percent of legal permanent residents visit the emergency department in a typical year, compared with 14.1 percent of the US-born population.[52] It is the case, however, that emergency visits by the unauthorized are less likely to result in payments to the hospital — 8.5 percent of those visits are uncompensated, compared to 6.2 percent of visits by the native born.

States have some leeway in how they define emergency care for the purposes of Emergency Medicaid support. For example, a few states cover ongoing (as opposed to emergent) kidney dialysis; New York covers chemotherapy and radiation. But the vast majority of Emergency Medicaid costs — perhaps 80 percent — support childbirth-related expenses for unauthorized immigrants.[53] It's estimated that only 8 percent of undocumented immigrants receive any direct public expenditure for healthcare in a given year.[54]

In addition to federal funding for expenses associated with childbirth, additional state options exist to provide prenatal care to immigrant women. The CHIP unborn-child option allows states to offer prenatal services to women regardless of immigration status. Another option allows states to waive the Medicaid five-year waiting period to offer prenatal care to newly arrived legal immigrants. Politically, these policies are supported largely because of the claim that the care in question will be offered to an unborn US citizen; such policies represent an uneasy meeting of minds between those seeking access to care for immigrants and those who wish to codify a protected status for the fetus that's separate from the status of the pregnant woman herself.

There is also indirect and less-transparent support for immigrant healthcare. For example, hospitals that serve large numbers of uninsured patients (a group increasingly dominated by the undocumented as insurance options expand among citizens) currently receive federal support through a program called the Disproportionate Share Hospital (DSH) program. Under the ACA, the DSH program is slated to be gradually phased out over time, a change that will affect hospitals serving many unauthorized immigrants. There are also large numbers of primary-care clinics providing basic care regardless of patients' immigration status; many of these clinics are partially supported with government funds.

In a 2019 *Forbes* magazine piece, a scholar affiliated with the conservative American Enterprise Institute, Chris Conover, estimated the direct government health expenditures on uninsured, undocumented immigrants at around $9.1 billion annually.[55] That figure includes Emergency Medicaid, state programs supporting unauthorized immigrants, DSH payments to hospitals, and payments to community health centers. Conover stretches his estimate of the costs to $17 billion by considering the fact that undocumented immigrants with employer-sponsored health insurance — like all people with such insurance — do not pay income taxes on this part of their compensation, and the fact that nonprofit hospitals get a tax break. (It is arguably unfair of him to tally these indirect "tax expenditures," which would exist even if no undocumented immigrants lived in the US.)

To be sure, even $9.1 billion is a lot of money, and healthcare does represent a significant share of the overall fiscal costs associated with undocumented immigration. But overall direct federal, state, and local government expenditures on health well exceed $1 trillion a year. As a share, healthcare for unauthorized immigrants barely registers. Some states and localities are certainly stretched by the fiscal burden of care for the undocumented population, but most are not. Concerns about the impact of health expenditures for the undocumented population are rooted mainly in notions of fairness rather than of affordability.

The Healthy Immigrant Paradox

Interestingly, despite lower levels of education and income and reduced access to care, studies over the past thirty years have consistently found that immigrants have better health outcomes than the US born. For example, Latin American immigrants experience lower rates of adult and infant mortality and give birth to fewer underweight babies than US natives — despite higher poverty rates and greater barriers to healthcare.[56] This phenomenon is sometimes known as the "healthy immigrant" paradox, the Latino paradox, or the epidemiological paradox. The finding is not limited to Latinos: Across racial and ethnic groups, immigrants have better health status on average.[57] Some of the literature has focused on the Latino population regardless of birthplace. Compared to non-Hispanic whites, Latinos in the US are healthier by many measures, and foreign-born Latinos have particularly strong health outcomes. The age-adjusted mortality rate for Latinos (combining US-born and foreign-born Latinos) in the US is 567 per hundred thousand compared to 747 per hundred thousand for non-Latino whites, a difference largely driven by lower rates of cancer and heart disease.[58] In data that looks at disease prevalence, 3.9 percent of non-Latino white adults ages eighteen to sixty-four have cancer compared with 2 percent of Latinos. For heart disease the prevalence is 7.5 percent versus 4.9 percent. These are surprising figures given that Latinos tend to have lower income and education levels than non-Latino whites.

Research also shows a tendency for health outcomes to worsen over the generations. For example, analysis by Francisca Antman at the University of Colorado Boulder, Brian Duncan at the University of Colorado Denver, and Stephen Trejo of the University of Texas examines the probability that those with Mexican ethnicity report being in poor health.[59] Compared to men with similar education levels, men born in Mexico are 6 percentage points less likely than third-plus-generation white Americans to say they are in poor health. Second-generation men (those with a parent born in Mexico) reported roughly the same health status as their white counterparts. By the third generation, men identifying as Mexican are 2 percentage points more likely to report poor health than similarly educated whites.

One explanation for the surprisingly good health outcomes of immigrants is selective migration — that is, healthier people choose to migrate whereas the less-healthy stay home. Similarly, the "salmon bias hypothesis," so called because of salmon returning to their place of birth to spawn, posits that Latino immigrants tend to leave the US and return home when they get sick. This would make for a healthier-than-average immigrant population remaining in the United States.

Some people also question whether data challenges might contribute to the paradox. For example, the choice of individuals to identify as Hispanic or Latino in survey questions may play a role. In the paper described above, Antman, Duncan, and Trejo study the question of "ethnic attrition" in the Mexican-born population and their descendants. They find that about 20 percent of "third-generation-Mexican" children (those with US-born parents and a Mexican-born grandparent) do not identify in survey data as having Mexican ethnicity. This choice not to identify as Mexican is usually related to the fact that one of their parents does not have Mexican heritage, which in turn is often correlated with family income (families with one white parent tend to be richer on average than families with two Mexican parents). Children who do identify as Mexican are in worse health on average, which the authors attribute to higher levels of socioeconomic disadvantage relative to other "third-generation-Mexican" children who do not identify as Mexican. The casual observer might look only at the children who identify as Mexican and mistakenly conclude that descendants of Mexican-born immigrants "downward assimilate" in terms of their health status more than they actually do. The larger point is that how individuals report their ethnicity to a survey enumerator can drive patterns in the data.

Another data issue arises from the fact that health is self-reported in most studies. Lack of access to care means that some immigrants are unaware that they have conditions like cancer or heart disease, so may report being healthier than they actually are. Research shows that immigrants from Mexico are less likely than the native born to be diagnosed with hypertension and diabetes if they have these diseases.[60] But given differential mortality rates, underdiagnosis is clearly not the full story.

Yet another possible reason for good health among immigrants may be cultural and lifestyle factors. Studies point to smoking as an example — the smoking rate among Latino immigrants is less than half that of non-Latino whites. Some researchers argue that smoking is the main driver of the healthy immigrant paradox.[61] As immigrants stay longer in the US they tend to adopt more typically American health behaviors, and Latinos born in the US generally have riskier health behaviors than those born abroad.

Studies have also found that neighborhoods matter. Latinos living in areas with a high density of other Latinos are in better health.[62] Like the immigrant paradox in general, this finding is unexpected because neighborhoods with concentrated minority populations tend to be economically disadvantaged. But the researchers conclude that positive health behaviors and social cohesion outweigh the absence of other resources.

Though the causes of the healthy immigrant paradox aren't completely settled, the paradox has implications for health policy regardless. Immigrants tend to have fewer medical needs on average, and therefore are comparatively cheap to include in a health system. So when the Affordable Care Act passed in 2010, it would have been financially beneficial to allow undocumented immigrants to purchase unsubsidized private insurance through the newly formed health insurance exchanges — as the inclusion of this group would have allowed companies to offer lower rates to everyone while still breaking even. The ultimate decision to exclude the unauthorized population was made on political rather than economic grounds.

Springfield, Massachusetts, 2018

Since the day her husband's van was pulled over by immigration agents, nobody else from the Massachusetts potato farm where Fatima Cabrera and her husband worked had been detained. ICE could have gone back to get more people, Fatima says. They could have, but they didn't. Meanwhile, four months later, Fatima, her ten-year-old daughter and her seven-year-old son were home in central Massachusetts, Fatima with a tracking device on her ankle. Their dad was back in Guatemala, thousands of miles away.

The kids are American citizens, and English is their primary language. "In Spanish I'm the one trying to explain to them what this word means, how it is supposed to sound," Fatima says. "They are more comfortable in English than Spanish." Fatima doesn't speak much English (our interviews with her were through a translator), but her husband can speak it with the kids. "We talk every day. Every day over Skype," Fatima says. "When he was here, he was the one that talked a lot of English with them. So he asks them how school's going, how's church going, what did you eat, if they are doing well."

Fatima spends a lot of time volunteering at the neighborhood Catholic church. At school, the kids talk to their friends in English. But at church they get Bible lessons in Spanish, and Fatima likes that it helps them get closer to the language. The priest likes the neighborhood kids to hang out at the church in their free time, she says, rather than sitting at home playing video games.

It upsets Fatima to think about having to take the kids to live in Guatemala. When she left for the US in 2004, she had just one relative in the United States, her cousin in Springfield. Now, she has more extended family here and Guatemala feels distant. In her home country, there are only opportunities for families with money; other kids don't have a chance, Fatima says. Plus, her two US-born kids don't know anything about Guatemala. They've never been there. How will they adapt to a strange culture, she asks? To the poverty, to the risk of going hungry?

The kids know now that their father has been deported, but Fatima hasn't fully explained that she, too, is under surveillance and at risk. Fatima is now the sole provider for her family. She's grateful that she can still work, but she wishes she had more time to spend with her kids. She wears the ankle monitor and checks in regularly with ICE. So many, many families are going through the same thing, she recognizes. "It's really hard to live like this. Sometimes you go [somewhere] and you think that they are behind you." she says. Her court date has been postponed twice. "The only option that I have is to wait."

In the meantime, she's preparing an asylum case. If that's not successful she may try to seek sanctuary in a nearby church. She worries constantly about her kids. If she is deported, she plans to bring them with her—she can't imagine being separated from them. But she doesn't think they will do well in Guatemala. "We can start all over again, but they can't because they are used to this country," Fatima says. "This is their country."

Chilling Effects of Enforcement

It is a long-standing question why many people eligible for public benefit programs do not enroll in them. Factors such as stigma, lack of information, and bureaucratic hassle are partly responsible for the incomplete participation in public programs, known as the "take-up" puzzle. Depending on the program, researchers commonly estimate that a quarter to a half of those eligible do not participate.[63] Take-up tends to be especially low among eligible immigrants. For example, children of noncitizens living below the poverty line are less likely to participate in public health insurance compared to children of citizens.

Why do immigrants have lower participation rates in public health programs? They may have particular difficulty obtaining information about programs and eligibility rules, completing English application forms, and navigating the complex administrative system. Research has also shown that social networks can be impactful. Immigrants who live near others who speak the same language tend to follow group norms about welfare use.[64] This tendency could arise because information flows across social networks, or because welfare use is stigmatized more in some groups than others. For some who came to the United States for economic opportunity, like Eduardo, needing to use benefits may be viewed as a sign of failure.

Recent research, including that of author Tara Watson, considers the role of immigration enforcement on the decision to access public benefits. As discussed earlier in this section, undocumented immigrants are excluded from most major safety net programs, but their children are often eligible by virtue of being citizens. What role does internal enforcement play in determining whether undocumented immigrants enroll their children in safety net programs like the Supplemental Nutrition Assistance Program (SNAP, also known as food stamps) and Medicaid?

One case study arises from the 1996 welfare reform bill known as the Personal Responsibility and Work Opportunity Reconciliation Act (PRWORA), the result of President Clinton's pledge to "end welfare as we know it." Like many citizens today, Congress in the 1990s was concerned that generous public benefits were causing immigrants to flock to the United States. PRWORA included a number of provisions targeted toward immigrants, and it aimed to de-incentivize immigration undertaken for the purpose of obtaining benefits. The law explicitly states that "self-sufficiency has been a basic principle of United States immigration law" and that "aliens within the Nation's borders [should] not depend on public resources to meet their needs"[65]

Under PRWORA, immigrant eligibility for public programs was restricted for legal noncitizens. The law banned the use of federal Medicaid funds for most post-enactment immigrants (those arriving after August 1996) for the first five years after arrival. In addition, the reform made it harder for states to use their own funds to provide benefits to undocumented immigrants, and it included a number of other provisions aimed at discouraging benefit use by immigrants. States did have the option to use their own funds to provide Medicaid to newly arrived *legal* immigrants, and about half of them chose to do so.

Despite the anti-immigrant language of the welfare reform bill, the actual number of immigrants made ineligible for Medicaid by its passage was quite small. Undocumented immigrants were ineligible both before and after reform, and eligibility restrictions for legal immigrants applied only to new arrivals and only in some states. Nevertheless, immigrant participation in Medicaid and other programs dropped sharply right after the 1996 reform, even among those still eligible.

Some observers hypothesize that indirect chilling effects may have discouraged immigrant participation in public programs for which they remained eligible. Even though most immigrants and their children did not experience a change in Medicaid eligibility following welfare reform, they might have been discouraged by the icy policy climate surrounding the welfare reform bill; in other words, their willingness to sign up for programs may have been "chilled."

Though the existence of chilling due to an icy policy climate is plausible, the fear and informal dissuasion that might lead to chilling are difficult to observe. One study by George Borjas found that, following welfare reform, Medicaid fell more in states with less-generous policies. But these falloffs in participation occurred even among those whose eligibility had not changed. Borjas attributed unexplained drops in program take-up to chilling at the state level.[66] Another paper looked at newly arriving immigrants—those people directly targeted by the policy change—and found that even in states that used their own funds to offer Medicaid to this group, new immigrants overwhelmingly avoided participation. The authors, economists Robert Kaestner and Neeraj Kaushal, attribute the *absence* of a difference between different kinds of states to chilling effects of the national welfare reform bill.[67] But neither of these early studies investigating immigrant program participation took into account another 1996 law, the IIRIRA (Illegal Immigration Reform and Immigrant Responsibility Act), which was passed just a month after welfare reform.

As described in part 2, IIRIRA legislation was a fairly major immigration reform which substantially increased financial resources for enforcement. Importantly, enforcement did not increase by the same amount everywhere. The Immigration and Naturalization Service (INS, a precursor to today's ICE), was divided into thirty-three districts for internal enforcement. Each district had a lot of autonomy, so when more funding became available, some districts rapidly increased their number of arrests whereas others saw little change.

So was it immigration enforcement rather than the welfare reform law that was responsible for declines in immigrant Medicaid participation? To investigate this question, author Tara Watson examines arrests in different INS districts before and after the 1996 immigration law.[68] What happened to the health insurance status of children of immigrants in those same areas? A striking relationship emerged: Children in places that ramped up enforcement were substantially less likely to be enrolled in Medicaid. This was true even for US-citizen children of immigrants, who are eligible for Medicaid regardless of their parents' immigration status.

That relationship is illustrated in figure 14, which looks at enforcement activity and Medicaid rates for two immigration enforcement districts. The Arizona/Nevada region had a steep increase in enforcement activity following the 1996 bill and simultaneously had a drop in Medicaid participation—from 40 percent of immigrant children enrolled in 1997 to 28 percent in 1999. (Medicaid participation rebounded by 2001 despite ongoing aggressive enforcement, perhaps because INS issued guidance that clarified that there wouldn't be "public charge"

FIGURE 14. Illustration of Medicaid enforcement relationship

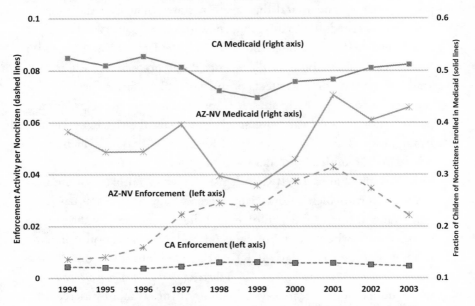

Source: Tara Watson, "Inside the Refrigerator: Immigration Enforcement and Chilling in Immigrant Medicaid Participation," *American Economic Journal: Economic Policy* 6 (2014): 313–38

implications for using the system.) California, by contrast, experienced a smaller uptick in enforcement activity following the 1996 law and a less dramatic decline in Medicaid enrollment for children of immigrants, from 51 to 45 percent. In fact, looking at the US as a whole, immigration enforcement was responsible for much of the overall decline in Medicaid participation around 1996.

In the Watson study based on Current Population Survey data, parents who reported their children's health as "very good" or "excellent" were the most sensitive to enforcement activity, whereas parents with children in poor health enrolled them in Medicaid regardless of enforcement levels. This finding is consistent with the notion that immigrants make calculated decisions in high-enforcement areas, perhaps deciding that it's worth risking deportation to get insurance coverage for a sick child but not for one who needs little more than an annual well-child visit.

The impact of enforcement has also been documented in ethnographic research. A focus group study of immigrants in Everett, Massachusetts, in 2009 found that many of them assumed their personal information would be shared with ICE if they tried to access health insurance or healthcare.[69] One Arabic-speaking participant said: "I was always afraid to go to the hospital, but I forced myself when my son got sick. I got Masshealth [public health insurance in Massachusetts], but as soon as I heard about the New Bedford incident [a 2007 ICE raid of a textile factory that led to more than three hundred arrests of unauthorized workers], I called Masshealth and told them I was moving to another state so they can cancel it. I wanted to minimize the risk of getting caught."

By early 2017, in the wake of rampant anti-immigrant rhetoric and stepped-up enforcement coming from the Trump administration, there were widespread reports of fear affecting health decisions among the undocumented. An article in *Modern Healthcare*, a healthcare industry trade publication, profiled a Woodburn, Oregon, community health center. Carlos Olivares, CEO of the YaParka Valley Farm Workers Clinic, had noticed a change in clinic use after an ICE raid targeted two vans full of flower-nursery workers: "Our no-show ratios increased, and we experienced a tremendous amount of phone calls and expressions of concern from patients."[70]

In truth, the risk of being deported from a doctor's office is low. ICE has a long-standing policy of avoiding (except in unusual circumstances) enforcement in "sensitive" locations including schools, places of worship, and healthcare facilities. This guidance was not officially changed in the Trump administration.[71] However, not all agents complied fully with the guidance, as was made clear by the story of one father, Romulo Avelica Gonzalez, who was arrested while dropping his thirteen-year-old daughter off at her Los Angeles school in 2017.[72] Fear of travel is a related — and probably more dire — concern. As we've seen, routine traffic stops are a common way that immigrants get caught up in the enforcement system. Ethnographic research suggests that government checkpoints and patrols reduce the willingness of undocumented migrants both to travel and to visit healthcare providers.[73]

Public-Charge Rule

The current policy landscape leaves many immigrants and community organizations unsure of the risks associated with accessing benefits. In 2019, the Trump administration implemented an expansion of the so-called public-charge doctrine, which allows immigration officials to use the past or potential future use of public benefits as grounds to deny admission to, deny citizenship to, or deport noncitizens living in the United States.

Rooted in colonial-era "poor laws," the notion of public charge was codified in an 1882 immigration law aiming to restrict entry to or in some cases deport individuals who would be a burden on the state.[74] At the time, the notion was often used as a way to target Irish immigrants, the mentally ill, and others viewed as undesirable.

In the modern era, the public-charge doctrine has almost never been used in deportation cases. It is instead used to determine whether someone should be admitted into the country or allowed to adjust their existing status and become a legal permanent resident. This standard was made explicit in 1999: The past use of cash welfare assistance can be considered in admission and status adjustment decisions, as can the question whether an immigrant is in long-term institutional care paid for by the government. In-kind public benefits such as healthcare or food assistance were not considered.

The new Trump-era public-charge rule expands the set of programs under consideration to include public health insurance, food assistance, and housing—all of which had, previously, long been excluded. Thus, the rule has the potential to affect a substantial fraction of the population—about twenty-three million noncitizens and another twenty-one million citizens who share households with them.[75] Because undocumented immigrants are ineligible for most programs, the direct impact of the rule should be small. But chilling effects may lead some immigrants to be newly reluctant to apply for benefits on behalf of citizen family members. This policy is yet another one whose direct effect is overshadowed by the impacts of the confusion and fear associated with the policy change.

The new policy also puts more emphasis on prospective determination, meaning that officials can deny admission to applicants perceived to be at high risk of using benefits in the future. While economic considerations have always been at play, the rule could lead to a shift in immigration admissions and status adjustments that would increasingly favor people with more economic resources. The actual impact of the guidance will depend on how it is implemented in the day-to-day decisions of bureaucrats.

The expansion of the public-charge rule also highlights the wide leeway the current system gives the executive branch to make important immigration policy decisions. The president always has some discretion in how much to enforce various laws and regulations. Legislative stalemate on the immigration issue has resulted in a lack of a cohesive or sensible immigration policy, and left even more authority in the hands of the presidential administration. The result is an immigration policy whiplash in which the on-the-ground implementation of the law can change radically every four to eight years. In early 2021, Biden ordered a review of the public-charge rule with the likely goal of making it less restrictive, though in reality a full unwinding of the rule will require a regulatory process and will not take place overnight.[76]

Immigration Enforcement, Stress, and Health

Immigration enforcement can affect health beyond its impact on immigrant participation in Medicaid and other public programs. It's well established that stress can have harmful effects on both physical and mental health—and the stress surrounding both the fear of enforcement and the family disruption associated with enforcement is no exception. "The fear is causing stress and depression," a Haitian participant in one focus group said. "People are afraid of police, afraid to go out, afraid to walk on the street. You don't want people to be scared of you, to call the police on you. How could you not have stress? I'm young. All my hair is falling out."[77] High-profile and broad enforcement actions are likely to be particularly salient to immigrants' stress levels.

A recent study by Jens Hainmueller, a political scientist at Stanford University, along with a team of coauthors, took a creative approach to looking at the relationship between mental health and enforcement. Using data from the state of Oregon, it compared 3,039 children of immigrant mothers born just before and just after the birthdate restriction for Deferred Action for Childhood Arrivals (DACA). Under DACA, immigrants with similar experiences ended up qualifying for work permits and protection from deportation—or not—simply because their birthdays were a few days or weeks before or after an arbitrary date. The study looked at families from 2013 to 2015 and found that DACA-eligible mothers had kids who were 50 percent less likely to suffer from adjustment and anxiety disorders.[78] From this study and others, there is strong and convincing evidence that DACA generates beneficial mental-health effects.

Another study examined the incidence of low-birthweight babies among Iowan Latina mothers, and found that the rate increased following a major raid at a meatpacking plant in Postville, Iowa, in 2008.[79] Looking at birth certificates for over 5,100 children born to Latina mothers, three researchers at the University of Michigan found that the incidence of low birthweight increased by 24 percent for babies born in the thirty-seven weeks following the raid, as compared to those born in the same period a year earlier. There were effects for births to both US- and foreign-born Latina women, but no similar effect was found for births to non-Latina mothers. The authors conclude that the psychosocial stress associated with the raid in the Latino community led to adverse health consequences for children at birth, another example of the far-reaching impacts of high-visibility enforcement.

Glendale, California, 2017

In the months after Trump's election, Mia Park compulsively checked her mailbox for a final confirmation of what she had thought in the fall was an all-but-approved DACA application. Finally, in March 2017, she got a letter from USCIS: Her application had been rejected. The dates of the legal status she'd once had through her F-2 visa—the type of visa granted to the family members of people with F-1 student visas—made her ineligible for the program, it said. Though there was no mention or threat of deportation in the brief, matter-of-fact government correspondence, Mia interpreted the letter as notice of her expulsion from the country. To Mia, the exact words of the letter weren't the source of its impact. During the presidential campaign Trump had promised to rescind DACA and to deport immigrants like her. Now she feared both promises might come true.

She frantically sought advice from the couple of community college professors she'd confided in about her status, and she wrote a heartfelt letter back to the government agency, pleading her case not by disputing the visa dates, but with the argument that she'd studied hard, learned English, and intended to help fill the gender gap in college mathematics by pursuing her PhD and becoming a university professor (she was then a sophomore math major). Unsurprisingly, this argument fell on deaf ears.

The semester before, Mia's brother, Michael, had transferred from the Kansas college where he was on a football scholarship to Texas Tech University, where he thought he would get a better education in the computer science courses that would allow him to eventually work in cybersecurity. He'd applied as a transfer student to Texas Tech, Georgia Tech, and New York University, and had gotten into all three. His decision was a practical one: Texas gave him the most scholarship money.

Michael had had DACA since before he started college in 2014. When he arrived in Texas his DACA status allowed him to get a job with the university. He'd known when he entered college that he wanted to major in computer science. He'd always liked tech support, and he enjoyed designing web sites, including a site for his aunt's textile business in Los Angeles. At Texas Tech, he worked his way up from student analyst to student technician to student supervisor and employee trainer. He calls the work "Tech Support 101 — when people call and vaguely ask us why their Wi-Fi isn't working — to Networking 401."

Academically, Michael preferred Texas Tech to his Kansas school. It was so much bigger — forty thousand undergraduates — and it had a lot of resources. Although he was in a very conservative part of a red state, the university itself was diverse, with many students who came from bigger cities and different places. After his first year in Texas, Michael spent the summer at an internship in Minneapolis, another place he'd never been before. He'd already had a profile on LinkedIn, and he'd spent time on the job site looking for businesses that interested him. He'd found an entrepreneur in Minneapolis who ran his own cybersecurity company made up of a lot of ex-military types. Michael reached out to him through the platform, and the CEO of the small business ended up offering Michael a summer internship. By the time the summer was over, Michael was confident he knew exactly what he wanted to do when he graduated.

But soon after Michael returned to campus in the fall of 2017, Trump made his promise to rescind DACA.[80] Michael submitted his paperwork to renew his status for the second time in September 2017. He knew he was at risk of losing his ability to work, to drive — to pursue the career goals that had solidified for him in the past couple of years. But there was nothing to do but keep moving ahead as if everything would be okay. In December of 2017 and January of 2018, he applied for more than seventy internships for the coming summer. "I made it a hobby," he says. "I have an Excel sheet. I applied everywhere from Walmart to Target to Microsoft and Facebook." He knew that between his coursework, his tech work with the university, and his previous internship at the business in Minneapolis, he was very qualified. He got a lot of interviews but he never heard back from any of them. Meanwhile, friends he worked with on campus who didn't have a security background were getting internship offers. "I don't know how far my status is going to get me because you need top security clearance for all the jobs, which I can't get."

On January 19, 2018, Michael's DACA status officially expired. He knew USCIS had received and was reviewing his renewal paperwork, but it hadn't arrived. He was placed on leave without pay from his campus jobs. He kept a motorcycle on campus with him. Driving it without a license wasn't an option he seriously considered. "We got immigration services down the street — a big building and bunch of vans outside, parked up. It's not anything like LA," he says. He didn't even look for under-the-table work since he wanted to keep his record clean. Illegal work, he reasoned, was too big a risk to his future career goals. "As somebody who wants to go into security field, I don't want to have a dirty background," he says. Instead, he started making some extra cash by donating plasma, two three-hour sessions each week. The process was tiring and time-consuming, but Michael was able to make $80 a week that way, enough to pay for food and utility bills.

Like in Kansas, he hadn't told anyone on the Texas campus—including roommates, professors, or coworkers—about his status. When his DACA expired, he didn't even tell his mom. "She's fighting her own battles and I don't want to be something else that she has to worry about," he explains. "She doesn't really have to know; she has no control over it." Though he was in a campus club with an outspoken undocumented grad student from Pakistan, he hadn't opened up to her about his situation. "She's very vocal about it. And honestly, I do think she really needs for me to open up to her and really help her out. But I don't know, I've been very hesitant." Michael just tried to push forward with school and life without thinking too far into the future. Because when he did try to think about the future, he found little to be hopeful about. "I don't even know what's going to happen," he says. "You know, to see someone like Donald Trump get elected, it still now shocks me every day."

The most realistic resolution Michael could see was going back to South Korea, a country he hadn't been in since he was ten years old. "What does that mean for me?" he wondered. "Do I have to start practicing the language again? Where am I going to live? How am I going to find a job?" As a twenty-two-year-old college student, Michael had already done a lot to start carving out a career path for himself in the US. "I don't even know how their system works, so what do I do? I haven't really thought it through. I kind of don't want to."

K–12 Education for Immigrant Kids

Education is a major component of the short-term costs of immigration, costs which are largely borne at the state and local level and are heavily concentrated in certain regions. These costs are mainly driven not by immigrants but by their children, who are most often United States citizens. At the same time, education is a means to increase the productivity of the future workforce and a way to promote integration of children of immigrants into the economic and social fabric of the broader society.

Access to free K–12 public education is guaranteed to all children regardless of legal status under the 1982 *Plyer vs. Doe* Supreme Court decision. The court case arose in response to a 1975 Texas law that allowed local districts to deny education to undocumented children or to charge them tuition. Lawyers for the national Mexican American Legal Defense and Educational Fund sought a test case to advocate against the policy in federal court. They settled on the small district of Tyler, Texas, about 100 miles east of Dallas, where the federal district court judge overseeing the case was known to have a progressive outlook. The lawsuit centered on a family in which siblings of different immigration statuses attended the local Tyler schools. To protect the children from deportation and harassment, their identities were not divulged.[81]

The case reached the Supreme Court in 1982, and in a 5–4 decision the court ruled that the Texas policy was in violation of the equal protection clause of the Fourteenth Amendment. Justice William Brennan authored the decision, noting that the state policy could not "be considered rational unless it furthers some substantial goal of the State." He wrote: "It is difficult to understand what the State hopes to achieve by promoting the creation and perpetuation of a subclass of illiterates within our boundaries."[82] The decision did not rule out differential treatment of undocumented individuals for other public benefits, and there is no similar legal precedent requiring equal access at the college level.

Because immigrants have more children on average than the US born, a disproportionate number of school-aged children have foreign-born parents. (As of the 2010 census, the average number of children ever born to a forty-to-forty-four-year-old woman averaged 1.84 for native-born women and 2.19 for foreign-born women.[83]) The Center for Immigration Studies, a research group aimed at reducing the number of immigrants, uses 2015 census data to calculate that 23 percent of K–12 public-school students have at least one foreign-born parent.[84] In a few metropolitan areas, including San Jose, Los Angeles, and Miami, more than half of public-school students are the children of immigrants. These figures include students with both documented and undocumented parents. According to the Pew Research Center, in 2014,

7.3 percent of all K–12 students in the United States were the children of unauthorized immigrants — about 3.9 million kids.[85]

Regardless of legal status, there are challenges associated with high immigrant populations in schools. One is that immigrant children, and children of noncitizens in particular, are more likely to live in poor families. According to analysis of 2017–2019 Current Population Survey data, the poverty rate of noncitizen children is 28 percent and the rate among citizen children living in mixed-citizenship households is 25 percent, compared to 15 percent for children in all-citizen households.[86] Interestingly, children with naturalized household members are *less* likely to live in poverty than children living with all US-born household members (13 percent versus 16 percent).

A second obvious fact that can add to the challenges facing educators is that the children of immigrants are often English-language learners (ELL), and therefore require specialized resources. The most recent numbers, from 2017, suggest that 10.1 percent of all public-school children in K–12 receive ELL services of some kind. The number ranges from less than 1 percent in West Virginia to 19.2 percent in California, highlighting the uneven fiscal consequences of providing K–12 education to children of immigrants.[87]

Services provided to ELL students vary. Students may be pulled out of regular instruction for part of the day to receive English instruction, or regular classes may be taught in two languages, integrating ELL students and fluent English speakers in a "dual language immersion" model. Alternatively, some districts offer a transitional bilingual program for ELL students, where a group of ELL students are separated from the mainstream classroom to learn in both languages for a period of several years.

Economists Aimee Chin of the University of Houston, N. Meltem Daysal of the University of Southern Denmark, and Scott Imberman of Michigan State University examined the effect of bilingual education by exploiting a quirky feature of Texas law. According to the legislation, transitional bilingual education for elementary students was mandated when there were at least twenty limited-English students in a grade who spoke the same home language.[88] The researchers were able to compare students in grades with just over the twenty-student threshold, who more often got bilingual education, to similar students in grades that didn't meet the cutoff, who typically used more-traditional English as a Second Language programs instead.

As it turns out, there wasn't much difference between the educational achievement of Spanish-speaking students in the two different groups, suggesting that no one approach is clearly better in terms of test scores. When judged solely by test scores, the presence of bilingual education for ELL students benefited English-proficient students who were left in a mostly-English-speaking classroom, but the exact reasons for this finding are unclear.

The question of which curricular approach is most appropriate remains one of considerable controversy both in educational circles and politically. The debate hinges not just on student academic achievement, but on questions about identity, culture, and parental autonomy. Though the United States has no official language, most people agree that teaching English fluency should be a key curricular goal of American school systems, and—as previously discussed—such fluency is also critical to students' future economic prospects. Some parents prefer partial instruction in the native language as a way to preserve or promote cultural heritage, while others make the case that improved content learning can result from a bilingual approach. The question of how to serve ELL students is part of a broader debate about the degree to which immigrants should be expected to adapt to the dominant English-speaking culture and the degree to which public institutions should reflect and accommodate a plurality of cultures.

Immigration and the response to it can also have broader impacts on schools and communities. In a 1998 paper, economist Jim Poterba of the Massachusetts Institute of Technology shows that public-school expenditures grow more slowly in places where the elderly population and the child-age population have more-divergent racial composition.[89] Though the study doesn't focus on immigration directly, it is plausible that support among white Americans for public education is affected by their perceptions of who is benefiting from that education, with consequences for children of immigrants and nonimmigrants alike.

Immigrant inflows can engender a new version of "white flight." The 2012 paper "Cracks in the Melting Pot" by Dartmouth economists Elizabeth Cascio and Ethan Lewis examines the experience of California between 1970 and 2000. For every additional household enrolling Latino children with limited English in a public school district, the typical district loses 1.4 households with non-Latino children to other districts in the same metropolitan area, their research found.[90]

Still another way that immigration may affect public schools stems from the complicated ways that funds are allocated to schools with more low-income students. Though most educational funding comes from state and local sources, the federal government provides supplemental funding to high-need schools through a program called Title I. Schools traditionally have relied on applications to the National School Lunch Program — which serves low-income students for free or at a reduced price regardless of student legal status — to document the prevalence of poverty for the purposes of claiming Title I funds.

Recently, some school districts have moved away from requiring each student to provide family income information in order to be eligible for free or low-cost school lunches; these school districts now opt for "community eligibility" instead. Schools or school districts now have the option to rely on census data or welfare-program participation rates to demonstrate that at least 40 percent of their students are high-need. In those cases, all students receive free school lunch.[91] Community eligibility expands access to food for disadvantaged students, including students from undocumented families who may have been hesitant to submit a school-lunch application.

The move away from school-lunch applications requires schools to use different means to demonstrate their eligibility for Title I funds. Some worry that Title I funds will be pulled away from certain low-income schools because children of immigrants are underrepresented in the census and are less likely to participate in welfare programs. One study from Massachusetts found that more than a quarter of all recent-immigrant students would have qualified for free-lunch benefits, but that these same students would not be recorded as "economically disadvantaged" for Title I under the new means of data collection—mainly because their families were ineligible for or did not use social service programs.[92]

Because recent-immigrant students are concentrated in particular school districts, the changes in funding allocation could—in some immigrant-dense schools—reduce the school resources available to low-income children of immigrants and nonimmigrants alike. Though the Massachusetts study could not separately identify children of undocumented parents, experts have expressed a concern that this group in particular is undercounted in the new funding allocation, which is systematically pulling federal Title I resources away from districts that serve large undocumented populations.

Schools also play a complex role in the enforcement environment, with some parents hesitating to send their children to school in times of heightened enforcement. A 2010 Urban Institute report suggests that children often experienced school disruption immediately following an immigration raid, for example—presumably because their parents were keeping them home out of fear or because their home life was disrupted. At the same time, the report highlights the role schools play as a source of strength and stability for immigrant families. School officials were instrumental in facilitating care for children whose parents were arrested, the Urban Institute report found, and in offering counseling to affected children. In addition, school provided positive structure and routine for children when other aspects of their lives became chaotic. One family member in the report described the school as a "refuge" for a child who had been affected by a worksite raid.[93]

Higher Education

An estimated one hundred thousand undocumented students graduate from US high schools each year, according to a 2019 Migration Policy Institute memo.[94] About 70 percent of all American high school graduates enroll in a two- or four-year college soon after graduating, and even though there are no current estimates, it's clear that undocumented students go to college in lower numbers.[95] There are quite a few college enrollees without papers, however. For example, there are tens of thousands of such students in California — an estimated 13,500 in the University of California and California State systems, and at least fifty thousand more in community colleges around the state.[96] Roughly half of these students have temporary protection under DACA.

The cost of college is obviously a hurdle for many young Americans — and particularly so for undocumented students. The undocumented and those with DACA are ineligible for federal student aid such as Pell grants and subsidized student loans, which are critical supports for most low-income college students in the United States. Citizen children of undocumented parents are eligible for federal support, but requesting aid requires reporting parental financial information and entering 000–00–000 if the parent lacks a social security number, potentially causing a chilling effect for some citizen students.[97] In practice, the lack of federal aid for college is another way in which the costs of unauthorized immigration are borne by receiving localities and states.

A key policy debate surrounds the question of whether the undocumented should qualify for the lower tuition granted to other in-state residents. According to researchers Catalina Amuedo-Dorantes at San Diego State University and Chad Sparber at Colgate University, the average yearly difference between the sticker price of in-state and out-of-state tuition across flagship universities in ten states is $12,197. Even at community colleges, the yearly difference averages $4,261.[98] In other words, in-state tuition makes a pretty big difference to the cost of college.

The 1996 Illegal Immigration Reform and Immigrant Responsibility Act (IIRIRA) attempted to curtail the practice of treating undocumented immigrants like any other residents for the purpose of determining in-state tuition, but there is disagreement about what exactly is permitted under the law. The main substantive ruling on the issue comes from a 2005 class-action lawsuit in California. Opponents of in-state tuition for undocumented immigrants argued that California's policy — which allows lower tuition for those who attended and graduated from high school in the state — operates unfairly as a backdoor way to provide undocumented residents with in-state tuition benefits, in violation of the spirit of IIRIRA. After a lengthy legal process, California's policy of offering in-state tuition to undocumented immigrants was allowed to persist.

As of 2019, about twenty states charge undocumented residents in-state tuition, including a few that have applied this policy just to so-called DACA-mented students. Seven states — California, Colorado, Minnesota, New Mexico, Oregon, Texas, and Washington — offer financial aid as well as discounted tuition. Another five states — Alabama, Arizona, Georgia, Indiana, and South Carolina — have laws that explicitly ban offering in-state tuition to undocumented students. Alabama and South Carolina further forbid the enrollment of undocumented students at public postsecondary institutions, even at full tuition rates.[99]

How much do these state policy differences matter? Their impacts may be felt even before students reach college age. Ethnographic research by UCLA's Leisy Abrego suggests that undocumented high school students are discouraged from achieving their full potential when they perceive legal barriers to college attendance. On the flip side, the educational benefits of in-state tuition laws may trickle down to the high school level, even for students who never directly use them. One study by researcher Robert Bozick at the RAND Corporation think tank and colleague Trey Miller supports this idea: Mexican-born noncitizen students in states with more-generous policies for undocumented students were substantially more likely to graduate from high school.[100]

Other research by Neeraj Kaushal at Columbia University, and separate research by Amuedo-Dorantes and Sparber, shows beneficial impacts on college enrollment as well as associate degree completion when in-state-tuition policies are in place. These benefits come without any detectable reductions in education for US-born students.[101]

Washington State, 2011

Jorge Ramirez and his wife, Yuuko, arrived back in Washington State as newlyweds, but there was no wedding reception and no honeymoon. "It was a really difficult time when I get out from detention because we basically start again," Jorge says. Their savings were gutted. Jorge had to report regularly to the local immigration office. Like Anabel Barron, Jorge had been granted a stay of removal, which he describes as "a kind of condition that allows you to stay for now, but without knowing what's going on." He was given a work permit. He was given a social security number. "So, I start paying my taxes with my real social security number now," he says.

For close to three years everything seemed stable for Jorge and Yuuko. They were both working long hours and rebuilding their savings. The couple's son, Akemi, was born in early 2013. The baby was a delight, a cheerful little boy with wide brown eyes and silky black hair whom Jorge and Yuuko imagined growing up in the suburbs, playing sports, taking music classes, and — of course — graduating from high school and going on to college.

With Yuuko's help and encouragement, Jorge had obtained his business license. His small stucco company was doing well. He and Yuuko had bought a home: a three-bedroom, one-bath place on a quiet suburban street. For years before, the couple had been living frugally in a tiny studio apartment. "We saved every penny," Yuuko says. The house was a foreclosure, one of the worst houses on the block when they bought it in 2013 for $275,000. "It was trashed, a total dump," Yuuko says. "It was so dirty we put plastic in the center of the living room and that's where we slept for a couple weeks."

For six months Yuuko and Jorge put countless hours of work into repainting and relandscaping, often working at night after the baby was asleep. They laid down new flooring, replaced the furnace, and worked to make the place homey with colorful curtains, wall hangings, and framed family photos. Sidewalks lined the neighborhood streets and there was a playground and playing fields at the end of the block. This was where they wanted their son to grow up.

Then one winter day in 2014 Jorge went to his routine immigration appointment and was told that ICE had decided to close his case — and that he was scheduled to be deported on June 30. "The reason they decided to give me was that my wife and my kid, they are good, they are healthy, so they don't need me here," Jorge says. "They say, 'You have to go.' And they give me ninety days to leave the country." The couple knew that if Jorge were deported, the fact that he had been previously caught crossing the border meant he would be ineligible to even apply for any type of US visa for at least ten years.

The "healthy family" reasoning seemed absurd to Jorge. The US government believed that a healthy family didn't need a father? Without Jorge's salary, Yuuko wouldn't be able to afford the mortgage or the other costs of raising a child alone. But those were just practicalities. They wanted — needed — to be together.

An ICE officer had attached a metal GPS monitor to Jorge's ankle. Twice a month a case worker visited his home. Every once in a while, he got an unannounced check-in call and was expected to answer the phone right away. When he was at work, Jorge tried to hide the tracking device under long pants, but it was bulky and almost impossible to keep inconspicuous. Friends would ask him about it, and he noticed strangers looking. The endless appointments interfered with his stuccoing work. Being under daily surveillance was a constant stress.

He felt like the entire system was broken. He'd known people who were into drugs, who had felonies, who had been given status to stay in the US. And he'd seen people just like him — people who were working hard, making a living, and never getting into trouble — being sent back. His own lawyer had described the situation as being like ICE throwing a pile of papers describing immigrant cases in the air. "Whatever lands on the table, they stay. Whatever is on the floor, they have to leave. It feels like it's like that," Jorge says.

But he didn't complain, at least not outside his own home: "We have been fighting this for more than three years. I don't want to do anything to ruin it," he said in 2014.

Meanwhile, the couple collected messages of support. One letter came from officials at the nonprofit where Jorge and Yuuko had volunteered helping people with tax preparation. Neighbors and people Jorge had worked for all contributed words of endorsement, too. All of it was submitted to ICE.

On May 29, 2014, Jorge and Yuuko got a new letter from the director of ICE's Seattle field office. Jorge was "expected to depart the United States on or before May 31, 2015, in compliance with the existing administratively final removal order," it read. He had another year. Another year in which, they hoped, some sort of federal legislation or action that would help them might be passed. The couple was grateful for the reprieve, but not at peace. "It is really scary how quick they can switch," Jorge says. "That means they can switch back any time that they want. They control your destiny."

The only way for the family to stay together might be for them to find a new home outside the United States. Yuuko researched the possibility of them all moving to Japan, though it is an option she finds unappealing. She was forced to give up her Japanese citizenship when she passed the American naturalization test (Japan is one of many countries that does not allow dual citizenship). She could take it back, but that would mean relinquishing her rights as an American.

The most obvious solution, perhaps, is for Jorge to bring his family back with him to his hometown in Mexico State. Sitting side-by-side on their living room couch with their infant son playing on the floor beside them, the couple seem to have divergent views of that possibility.

"We've been talking about it ever since he received the deportation order," Yuuko says. "We were planning to move to Mexico. That was our plan." She pauses. "But having a child I think makes it a little bit different. We purchased this house hoping that Jorge could stay, immigration reform happens, and then we can stay here, and we can raise Akemi here in a good school district. . . . Education is very important to me. I think it's very, very important for him."

"In Mexico, most of Jorge's family are only elementary-school graduates," Yuuko continues. "High school was very difficult for Jorge to finish financially. Even though it's important to be close to his parents because they are getting older, when I think about Akemi it's very difficult to plan on that."

"To be honest, I don't think about Yuuko or Akemi going to Mexico," Jorge says. "I don't think that is a place for them. I don't think I can get a job that I can support my family. Over here, you work hard, you can make something happen. I know my kid has more possibilities to do something good being here."

"We always have somewhere in our heads that we need to be prepared, but we don't actually realistically plan things yet," Yuuko says. "That's something that ICE accuse us of, that we don't prepare anything. But who could do that? We have a life here already."

Unauthorized Taxpayers

Even before Jorge Ramirez became an independent business owner, he was paying US taxes. As a minimum-wage worker at the Wendy's fast-food restaurant in Nevada, he worked under a fake social security number. Every week, he paid payroll taxes like any other worker. Later, as the owner of his own licensed stuccoing business, he filed taxes with a legal ITIN number. He's far from alone.

It is perhaps obvious that immigrants pay state sales and excise taxes as they shop for goods and services. Like all residents of the United States, immigrants pay taxes every time they buy clothes, put gas in their car, or eat at a restaurant. The left-leaning Institute on Taxation and Economic Policy estimates that unauthorized immigrants contribute about $7 billion annually to state and local governments in sales and excise taxes.[102]

In addition, about a third of unauthorized immigrants own their homes, meaning they contribute property-tax revenue to their local communities.[103] Some undocumented immigrants purchase homes in cash; others obtain a so-called ITIN mortgage—which uses not a standard social security number, but, rather, the identification number generated for the purpose of paying federal taxes—to acquire a home loan. Even renters indirectly support property-tax payments to their local governments. The Institute on Taxation and Economic Policy estimates that unauthorized immigrants contribute $3 billion in property taxes to their local communities.[104]

Immigrants also contribute significant tax revenue through federal payroll taxes. In general, separately from what the pay in annual income taxes, almost all W-2 workers in the United States have 6.2 percent of their earnings deducted from their paycheck for social security contributions; another 1.45 percent is deducted to go toward Medicare. The employer pays an equivalent additional amount into those systems. In the formal sector, employers collect SSNs for all workers—through the W-9 form new workers are required to complete—and deduct payroll taxes from each paycheck, even for those with invalid social security numbers.

What happens when employees use a social security number that belongs to someone else, or make one up? Historically, employers have sometimes received "no-match" letters from the Social Security Administration when submitting payroll taxes associated with an invalid SSN. In theory, the employer is supposed to try to get more information to resolve the issue, though historically penalties for ignoring the letters have been minor. Employers also need to be careful to avoid terminating employees who are authorized to work in the United States but may have paperwork issues; legally, employers cannot fire an employee simply because of the no-match letter. The practice of sending the letters has been the subject of litigation, and the Obama administration suspended them in 2012. The Trump administration resumed sending the letters in 2019.[105]

Regardless of the risk of no-match letters, it's clear that many unauthorized immigrants contribute to the federal coffers through payroll taxes. Using 2010 data, the Social Security Administration estimated that about 3.1 million unauthorized workers contributed to the social security system through the payroll tax, just under half of all unauthorized workers. Of these 3.1 million, an estimated 1.8 million worked using a nine-digit number that was not a valid SSN or was a valid SSN attributed to a name other than that of the worker.

Payments linked to these SSNs are recorded in a so-called Earnings Suspense file and — because the social security system is largely a pay-as-you-go system — they are used to fund benefits for current retirees. The Earnings Suspense file also includes contributions from authorized workers with paperwork issues (from a delayed name change or typo, for example), and on an annual basis represents payroll tax associated with 1 to 2 percent of all wages.[106]

Another 1.3 million unauthorized workers are estimated to have social security payments attached to their own names, either because they obtained an SSN in their name with a fraudulent birth certificate or because they overstayed a temporary work visa with a once-valid SSN.[107] All told, unauthorized workers added about $13 billion to the social security system in 2010, roughly 2 percent of all payroll taxes contributed.

When the undocumented are successful in normalizing their status, they sometimes are able to receive credit for past social security contributions that are recorded in the Earnings Suspense file. These workers must be able to show that they were responsible for the social security contributions that were made under a different name. In most cases, however, undocumented immigrants paying into the social security system are unlikely to receive social security benefits. This is one reason the Social Security Trustees Report describes immigration, including undocumented immigration, as a net positive for the long-run financial health of the social security system. A higher net immigration rate postpones the date of Social Security Trust Fund depletion, currently expected in the year 2034.[108] Immigrants in informal under-the-table jobs — of whom there were about 3.9 million in 2010, according to Social Security Administration estimates — generally do not contribute payroll taxes, though.[109]

Perhaps surprisingly, many undocumented immigrants also file state and federal income taxes. Undocumented immigrants are legally required to pay income taxes according to the usual filing rules, even if they were not legally eligible to be in the United States or to do the work that generated the income. Filing taxes with a fake social security number or someone else's SSN is a serious offense. This presents a legal conundrum, but the Internal Revenue Service (IRS) has a solution: It offers ITINs (Individual Taxpayer Identification Numbers) as a means for anyone who isn't eligible for a social security number, including undocumented immigrants, to pay taxes. ITINs are nine digits, like SSNs, but begin with the number 9 and have a 7 or 8 in the fourth digit. Officially, ITINs are meant to be used only for tax filing. They cannot be used in lieu of a social security number for employment verification. However, some banks have allowed ITIN holders to open accounts or obtain a mortgage using the ITIN.

The IRS has a strong commitment to privacy, maintaining a firewall between itself and those responsible for enforcing immigration law. As noted in a 2018 report by the Bipartisan Policy Center, a centrist think tank that aims to improve dialogue across party lines: "Agencies are singularly focused on their own mandates: the IRS is interested in maintaining a broad tax base and collecting all taxes owed to the government, regardless of the source, whereas immigration enforcement officials want to enforce the law against unauthorized work. . . .

Addressing these conflicting interests would require legislative change and implicate millions of taxpayers, which means the current state of affairs will likely prevail for the foreseeable future."[110] In terms of immigration enforcement, there is minimal risk to an immigrant from paying taxes, and arguably a more-significant tax-enforcement risk from not paying them.

In addition to fear of tax authorities, some unauthorized immigrants pay taxes in hopes that it will help them secure legal status in the future.[111] Tax filings can be used to support the case that an immigrant is of "good moral standing" and to establish a history of work and residence within the United States. These factors are sometimes considered in individual cases of status adjustment and deportation; they could also be relevant in the event of a comprehensive immigration reform bill in the future. For example, the proposed DREAM Act requires "good moral character" as one condition for a pathway to citizenship.

Another reason some immigrants file an income tax return is that doing so can directly benefit them financially. If a worker had income tax withheld under a false social security number, they can file a return with an ITIN and list the SSNs they used for employment.[112] This allows the IRS to properly credit the withheld income taxes to the undocumented worker, allowing them to get a refund if appropriate. (It also helps the IRS avoid penalizing the rightful owner of the SSN if there is one.)

Those using ITINs are not eligible to claim the Earned Income Tax Credit, which operates like a negative income tax for low-income working families. ITIN filers also did not get the coronavirus-related relief (up to $1,200) that was issued in the spring of 2020. (Those who jointly filed taxes with ITIN filers, including citizen spouses, were also denied coronavirus relief.)

However, until recently ITIN filers have been eligible for the Child Tax Credit (CTC) and the Additional Child Tax Credit (ACTC), which represented over $4 billion in outflows to that group in 2010.[113] The ACTC was a refundable program, meaning that low-income individuals with children could get more from the credit than they paid in taxes. For example, a single mother with two children earning $17,000 would not owe any federal income taxes after taking the standard deduction and the usual personal exemptions for three people. However, she could claim the ACTC and—prior to 2017 tax reform—could get up to $1,000 back from the government per child. (The ACTC and CTC are now combined into one refundable tax credit called the CTC.)

The ability of unauthorized immigrants to claim the ACTC has been described as "paying illegal aliens federal dollars to stay in the United States" by the Center for Immigration Studies, a think tank that promotes low levels of immigration.[114] Perhaps in response to this point of view, the 2017 tax bill for the first time restricts refundable CTC credits to those who have children with SSNs (previously the credit could also be claimed for minors who were themselves undocumented). However, unauthorized immigrants will still be able to claim the child credit on behalf of their citizen children. Given that the majority of children of noncitizens are US born, and given a general increase in the maximum amount of the refundable credit from $1,000 to $1,400 per child under the 2017 tax law, it is unclear how much the revision of the CTC will reduce outflows to ITIN filers.

Yet another reason unauthorized immigrants might file a federal tax return is to obtain health insurance for their children. The Affordable Care Act (ACA, also known as Obamacare) implements its individual insurance mandate and its health insurance subsidies through the tax code. Undocumented immigrants are not eligible for ACA-related insurance subsidies, and they were not subject to tax penalties for being uninsured even before the Trump-era tax law that eliminated those penalties for all taxpayers starting in tax year 2019. However, the US-born children of undocumented immigrants are required to have insurance, and they are eligible for insurance subsidies under the ACA if the family meets certain income guidelines (subsidies are offered for those households at 100 to 400 percent of the federal poverty level). Filing a tax return can help parents access health insurance subsidies on behalf of their citizen children.

In 2010, the most recent year for which data is available, about three million households used an ITIN rather than an SSN to file their income tax returns. These ITIN returns are associated with $870 million in income tax revenue to the federal government (separate from and in addition to the $13 billion contributed by unauthorized immigrants to social security and Medicare through payroll taxes).[115] Though not every ITIN represents a filing by an undocumented immigrant, this figure suggests that a substantial fraction of unauthorized immigrants file income taxes. Many such filers receive net benefits for their families as a result of tax filing due to the refundable ACTC and to ACA insurance subsidies for citizen children.[116]

Of course, not all undocumented workers employed under a false SSN decide to file a tax return. The IRS reports that there are about a million people a year who have had income taxes withheld by their employer and are likely owed a refund but do not file. The money left unclaimed totals about $1 billion.[117] These one million people may include native-born individuals who haven't made the effort to file, but the number certainly also includes undocumented immigrants who had income taxes withheld under a false SSN.

So how much do unauthorized immigrants contribute in tax revenue? If one considers the CTC as part of the calculation, unauthorized workers pay negative federal *income* taxes in aggregate. But this loss is more than offset by their federal *payroll* taxes for social security and Medicare, and their state and local contributions are also substantial. Overall, after tax credits are added into the equation, best estimates are that unauthorized immigrants may contribute somewhere between $10 and $20 billion in tax revenue each year.

The participation of unauthorized immigrants in the tax system is illustrative of a more general theme: Disparate federal agencies, states, and localities are empowered to make policies that affect the lives and decisions of unauthorized immigrants, but there is little cohesion across them. The rules an undocumented immigrant contends with are often contradictory. It's illegal to use a false social security number to work, for example, but workers are encouraged to report the fact that they did so to the IRS, and in some cases receive greater financial benefits when they do so relative to those they would have gained by working in the informal sector. The government officially bans employment of the undocumented, but it pulls in billions in dollars in tax revenue from that employment. With each agency working in its own silo, it's little wonder that so many observers across the political spectrum view the system as broken.

Net Fiscal and Economic Impacts

Immigrants pay taxes, and they benefit from public expenditures. The difference between the total dollar amount of each category is called the net fiscal impact. Separate from broader economic impacts, how much do the foreign born get out of the government coffers compared to what they put in?

Answering this question is a challenging task. It requires considering some key questions, such as: Should we focus on the current year, or project ahead to the longer run? How should one factor the US-born children of the foreign born into the calculations? Should a portion of expenditures that in theory benefit everyone living in the United States — such as those spent on national defense — be considered as an outlay partially attributable to immigrants, or should we focus only on the incremental impacts of immigrants on spending? How does one incorporate the indirect effects of immigration on tax revenues generated by economic growth? The challenge is further complicated by incomplete data on both sides of the equation.

In 2017, the National Academies of Sciences, Engineering, and Medicine put together a comprehensive report assessing the fiscal impact of immigration overall (regardless of immigrants' legal status).[118] The report documents some interesting findings. First, it notes that fiscal impacts vary as a person ages and advises that one should consider fiscal impact over an individual's entire life in the United States. Unsurprisingly, tax revenues contributed by the foreign born are highest in midlife, and public expenditures are highest in childhood and old age. This pattern mimics what we see for US-born individuals, and it's largely driven by educational costs at the young end and retirement benefits at the older end. To partially address this issue, the analysis attributes expenditures for dependent children to their parents.

The National Academies report points out that *both* immigrants and US natives generate net fiscal cost in any given year. This is because in aggregate the government tends to run a deficit, spending more than it collects in revenue. On a per person annual basis, first-generation immigrants and their dependent children contribute an estimated $10,887 in government revenue and receive $15,908 in services and benefits, according to baseline estimates in the report — creating a net loss of $5,021. (This baseline estimate apportions collective costs like those for national defense to each person regardless of immigration status, so in that sense overstates the marginal impact of adding one more immigrant to the population.)

The estimated net fiscal cost of about $5,000 for an average first-generation immigrant is substantially larger than that of the average member of the third-plus generation (i.e., an adult whose parents were born in the United States); this third-plus group is estimated to generate a net fiscal loss of around $3,600 per person annually. Compared to first-generation immigrants, the third-plus generation received about $2,000 more in government benefits, but also contributed $3,400 more in revenue on an annual per capita basis. Arguably, according to these estimates, the main fiscal concern associated with immigration is not what the foreign born receive in government services, an amount which is comparatively low, but instead the lower amount contributed in taxes. The total fiscal shortfall associated with these estimates is $279 billion for the first-generation group and $109 billion for the second-generation group. Because Americans with grandparents born in the United States are the largest group studied, they also have the largest aggregate shortfall: $856 billion annually.

The story changes if one considers a longer horizon. Immigrants are younger than the average US resident and therefore will contribute more revenues over the coming decades during their peak earnings years. Furthermore, at almost every age, the second generation (adult children of immigrants) have a higher fiscal benefit than either the immigrant generation or the third-plus generation. Over the course of their lives, children of immigrants are better for the government coffers than the children of the US born.

Estimates of the seventy-five-year fiscal impact of one additional immigrant is positive; including descendants as part of the calculation makes the estimate even more positive. Over a seventy-five-year horizon, the net benefit to the government budget of a typical immigrant arrival is $173,000 to $259,000 in present value, depending on modeling assumptions. The figures do vary by education: Immigrants without a high school degree represent a net fiscal cost of $117,000 to $200,000, while immigrants with only a high school degree have roughly a zero net impact. Immigrants with more than a high school education are estimated to contribute more in taxes than they use in services over the course of seventy-five years.

The 2017 report is not the first to note that the fiscal costs of immigration largely accrue to state and local governments, since state and local governments bear the costs of education for the children of immigrants, as well as the costs of some health and safety net programs. By contrast, a substantial share of the tax revenues collected from immigrants accrues to the federal government (and to the social security system in particular). Around 95 percent of the estimated $1,400 in "excess" annual net fiscal cost of a first-generation resident compared to a third-plus generation resident is at the state and local level.

This finding highlights a fiscal mismatch: A small number of states and localities bear the bulk of the fiscal costs associated with immigration, largely by supporting educational and health expenditures for immigrants' children, while immigration's fiscal benefits take the form of federal tax benefits which are shared across the country. In other words, states with few immigrants enjoy the greatest net fiscal benefit from immigrants' presence in the United States.

The National Academies report doesn't distinguish by legal status, so it's hard to know how these numbers compare for the undocumented population. Relative to immigrants overall, undocumented immigrants contribute less on the revenue side (because they generally have lower incomes than their documented counterparts) and cost less on the expenditure side (because of their lack of eligibility for many programs). On net, because of lower average educational levels, a typical undocumented immigrant almost certainly generates a larger short-run fiscal cost than the typical authorized immigrant. As noted earlier, one of the main expenditures associated with the unauthorized population is public education for children, who are sometimes also undocumented but are more often US born.

Not much evidence exists for the fiscal impacts of the unauthorized population specifically. One 2006 study conducted by the Texas Office of the Comptroller attempted to analyze the overall impact of unauthorized workers on the state's economy, including comparing the total taxes paid by unauthorized immigrants to the costs those immigrants imposed on state and local government by driving up demand for services like education and healthcare.[119] The report found that undocumented immigrants in Texas paid $1.6 billion in state taxes in fiscal year 2005; they consumed $1.2 billion in state services, particularly in education. Thus, the net impact was positive at the state level. However, the net effect was negative for local governments, who spent $1.4 billion more than they collected for this population, primarily due to healthcare costs. At the state and local levels combined, the direct costs associated with services to unauthorized immigrants that year exceeded what they generated in tax revenue by about $1 billion.

Thus, the combined direct fiscal impact of unauthorized immigration to Texas taxpayers in 2005 was negative, a finding in keeping with the National Academies estimate for the immigrant populations with the lowest levels of education. However, the Texas report concluded that those costs were "more than offset by the boost to the size of the Texas economy"—a finding consistent with other state studies. For example, a 2014 study conducted by researchers at the University of North Carolina revealed that immigrants (both documented and undocumented) generated tax revenues roughly equivalent to expenditures, but that including the indirect benefits to the economy in the overall calculations yielded an estimate of almost $1 billion in net fiscal benefit.[120]

As another approach to understanding the big-picture fiscal impacts of unauthorized immigration, we can exploit Congressional Budget Office (CBO) scoring of immigration reform bills. The CBO is tasked with performing objective analysis of the fiscal impact of proposed legislation over ten years' time. Rather than assessing the overall impact of unauthorized immigration, the CBO approach has often addressed a different question: What is the fiscal impact of granting legal status to those who are unauthorized? For example, the CBO estimated a net $44 billion fiscal benefit to the 2006 Comprehensive Immigration Reform Act (a bipartisan bill that passed the Senate but failed in the House). The agency concluded that higher expenditures on immigrants newly eligible for Medicaid and the Earned Income Tax Credit under the proposed law, as well as increased spending on enforcement, would be more than offset with increased tax revenue.[121]

The CBO also scored the 2013 Border Security, Economic Opportunity, and Immigration Modernization Act (the bipartisan "Gang of Eight" reform bill that passed the Senate and was not brought for a vote in the House). The bill was projected to have a net fiscal benefit over ten years of $197 billion.[122] The bill includes a number of provisions that make isolating the impacts of legal status difficult, but it seems clear that most compromise immigration reform bills would improve the government's fiscal health.

The Social Security Administration points out that the biggest impact immigrants make to the financial health of the social security system comes from their contribution to population growth. The system is structured such that younger generations pay for the retirement of older generations, and the burden is less when the younger generation is sufficiently large in size relative to the older generation. As Americans live longer and have fewer children, the ability to sustain such a system is in jeopardy. Immigrants and their children help offset the demographic shift that would otherwise exacerbate the social security solvency challenge.

Overall, the direct fiscal impact (the difference between taxes paid and public expenditures, not accounting for indirect impacts on economic activity) of unauthorized immigration is likely negative in the short run—particularly for localities with a large number of immigrants. But as the children of immigrants are successfully integrated into society, the overall fiscal impact is much less negative and may well move into the positive range. Regardless, the overall fiscal impact may not be the number that is most relevant for policy. Immigrants, even unauthorized immigrants, are a net positive for the health of the economy overall if one considers their impact on economic activity and growth.

Lorain, Ohio, 2017

Anabel Barron's four kids spent much of their childhood living with the fear that their mom could be deported at any moment—and that fear only intensified after Donald Trump's election. But in some ways, life improved in the years after Anabel's 2013 traffic stop. She got a better job with a higher, more stable income; she made new friends; and she became involved with community organizations. She also began a romance with a man she'd known since she was seventeen years old. They'd been neighbors, and he was a support after the domestic violence incident with her ex. He was also an immigrant, originally from Honduras, and made his living working construction. They got married in December 2016.

Following her traffic stop, Anabel became accustomed to annual check-ins with ICE. Each one was incredibly stressful, but in a way they became routine. After Trump's election, things changed. Anabel had advocates attempting to support her, including a contact in her local Congresswoman's office. In the past, the woman had told her not to worry, but before her March 2017 check-in the message was different. "This time she just say, 'Anabel, prepare for the worst. They want to detain you,'" Anabel recalls. She was advised to secure passports for her minor children so that they would be ready to leave the country along with her. Getting those passports was difficult, though, given that legally the kids' dad still had partial custody. "I went with the proof that I couldn't get the passports," Anabel says. "My lawyer was able to negotiate that, instead of them putting me in the detention center, I should be wearing this ankle monitor so I can prepare for self-deportation."

Compared to detention and deportation the ankle monitor was a "blessing," as Anabel puts it, since every day she wore it was a day she would remain in her home with her kids. Still, it ravaged her life. "People think I'm a criminal, and that's the way I feel," she says. The tracker could never come off. She slept in it, and showered it in. Every morning and every night she had to plug it in so it could recharge.

Anabel had always been attentive to her appearance. "I like heels, and skirts, and dresses." But after the monitor, she says, "I can't wear a dress. All I've been doing is wearing dress pants. I feel if I show it, they will think that I'm a criminal. That's in my mind, so I change the way I dress." Her employer contacted the hospital where she worked as a translator as part of her job at the community nonprofit, explaining the situation and advising patients not to be alarmed that their translator was wearing a criminal tracking device.

"They sent out a memorandum about me every time I was going," Anabel says. "And nobody asked when I was in the hospital. But when I was getting groceries, activity with my kids, people would ask me, 'What did you do to wear that big ankle monitor?'" At her kids' elementary school, teachers and other parents would stare at her feet. "I just got so tired and frustrated," she says. Anabel was humiliated to have to wear the monitor to bed with her new husband. She was always kicking him with it. Her other foot was all bruised up from bumping into it. She found herself deeply depressed: "I had to seek professional mental-health services for myself. This was beyond what I could take."

In the meantime, her kids were growing up. Her eldest daughter, Leslie, had graduated from high school and enrolled at a college in Oklahoma close to where her aunt and godmother, Anabel's sister, had lived for many years. She had scholarship money and a job at a credit-card call center where she answered mostly Spanish-language phone calls. But it was still hard to make ends meet and after a couple years she transferred back to a school closer to home to save money.

Leslie's plan was to attend the local Police Academy after graduation, with the dream of someday becoming an FBI agent. At twenty-one, she married her college boyfriend. She'd met him in Oklahoma, where he grew up. His parents were also from Mexico, and he'd been born there and brought to the US as a toddler. He'd had DACA when they met, but Leslie petitioned for him in Ohio, and he was approved for a green card.

Anabel's second daughter had a baby when she was still a teenager, and then another one. She had a job as a manager of a department at Walmart. Her high school boyfriend, the kids' dad, joined the military, and Anabel's daughter eventually followed his lead, enlisting with the Army Reserve. Anabel's youngest two kids sometimes struggled being among the only nonwhite kids at their suburban Ohio school. Anabel's youngest daughter, especially, suffered from bullying, and had ongoing mental-health struggles that Anabel attributes to the stress of her early childhood.

It took years from when she first applied, but eventually, in July 2018, Anabel was granted deferred-action status associated with her U visa application. She didn't actually have the U visa — not yet. There's a cap of ten thousand U visas issued per year — and with three times that many people applying annually in recent years, the waiting list is daunting. Between 2015 and 2018 the wait time increased from an average of 11.4 months to three years and eight months.[123] Anabel is on the list, in line. Thanks to her pending application she has a new work number to replace the one she was given after her first stay of deportation. She still has to renew it, but instead of paying a $480 fee each year — as she did for her previous work permit, the one associated with her stay of removal — she'll now pay the $480 fee every two years.

More importantly, when her visa is issued, she'll have three years before she can apply for a green card. Five years after that, perhaps fifty years after she first arrived in the US as a young child, she'll be able to apply for United States citizenship.

CONCLUSIONS

This book has outlined the stories of six families caught up in the United States' immigration enforcement system. What stands out is the degree to which the arbitrary, fear-inducing enforcement environment causes stress and hardship for these families, including for the citizen children and partners of undocumented immigrants. The enforcement system is expensive to operate — and the human costs significantly outweigh the promised benefits.

Early in this book, we examined the impacts that immigration has on the American job market and the economy more broadly. The evidence shows economic benefits to immigration. Though some disadvantaged American workers likely face worse employment opportunities because of immigration, on net immigration is good for the labor-market prospects of US workers. Immigrants tend to expand job opportunities for highly educated US natives and to lower the costs of goods and services for everyone. The survival of some industries depends on foreign-born workers.

It's true that in the short run there are governmental costs associated with new arrivals, especially when it comes to schooling and other services for children. But over the long run, immigrants are a net positive for the government coffers. Lifetime economic contributions of second-generation immigrants exceed the level of those who have been in the United States for generations. Noncitizens tend to use social services at a lower rate than native-born Americans, and undocumented immigrants are in fact ineligible for many of the programs they are often accused of abusing. And despite the anti-immigrant rhetoric that's become both louder and crueler in the years since we began researching this book, immigrants do not raise crime rates. Many Americans are concerned about the impact of immigrants on economic vitality and violent crime, but the evidence simply does not support those fears.

There are two major issues that do warrant concern and further consideration. One is the adverse impact of immigrants on less-educated workers. Economists disagree on *how much* immigration drives down wages and employment opportunities for those at the bottom of the US income distribution, and we believe the effect is small—but it is real. When less-educated immigrants move into a region it tends to be disadvantaged workers, often US-born Black men, who suffer the most. The other group most affected is previous waves of less-educated immigrants. This adverse effect would increase with significant expansions in immigration. In an era of rising inequality and economic stagnation for the bottom half of American households, this particular adverse impact poses a serious concern.

The second issue relates to the value some native-born Americans put on preserving what they see as a traditional American identity. In the eyes of those who most strongly believe the social order is threatened by immigration, this identity is white and speaks English without an accent. According to Pew Research surveys, a majority of Americans view welcoming immigrants as core to the American ideal. But there is no doubt that immigration affects the racial and cultural makeup of our country—and that a significant minority of voters view that effect as negative.

Due to both current political will and economic realities, then, fully open borders are not a viable option. Increased *legal* immigration would be a positive for the economy, but as noted earlier in the book, a modest expansion in legal immigration would do little to curtail unauthorized migration. The upshot is the need to build a humane and effective enforcement strategy. Today's immigration enforcement policy—which is marked by capriciousness and cruelty—is neither.

What are the impacts of aggressive interior enforcement? The billions of dollars we spend result in fewer than a hundred thousand individuals deported each year, less than 1 percent of the unauthorized population. Those deportations are deeply harmful to hundreds of thousands of individuals and families, and they heighten fear and uncertainty for millions more—but they do not meaningfully change the labor market for American workers or even the demographic composition of the country.

Viewed through this lens, it seems that the goal of aggressive enforcement is not to deport enough immigrants to make a significant dent in the unauthorized population. Instead, by increasing the fear and stress that undocumented immigrants live with, perhaps it is hoped that individuals might choose to relocate (sometimes known as a "self-deportation") and that future migrants will be deterred from coming to the United States.

In part 2, we reviewed the evidence on whether interior enforcement achieves these goals. For the most part, unauthorized immigrants do not appear to move away from where they are living in response to aggressive enforcement. This finding is hardly surprising, given that a majority of such immigrants have lived in the US for more than a decade, and a large number of them have citizen children (or noncitizen children who have spent their entire childhoods in the United States). And a big downside to deportation—being banned from future entry—has little bite for the many who never had a hope of legal migration in their lifetimes anyway.

For a would-be immigrant, the expectation of possibly being harassed or deported might make the US a less appealing destination. At the same time, an immigrant might figure they have little to lose by working in the United States for a while and then being deported. The full hardship of deportation might become evident only once an individual has settled into life in the US and started a family. There is no clear evidence on how effective aggressive interior enforcement is at reducing future unauthorized migration. Though some immigrants are surely deterred, many others will be willing to risk deportation down the line as long as better jobs are available in the United States.

If we are correct that aggressive enforcement does little to reduce the current undocumented population and doesn't deter future migrants very much either, why has the US doubled down on this ineffective strategy? We have a cynical view. As we saw earlier in this book, some of the strongest advocates for immigration restrictions are Republicans who view immigrants as a threat to their vision of a traditional American identity. But these views are at odds with the pro-business wing of the party, which recognizes the critical role both undocumented and legal immigrants play in the competitiveness of US industry. The Republican Party's immigration policies aim to appeal to their socially conservative voting base without choking off the workers that business leaders—including Donald Trump himself, as evidenced by the forty-three undocumented Trump-property workers interviewed by the *Washington Post* in 2019—rely upon.[1]

Harassing, detaining, and deporting immigrants in a highly visible manner heightens the anxiety of those living in the United States without papers, and asserts a particular white, English-speaking American identity. It has virtually no impact on the ability of businesses to hire unauthorized workers. The Trump-era approach—one which emphasizes performative enforcement actions that don't necessarily lead to substantive reductions in the immigrant labor force—is a predictable consequence of a politics built on white nationalism but funded by those who profit from immigrant labor.

It would be a mistake to suggest the Trump administration was the first in recent history to pursue an aggressive enforcement regime. Obama was known as the "Deporter-in-Chief" because his administration moved to a harsher border policy in which attempted border crossers were officially deported, rather than simply returned to the other side of the border without a paper trail. He also oversaw a massive expansion of the Secure Communities program, which facilitated immigration enforcement through local jails. As described in part 2, the Obama administration aimed to show they were serious about enforcement of immigration violations as they sought comprehensive immigration reform—a futile effort, as it turned out—and congressional approval of protections for sympathetic categories of unauthorized residents like so-called Dreamers and their parents.

As the stories of the immigrant families interviewed for this book—as well as so many others—tell us, there is an enormous human cost to deporting immigrants who have long been settled in the country.

The current level of immigration in the United States is a net positive for the economy. Still, the unauthorized immigrant population does have negative impacts on the economic prospects of some of the most vulnerable Americans, and unfettered immigration would be likely to make those impacts worse. But if aggressive interior enforcement is not the most effective strategy for keeping unauthorized immigration in check, what is?

There are clearly no easy answers. Border security is one important component. Visa recipients, who represent a growing proportion of those in the country illegally, could be more closely monitored to deter overstays. There could be increased consequences for employers who hire unauthorized immigrants; at present, these employers frequently get a pass, while the workers they hired have their families torn apart. But internal enforcement is also part of the picture. An ideal internal enforcement approach would meet the following goals:

- It would be a consistent policy developed as a legislative compromise and not subject to radical change each time the president changed. A federal immigration policy governed through executive action is destined to fail.
- It would be broadly equitable, in the sense that individuals in similar circumstances would be treated similarly.
- It would be transparent and consistently enforced both so that individuals would have a good sense of what to expect, and so that there would be a general sense that the law was being upheld. Due-process protections would be in place.
- It would recognize the humanitarian costs of forcibly removing someone who has lived in the United States for a long time.
- It would recognize the particular social value and positive impacts on physical and mental health associated with keeping families intact, especially when the immigrant is a primary caretaker of someone living in the United States or the family includes United States citizens.
- It would reward undocumented immigrants who are social contributors in the sense that they pay taxes, avoid criminal activity, and support their communities.

- It would focus on a narrow, clearly defined set of goals, and avoid creating fear and a sense of vulnerability as an end or a means to an end.

In today's enforcement system, the costs far outweigh the benefits. Each year the United States spends billions on detention and deportation, all without economic gain and at great human cost. Though ICE is not exclusively focused on deportations, the cost of ICE's budget to the US taxpayer is more than $25,000 per immigrant removed.[2] Overzealous enforcement and deportation policies are leading to more broken families, in both the short and long terms. Families are economically destabilized. Some become dependent on social services they would not need if their family had remained intact. And while it might be tempting to think of enforcement as affecting "immigrant" families alone, the reality is that two-thirds of noncitizens live in mixed-citizenship households.

The broken system is also destructive on a broader political level. Immigration laws are inconsistently and inequitably enforced, leading both to a sense that immigration is out of control for those who oppose it, and to a general sense of anxiety and danger for those who live under the shadow of enforcement. The current system reflects neither the shared values of Americans nor good governance, leading to institutional mistrust from all sides of the political spectrum — a mistrust that bleeds into broader issues beyond immigration.

*　*　*

The 2013 Border Security, Economic Opportunity, and Immigration Modernization Act was one attempt to reach a compromise, negotiated by a bipartisan group of senators known as the Gang of Eight. In addition to some changes to the legal immigration system, the bill would have tightened border security and offered a pathway to citizenship. Almost any compromise bill would incorporate elements of increased border security in exchange for a more-humanitarian enforcement regime for those who are settled in the US already.

A feature of the bill was the creation of a new immigration status:

"Registered Provisional Immigrant." To apply for this status, immigrants would have needed to pay a $500 fine plus any back taxes that they owed. An immigrant's criminal record would also have been taken into account, and the individual would have had to have been living in the country since 2011 or earlier. The status would last for six years and would be renewable. After thirteen years, someone who met certain criteria (English fluency, among others) could apply for legal permanent residency. The permanent-residency component of the proposed 2013 law was conditional on successfully reducing the number of border crossings—a built-in incentive for future pro-immigrant administrations to take the enforcement component seriously.[3]

The Congressional Budget Office, a nonpartisan agency that evaluates the budget implications of proposed legislation, predicted that the 2013 reform would have reduced the federal deficit by almost $200 billion over a decade. Though wages would have been depressed in the short term, the bill would have had a positive effect on wages over the longer run.[4] The 1986 IRCA reform—involving amnesty for undocumented workers—improved wages for those workers; it also encouraged immigrants to spend more of their income in the United States, rather than sending it to relatives in home countries in the form of remittances. Overall, a compromise bill like the "Gang of Eight" reform was likely to have a positive impact on the overall economy.

The bill was passed in the Senate by a 68–32 margin, leaving little doubt that a politically feasible compromise could exist. Ultimately, though it was widely assumed that the bill could also pass in the House on a bipartisan basis, it was never brought to a vote: There simply was not adequate support among the House Republican leadership at that time.

This political failure represents the worst of our polarized system. A majority of Americans support a sensible compromise. And while such a bill would not have helped all the families profiled in this book, for most of them it would have made a life-changing difference. Jorge Ramirez would be investing in his business rather than retreating from society, living with the fear that he could be separated from his family and deported at whim. The constant anxiety that has enveloped Eduardo Lopez's and Anabel Barron's families for years would be dissipated. And Michael and Mia Park, who arrived in the US as young children and have lived their entire adult lives uncertain that their investments in their education will ever pay off, would have a clear path ahead for their future.

Such a legislative compromise would have left activists on both sides dissatisfied. Those opposed to immigration would prefer to see punitive measures taken against people who crossed the border illegally long ago, while immigrant advocates would prefer to see less border control — or none at all — and an easier pathway to citizenship. But for most of the regular families we interviewed for this book, a fast track to citizenship is far less important than a sense of certainty about the future — for themselves and their children.

The new Biden administration has pledged to reverse much of Trump-era immigration policy — including unwinding the public-charge rule, scaling back detention, and reinstating the DACA program. Some changes will be easier to make than others: Law professor Lucas Guttentag documented hundreds of small and large changes in immigration policy made between 2017 and 2020.[5] But meaningful change cannot be limited to the executive branch, where a political roller coaster upends lived realities for immigrants every four years. Instead, it is time for Americans to recognize the damage caused by a policy rooted in fear and uncertainty, and to come together to enact sensible reform.

Ultimately, the solution might be something like the 2013 Gang of Eight bill, or it might be legislation with different contours that moves us toward the goals articulated above in a different way. Virtually any bill that offers consistency, transparency, and humanity will be an improvement over the legislative vacuum we have now. With a new administration, there is an opportunity for meaningful progress, progress that is supported by a majority of Americans, if Congress stands ready to act. Immigrants and nonimmigrants alike would benefit from a fairer, clearer, and kinder approach. It's time we take concrete legislative action to make sense of a senseless system.

ACKNOWLEDGMENTS

Above all, we want to thank the families whose stories appear in this book. Most we met for the first time many years ago now. In some cases, circumstances changed drastically over the years we were intermittently in touch, calling with a few more questions or emailing for a few points of clarification. We believe that most of the people interviewed were motivated by a desire to increase understanding of the challenges of their lives. We hope we've done their stories justice.

We also want to thank the many undocumented individuals and families we interviewed whose stories ultimately did not end up in this book, but whose spirit and insights influenced the final result nonetheless. Each story was moving and informative in its own way.

In the course of researching, we also spoke with a number of academics, lawyers, activists, and other professionals who helped us make further connections and shared their expertise and knowledge from years in the field. Thank you to Trista Beard, Melissa Chua, Arturo Corso, Veronica Dahlberg, Richardo Elford, Lili Farhang, Sam Freeman, Katy Green, Talia Inlender, Josh Lamel, Carrie Love, Javier Luengo-Garrido, Brooke Mead, Christine Neumann-Ortiz, Jennie Pasquarella, Jacob Sapochnick, Michele Sisselman, and Carmen Whalen.

Thank you to our Williams College research assistants who directly or indirectly contributed to the effort: Lei Brutus, Anand Butler, Arno Cai, Nick Harrington, Catherine Jiang, Ryan Kelley, Mie Mizutani, and Yinga Xia. Bashudha Dhamala and Argenis Herrera at Williams provided a fresh read of the nearly finished manuscript and Bashudha

Dhamala methodically fact-checked statistics, citations, and so much more. We are grateful to Keith Watson and to the students in Wellesley College Economics 311 along with their professor, Kristin Butcher, for offering helpful feedback.

Los Angeles writer friends Maraya Cornell, Maggie Flynn, Michal Lemberger, Rachel Levin, and Elline Lipkin provided valuable feedback on early drafts. Thank you to Elizabeth Bryer, who offered a careful late-stage read and generous emotional support at every stage along the way.

This book was originally suggested by Joe Jackson, then the economics editor at the University of Chicago Press. Editors Christie Henry, Jane Macdonald, and Chuck Myers all provided helpful insights in following years. Editor Chad Zimmerman saw the project to the finish line with great care and support. Thank you as well to Tamara Ghattas, Noor Shawaf, and Alicia Sparrow, who helped with all the final details, and to Jessica Wilson, who provided a thorough and thoughtful copy edit. Laurie Liss at Sterling Lord contributed steady enthusiasm over many years.

Finally, thank you to our husbands, Rob and Dan, and our kids, Emma, Piper, Corin, Otto, and Laszlo. We are grateful for your unwavering support and encouragement.

NOTES

Prologue

1   William A. Kandel, *Permanent Legal Immigration to the United States: Policy Overview*, Congressional Research Service, May 11, 2018, https://fas.org/sgp /crs/homesec/R42866.pdf.

2   US Department of State Bureau of Consular Affairs, *Diversity Visa Program, DV 2016–2018: Number of Entries Received During Each Online Registration Period by Country of Chargeability*, accessed February 29, 2020, https://travel.state.gov /content/dam/visas/Diversity-Visa/DVStatistics/DV%20AES%20statistics %20by%20FSC%202016-2018.pdf.

3   US Department of State Bureau of Consular Affairs, *Visa Bulletin: Immigrant Numbers for January 2019*, no. 25, vol. X, January 2019, https://travel.state.gov /content/travel/en/legal/visa-law0/visa-bulletin/2019/visa-bulletin-for-janu ary-2019.html.

4   Jynnah Radford, "Fact Tank: Key Findings about U.S. Immigrants," Pew Research Center, June 17, 2019, https://www.pewresearch.org/fact-tank/2019/06 /17/key-findings-about-u-s-immigrants/.

5   John Kelly, "Statement by Secretary of Homeland Security John Kelly on Southwest Border Security," US Department of Homeland Security Office of the Press Secretary, March 8, 2017, https://www.dhs.gov/news/2017/03 /08/statement-secretary-homeland-security-john-kelly-southwest-border -security.

6   Frank Askin, "Chilling Effect," *First Amendment Encyclopedia* (Murfreesboro, TN: Free Speech Center, Middle Tennessee State University, 2009), accessed November 14, 2020, https://www.mtsu.edu/first-amendment/article/897/chil ling-effect.

7   Patrick Ettinger, *Imaginary Lines: Border Enforcement and the Origins of Undocumented Immigration, 1882–1930*. Austin: University of Texas Press, 2009.

8   Data through 2000 based on Campbell Gibson and Kay Jung, "Historical Cen-

sus Statistics on the Foreign-Born Population of the United States: 1850–2000" (US Census Bureau working paper no. POP-WP081, February 1, 2006), https://www.census.gov/library/working-papers/2006/demo/POP-twps0081.html. Data after 2000 based on Jynnah Radford, "Fact Tank: Key Findings about U.S. Immigrants."

9   Origin data based on authors' analysis of IPUMS decennial census and American Community Survey data. Data obtained from Steven Ruggles, Sarah Flood, Ronald Goeken, Josiah Grover, Erin Meyer, Jose Pacas, and Matthew Sobek, *IPUMS USA: Version 10.0* [data set] (Minneapolis, MN: IPUMS, 2020), http://doi.org/10.18128/D010.V10.0.

10 Authors' calculations based on US census data.

11 Lyndon B. Johnson, "Remarks at the Signing of the Immigration Bill," Liberty Island, New York, October 3, 1965, http://www.lbjlibrary.org/lyndon-baines -johnson/timeline/lbj-on-immigration, citing *Public Papers of the Presidents of the United States: Lyndon B. Johnson, 1965*, vol. II, entry 546: 1037–40 (Washington, DC: Government Printing Office, 1966).

12 Authors' calculations based on IPUMS census and American Community Survey data. Data obtained from Steven Ruggles, Sarah Flood, Ronald Goeken, Josiah Grover, Erin Meyer, Jose Pacas, and Matthew Sobek, *IPUMS USA: Version 9.0* [data set] (Minneapolis, MN: IPUMS, 2019), https://doi.org/10.181 28/D010.V9.0.

13 Pew Research Center, "Unauthorized Immigrant Population Trends for States, Birth Countries and Regions," June 12, 2019, https://www.pewresearch.org /hispanic/interactives/unauthorized-trends/.

14 Migration Policy Institute Data Hub, "Profile of the Unauthorized Population: United States," accessed July 31, 2019, https://www.migrationpolicy.org/data /unauthorized-immigrant-population/state/US#.

15 Randy Capps, Michael Fix, and Jie Zong, "A Profile of U.S. Children with Unauthorized Immigrant Parents," Migration Policy Institute fact sheet, January 2016, https://www.migrationpolicy.org/research/profile-us-children-unautho rized-immigrant-parents.

16 Pew Research Center, "Unauthorized Immigrant Population Trends for States, Birth Countries and Regions," June 12, 2019, https://www.pewresearch.org /hispanic/interactives/unauthorized-trends/.

17 US Department of Homeland Security, *Fiscal Year 2019 Entry/Exit Overstay Report*, March 30, 2020, https://www.dhs.gov/sites/default/files/publications/20 _0513_fy19-entry-and-exit-overstay-report.pdf.

18 Robert Warren, "US Undocumented Population Continued to Fall from 2016 to 2017 and Visa Overstays Significantly Exceeded Illegal Crossings for the Seventh Consecutive Year," *Journal on Migration and Human Security* 7, no. 1

(2019): 19–22, https://journals.sagepub.com/doi/pdf/10.1177/23315024198
30339.

19 Migration Policy Institute Data Hub, "Profile of the Unauthorized Population:
United States."

20 US Department of Agriculture Economic Research Service, "Farm Labor," last
updated April 22, 2020, https://www.ers.usda.gov/topics/farm-economy/farm
-labor/#legalstatus.

21 Migration Policy Institute, "Profile of the Unauthorized Population: United
States," accessed June 29, 2020, https://www.migrationpolicy.org/data/unau
thorized-immigrant-population/state/US#.

22 Donald Kerwin, Mike Nicholson, Daniela Alulema, and Robert Warren, *US
Foreign-Born Essential Workers by Status and State, and the Global Pandemic*,
Center for Migration Studies of New York report, May 1, 2020, https://cmsny
.org/publications/us-essential-workers/.

23 US Department of Homeland Security, *FY 2021 Budget in Brief*, accessed February 15, 2021, https://www.dhs.gov/sites/default/files/publications/fy_2021
_dhs_bib_0.pdf.

24 Doris Meissner, Donald M. Kerwin, Muzaffar Chishti, and Claire Bergeron, *Immigration Enforcement in the United States: The Rise of a Formidable Machinery*,
Migration Policy Institute report, January 2013: 9, https://www.migrationpol
icy.org/research/immigration-enforcement-united-states-rise-formidable-ma
chinery.

25 US Department of Homeland Security, FY 2021 Budget in Brief."

26 US Department of Justice, "Summary of Budget Authority by Appropriation,"
accessed February 15, 2021, https://www.justice.gov/doj/page/file/1246636
/download.

27 Paul Colford, "'Illegal Immigrant' No More," AP Style Guide blog, April 2,
2013, https://blog.ap.org/announcements/illegal-immigrant-no-more.

Part One: Arrivals

1 National Immigration Forum, "Push or Pull Factors: What Drives Central
American Migrants to the U.S.?" July 23, 2019. https://immigrationforum.org/ar
ticle/push-or-pull-factors-what-drives-central-american-migrants-to-the-u-s/.

2 Gordon H. Hanson, "Illegal Migration from Mexico to the United States," *Journal of Economic Literature* 44, no. 4 (2006): 869–924.

3 Gordon H. Hanson and Antonio Spilimbergo, "Illegal Immigration, Border
Enforcement, and Relative Wages: Evidence from Apprehensions at the U.S.–
Mexico Border," *American Economic Review* 89, no. 5 (1999): 1337–57.

4 Jens Manuel Krogstad, Jeffrey S. Passel, and D'Vera Cohn, "Fact Tank: 5 Facts

about Illegal Immigration in the U.S.," Pew Research Center, June 12, 2019, https://www.pewresearch.org/fact-tank/2019/06/12/5-facts-about-illegal-immigration-in-the-u-s/.

5   Randall Akee and Maggie R. Jones, "Immigrants' Earnings Growth and Return Migration from the U.S.: Examining their Determinants Using Linked Survey and Administrative Data" (US Census Bureau Center for Economic Studies Working Paper no. 19–10, 2019), https://luskin.ucla.edu/wp-content/uploads/2020/04/CES-WP-19-10-Immigration-Earnings.pdf.

6   Brian C. Cadena and Brian K. Kovak, "Immigrants Equilibrate Local Labor Markets: Evidence from the Great Recession," *American Economic Journal: Applied Economics* 8, no. 1 (2016): 257–90.

7   Jens Manuel Krogstad, "Fact Tank: On Views of Immigrants, Americans Largely Split Along Party Lines," Pew Research Center, September 30, 2015, http://www.pewresearch.org/fact-tank/2015/09/30/on-views-of-immigrants-americans-largely-split-along-party-lines/.

8   Jennifer Van Hook, "Analysis: Why the 2020 Census Doesn't Need a Citizenship Question to Count the Undocumented," PBS News Hour, July 17, 2019, https://www.pbs.org/newshour/science/analysis-why-the-2020-census-doesnt-need-a-citizenship-question-to-count-the-undocumented.

9   Barry R. Chiswick, "The Effect of Americanization on the Earnings of Foreign-Born Men," *Journal of Political Economy* 86, no. 5 (1978): 897–921.

10 George J. Borjas, "Self Selection and the Earnings of Immigrants," *American Economic Review* 77, no. 4 (1987): 531–53.

11 Authors' calculations based on IPUMS census and American Community Survey data. Data obtained from Steven Ruggles, Sarah Flood, Ronald Goeken, Josiah Grover, Erin Meyer, Jose Pacas, and Matthew Sobek, *IPUMS USA: Version 9.0* [data set] (Minneapolis, MN: IPUMS, 2019). https://doi.org/10.18128/D010.V9.0.

12 Authors' calculations based on IPUMS census and American Community Survey data. Data obtained from Steven Ruggles et al., *IPUMS USA: Version 9.0* [data set].

13 Hoffman Plastic Compounds, Inc. v. National Labor Relations Board, 535 US 137 (2002), https://supreme.justia.com/cases/federal/us/535/137/.

14 Christoph M. Schmidt, Anette Stilz, and Klaus F. Zimmerman, "Mass Migration, Unions, and Government Intervention," *Journal of Public Economics* 55, no. 2 (1994): 185–201.

15 See Henning Finseraas, Marianne Røed, and Pål Schøne, "Labour Immigration and Union Strength," *European Union Politics* 21, no. 1 (March 2020): 3–23.

16 Adeel Hassan, "Witness in Hard Rock Hotel Collapse Is Deported," *New York Times*, November 29, 2019, https://www.nytimes.com/2019/11/29/us/hard-rock-hotel-worker-immigration.html.

17   Roger Lowenstein, "The Immigration Equation," *New York Times Magazine*, July 9, 2006, https://www.nytimes.com/2006/07/09/magazine/09IMM.html.

18   Ethan Lewis and Giovanni Peri, "Immigration and the Economy of Cities and Regions" (National Bureau of Economic Research Working Paper no. 20428, August 2014), https://www.nber.org/system/files/working_papers/w20428/w20428.pdf.

19   David Card, "Immigrant Inflows, Native Outflows, and the Local Labor Market Impact of Immigration," *Journal of Labor Economics* 19, no. 1 (2001): 22–64.

20   Authors' calculations based on IPUMS census and American Community Survey data. Data obtained from Steven Ruggles et al., *IPUMS USA: Version 9.0* [data set].

21   This approach has faced recent criticism because flows are fairly persistent decade after decade, so it is difficult to separate long-run effects of immigration in the 1990s versus the short-run impacts of later immigration. See David A. Jaeger, Joakim Ruist, and Jan Stuhler, "Shift-Share Instruments and the Impact of Immigration" (National Bureau of Economic Research Working Paper no. 24285, February 2018), https://www.nber.org/system/files/working_papers/w24285/w24285.pdf.

22   Card, "Immigrant Inflows, Native Outflows, and the Local Market Impacts of Higher Immigration."

23   Ran Abramitzky, Phillip Ager, Leah Platt Boustan, Elior Cohen, and Casper Hansen, "The Effects of Immigration on the Economy: Lessons from the 1920s Border Closure" (National Bureau of Economic Research Working Paper no. 26536, December 2019), https://www.nber.org/system/files/working_papers/w26536/w26536.pdf.

24   Pia Orrenius and Madeline Zavodny, "Does Immigration Affect Wages? A Look at Occupation-Level Evidence," *Labour Economics* 14, no. 5 (2007): 757–73.

25   US Department of Homeland Security, "Persons Obtaining Lawful Permanent Resident Status by Type and Major Class of Admission: Fiscal Years 2016 to 2018," Table 6 in the *2018 Yearbook of Immigration Statistics*, accessed May 26, 2020, https://www.dhs.gov/immigration-statistics/yearbook/2018/table6.

26   David Card, "The Impact of the Mariel Boatlift on the Miami Labor Market," *Industrial and Labor Relations Review* 43, no. 2 (1990): 245–57.

27   Mette Foged and Giovanni Peri, "Immigrants' Effect on Native Workers: New Analysis on Longitudinal Data," *American Economic Journal: Applied Economics* 8, no. 2 (April 2016): 1–34.

28   George Borjas, "The Labor Demand Curve Is Downward Sloping: Reexamining the Impact of Immigration on the Labor Market," *Quarterly Journal of Economics* 118, no. 4 (2003): 1335–74.

29   George Borjas, Jeffrey Grogger, and Gordon H. Hanson, "Immigration and

the Economic Status of African-American Men," *Economica* 77, no. 306 (April 2010): 255–82.

30 Evan Peacutrez and Corey Dade, "An Immigration Raid Aids Blacks—For a Time," *Wall Street Journal*, January 17, 2007, https://www.wsj.com/articles /SB116898113191477989 (paywall).

31 George J. Borjas and Richard B. Freeman, "From Immigrants to Robots: The Changing Locus of Substitutes for Workers," *RSF: The Russell Sage Foundation Journal of the Social Sciences* 5, no. 5 (Fall/Winter 2019): 22–42.

32 David H. Autor, David Dorn, and Gordon H. Hanson, "The China Syndrome: Local Labor Market Effects of Import Competition in the United States," *American Economic Review* 103, no. 6 (2013): 2121–68.

33 Giovanni Peri, "Rethinking the Area Approach: Immigrants and the Labor Market in California," *Journal of International Economics* 84, no. 1 (2011): 1–14.

34 Anna Maria Mayda, Giovanni Peri, and Walter Steingress, "The Political Impact of Immigration: Evidence from the United States," *American Economic Journal: Applied Economics* (forthcoming 2021), https://www.aeaweb.org/arti cles?id=10.1257/app.20190081&&from=f.

35 Julie Hotchkiss, Myriam Quispe-Agnoli, and Fernando Rios-Avila, "The Wage Impact of Undocumented Workers: Evidence from Administrative Data," *Southern Economic Journal* 81, no. 4 (2015): 874–906.

36 Sarah Bohn, Magnus Lofstrom, and Steven Raphael, "Do E-Verify Mandates Improve Labor Market Outcomes of Low-Skilled Native and Legal Immigrant Workers?: E-Verify and Legal Worker Outcomes," *Southern Economic Journal* 81, no. 4 (April 2015): 960–79.

37 Annie Laurie Hines and Giovanni Peri, "Do Apprehensions of Undocumented Immigrants Reduce Crime and Create Jobs? Evidence from U.S. Districts 2000–2015," *UC Davis Law Review* 52, no. 1 (November 2018): 255–98.

38 Chloe East, Philip Luck, Hani Mansour, and Andrea Velasquez, "The Labor Market Effects of Immigration Enforcement" (IZA Discussion Paper no. 11486, April 2018), http://ftp.iza.org/dp11486.pdf.

39 Authors' calculations based on IPUMS census and American Community Survey data. Data obtained from Steven Ruggles et al., *IPUMS USA: Version 9.0* [data set].

40 Francesca Mazzolari and David Neumark, "Immigration and Product Diversity," *Journal of Population Economics* 25, no. 3 (2012): 1107–37.

41 World Bank, "Annual Remittances Data," updated April 2020, https://www .worldbank.org/en/topic/migrationremittancesdiasporaissues/brief/migra tion-remittances-data.

42 Dean Yang, "Migrant Remittances," *Journal of Economic Perspectives* 25, no. 3 (2011): 129–52.

43 William W. Olney, "Remittances and the Wage Impact of Immigration," *Journal of Human Resources* 50, no. 3 (2014): 694–727.

44 Catalina Amuedo-Dorantes and Francesca Mazzolari, "Remittances to Latin America from Migrants in the United States: Assessing the Impact of Amnesty Programs," *Journal of Development Economics* 91, no. 2 (2010): 323–35.

45 Brian C. Cadena and Brian K. Kovak, "Immigrants Equilibrate Local Labor Markets: Evidence from the Great Recession," *American Economic Journal: Applied Economics* 8, no. 1 (2016): 257–90.

46 Abigail Wozniak, "Are College Graduates More Responsive to Distant Labor Market Opportunities?," *Journal of Human Resources* 45, no. 4 (2010): 944–70.

47 George J. Borjas , "Does Immigration Grease the Wheels of the Labor Market?," *Brookings Papers on Economic Activity* 32, no. 1 (2001): 69–134.

48 Olivier Blanchard and Lawrence Katz, "Regional Evolutions," *Brookings Papers on Economic Activity* 23, no. 1 (1992): 1–75.

49 Brian C. Cadena, "Native Competition and Low-Skill Immigrant Inflows," *Journal of Human Resources* 48, no. 4 (Fall 2013): 910–44.

50 Amy A. Fowler and Douglas J. Bersharov, "The End of Welfare as We Know It?," *Public Interest* 111(Spring 1993): 95–108.

51 Authors' analysis of 2017 American Community Survey data: list of most common occupations for noncitizens ages 18–64 with less than 12 years of schooling. Data obtained from Steven Ruggles, Sarah Flood, Ronald Goeken, Josiah Grover, Erin Meyer, Jose Pacas, and Matthew Sobek, *IPUMS USA: Version 10.0* [data set] (Minneapolis, MN: IPUMS, 2020), http://doi.org/10.18128/D010 .V10.0.

52 Lewis and Peri, "Immigration and the Economy of Cities and Regions."

53 Hernan Ramirez and Pierrette Hondagneu-Sotelo, "Mexican Immigrant Gardeners: Entrepreneurs or Exploited Workers?," *Social Problems* 56, no. 1 (2009): 70–88.

54 Ramirez and Hondagneu-Sotelo, 70, 72.

55 Ramirez and Hondagneu-Sotelo, 72.

56 Ramirez and Hondagneu-Sotelo, 72.

57 Ramirez and Hondagneu-Sotelo, 84.

58 Ramirez and Hondagneu-Sotelo, 85.

59 US Department of Agriculture Economic Research Service, "Farm Labor," last updated April 22, 2020, https://www.ers.usda.gov/topics/farm-economy/farm -labor/#legalstatus.

60 Steven Zahniser, Tom Hertz, Peter Dixon, and Maureen Rimmer, *The Potential Impact of Changes in Immigration Policy on U.S. Agriculture and the Market for Hired Farm Labor: A Simulation Analysis* (US Department of Agriculture Economic Research Service Report no. 135, May 2012), https://www.ers.usda

.gov/webdocs/publications/44981/20515_err135_reportsummary_1_.pdf?v
=760.5.

61 David J. Bier, "H-2A Visas for Agriculture: The Complex Process for Farmers to
Hire Agricultural Guest Workers" (Cato Institute Immigration Research and
Policy Brief no. 17, March 2020), https://www.cato.org/publications/immigra
tion-research-policy-brief/h-2a-visas-agriculture-complex-process-farmers
-hire.

62 Mette Foged and Giovanni Peri, "Immigrants' Effect on Native Workers: New
Analysis on Longitudinal Data," *American Economic Journal: Applied Economics* 8, no. 2 (April 2016): 1–34.

63 Joshua D. Angrist and Adriana D. Kugler, "Protective or Counter-Productive?
Labour Market Institutions and the Effect of Immigration on EU Natives," *Economic Journal* 113, no. 488 (2003): F302–31.

64 Giovanni Peri, "The Effect of Immigration on Productivity: Evidence from U.S.
States," *Review of Economics and Statistics* 94, no. 1 (2012): 348–58.

65 Patricia Cortes and Jose Tessada, "Low-Skilled Immigration and the Labor
Supply of Highly Skilled Women," *American Economic Journal: Applied Economics* 3, no. 3 (2011): 88–123.

66 Catalina Amuedo-Dorantes and Almudena Sevilla-Sanz, "Low-Skilled Immigration and Parenting Investments of College-Educated Mothers in the United
States: Evidence from Time-Use Data," *Journal of Human Resources* 49, no. 3
(2014): 509–39.

67 Jeanne Batalova, "Spotlight: Immigrant Health-Care Workers in the United
States," Migration Policy Institute, May 14, 2020, https://www.migrationpolicy
.org/article/immigrant-health-care-workers-united-states.

68 Leah Zallman, Karen E. Finnegan, David U. Himmelstein, Sharon Touw, and
Steffie Woolhandler, "Care For America's Elderly And Disabled People Relies
On Immigrant Labor," *Health Affairs* 38, no. 6 (2019): 919–26.

69 Kristin Butcher, Kelsey Moran, and Tara Watson, "Immigrant Labor and the Institutionalization of the U.S.-Born Elderly," (unpublished manuscript, December 3, 2020), PDF file.

70 Delia Furtado and Francesc Ortega, "Does Immigration Improve Quality of
Care in Nursing Homes?" (IZA Discussion Paper no. 13552, July 2020), http://
ftp.iza.org/dp13552.pdf.

71 Katherine Magnuson, Claudia Lahaie, and Jane Waldfogel, "Preschool and
School Readiness of Children of Immigrants," *Social Science Quarterly* 87, no. 5
(2006): 1241–62.

72 William W. Olney, "Immigration and Firm Expansion," *Journal of Regional Science* 53, no. 1 (2013): 142–57.

73 Nikolaj Malchow-Moller, Jakob Roland Munch, Klaus Aastruo Seidelin, and

Jan Rose Skasken, "Immigrant Workers and Farm Performance: Evidence from Matched Employer-Employee Data," *American Journal of Agricultural Economics* 95, no. 4 (2013): 819–41.

74 Ethan Lewis, "Immigration, Skill Mix, and Capital Skill Complementarity," *Quarterly Journal of Economics* 126, no. 2 (2011): 1029–69.

75 Douglas S. Massey and Zai Liang, "The Long-Term Consequences of a Temporary Worker Program: The US Bracero Experience," *Population Research and Policy Review* 8, no. 3 (September 1989): 199–226.

76 Abramitzky, Ager, Boustan, Cohen, and Hansen, "The Effects of Immigration on the Economy: Lessons from the 1920s Border Closure."

77 Allison O'Connor and Jeanne Batalova, "Spotlight: Korean Immigrants in the United States," Migration Policy Institute, April 10, 2019, https://www.migra tionpolicy.org/article/korean-immigrants-united-states#DistributionState Cities.

78 Jie Zong and Jeanne Batalova, "How Many Unauthorized Immigrants Graduate from U.S. High Schools Annually?," Migration Policy Institute fact sheet, April 2019, https://www.migrationpolicy.org/research/unauthorized-immigrants -graduate-us-high-schools.

79 Robert Barro and Jong-Wha Lee, "A New Data Set of Educational Attainment in the World, 1950–2010," *Journal of Development Economics* 104 (2013): 184–98.

80 Robert Kaestner and Ofer Malamud, "Self-Selection and International Migration: New Evidence from Mexico," *Review of Economics and Statistics* 96, no. 1 (March 2014): 78–91.

81 Barry R. Chiswick, "The Effect of Americanization on the Earnings of Foreign-Born Men," *Journal of Political Economy* 86, no. 5 (1978): 897–921.

82 George J. Borjas, "The Slowdown in the Economic Assimilation of Immigrants: Aging and Cohort Effects Revisited Again," *Journal of Human Capital* 9, no. 4 (2015): 483–517.

83 Ethan G. Lewis, "Immigrant-Native Substitutability and the Role of Language," in *Immigration, Poverty, and Socioeconomic Inequality*, eds. David Card and Steven Raphael (New York: Russell Sage Foundation, 2013): 60–97.

84 E. Scott Reckard and Andrew Khouri, "Wealthy Chinese Home Buyers Boost Suburban L.A. Housing Markets," *Los Angeles Times*, March 24, 2014, http:// www.latimes.com/business/la-fi-chinese-homebuyers-20140324-story.html.

85 David M. Cutler, Edward L. Glaeser, and Jacob L. Vigdor, "Is the Melting Pot Still Hot? Explaining the Resurgence of Immigrant Segregation," *Review of Economics and Statistics* 90, no. 3 (2008): 478–97.

86 Alejandro Portes and Alex Stepick, "Unwelcome Immigrants: The Labor Market Experiences of 1980 (Mariel) Cuban and Haitian Refugees in South Florida," *American Sociological Review* 50, no. 4 (1985): 493–514.

87   Matthias Gafni, "Orinda: District Hires Private Investigator, Kicks Live-In Nanny's Daughter Out of School," *Mercury News*, November 27, 2014, http://www.mercurynews.com/my-town/ci_27024371/orinda-district-hires-private-investigator-kicks-live-nannys.

88   California Department of Education, "Fingertip Facts on Education in California, 2018–19 School Year," accessed July 31, 2019, http://www.cde.ca.gov/ds/sd/cb/ceffingertipfacts.asp.

89   Marianne Bertrand, Erzo F. P. Luttmer and Sendhil Mullainathan, "Network Effects and Welfare Cultures," *Quarterly Journal of Economics* 115, no. 3 (August 2000): 1019–55.

90   Paul Collier, *Exodus: How Migration Is Changing Our World* (New York: Oxford University Press, 2013).

91   Claire Brockaway and Carroll Doherty, "Fact Tank: Growing Share of Republicans Say U.S. Risks Losing Its Identity If It Is Too Open to Foreigners," Pew Research Center, July 17, 2019, https://www.pewresearch.org/fact-tank/2019/07/17/growing-share-of-republicans-say-u-s-risks-losing-its-identity-if-it-is-too-open-to-foreigners/.

92   Pew Research Center, "U.S. Unauthorized Immigrant Population Estimates by State, 2016," February 5, 2019, https://www.pewresearch.org/hispanic/interactives/u-s-unauthorized-immigrants-by-state/.

93   US Department of Homeland Security, "REAL ID Frequently Asked Questions for the Public," April 25, 2019, https://www.dhs.gov/real-id-public-faqs.

94   National Conference of State Legislatures, "States Offering Driver's Licenses to Immigrants," February 2020, https://www.ncsl.org/research/immigration/states-offering-driver-s-licenses-to-immigrants.aspx.

95   Sarah E. Hendricks, *Living in Car Culture without a License*, American Immigration Council Special Report, April 24, 2014, https://www.americanimmigrationcouncil.org/research/living-car-culture-without-license. Hendricks cites Steven Raphael and Lorien Rice, "Car Ownership, Employment and Earnings," *Journal of Urban Economics* 52, no. 1 (July 2002): 109–30.

96   National Immigration Law Center, "Access to Driver's Licenses for Immigrant Youth Granted DACA," July 22, 2020, https://www.nilc.org/wp-content/uploads/2020/06/access-to-DLs-for-immigrant-youth-with-DACA.pdf.

97   Insurance Information Institute, "Background on: Compulsory Auto/Uninsured Motorists," June 20, 2019, https://www.iii.org/article/background-on-compulsory-auto-uninsured-motorists.

98   Kalee Thompson, "The Fight to Keep Sanctuary Cities for Undocumented Immigrants in Wisconsin," *Vice*, April 3, 2016, https://www.vice.com/en_us/article/jma7d7/the-fight-to-keep-sanctuary-cities-for-undocumented-immigrants-in-wisconsin.

99 Sukhvir S. Brar, *Estimation of Fatal Crash Rates for Suspended/Revoked and Unlicensed Drivers in California,* California Department of Motor Vehicles report, September 2012, https://www.dol.wa.gov/about/docs/UnlicensedDriverStudy.pdf.

100 Tatiana Sanchez, "DMV Licensed 800,000 Undocumented Immigrants under 2-Year-Old Law," *Mercury News,* December 28, 2016, http://www.mercurynews.com/2016/12/28/dmv-licensed-800000-undocumented-immigrants-under-2-year-old-law/.

101 David Seminara, "Oregon Voters Oppose Driver's Licenses for Illegals," Center for Immigration Studies, October 22, 2014, https://cis.org/Seminara/Oregon-Voters-Oppose-Drivers-Licenses-Illegals.

102 US Customs and Border Protection, "U.S. Border Patrol Fiscal Year Southwest Border Sector Deaths (FY 1998–FY 2019)," last modified January 29, 2020, https://www.cbp.gov/document/stats/us-border-patrol-fiscal-year-southwest-border-sector-deaths-fy-1998-fy-2019.

Part Two: Arrests

1 Patrick Ettinger, *Imaginary Lines: Border Enforcement and the Origins of Undocumented Immigration, 1882–1930* (Austin: University of Texas Press, 2009).

2 Ettinger, *Imaginary Lines* 8, quoting historian Patricia Limerick.

3 Ettinger, *Imaginary Lines.*

4 Roy Rosenzweig Center for History and New Media Bracero History Archive, "About," accessed July 31, 2019, http://braceroarchive.org/about.

5 Library of Congress Classroom Materials, "Immigration and Relocation in U.S. History: Mexican: Expansion and Expulsion," accessed July 30, 2019, http://www.loc.gov/teachers/classroommaterials/presentationsandactivities/presentations/immigration/mexican8.html.

6 Erin Blakemore, "The Largest Mass Deportation in American History," History Channel History Stories, last updated June 18, 2019, https://www.history.com/news/operation-wetback-eisenhower-1954-deportation.

7 Authors' calculations based on US Department of Homeland Security, "Aliens Removed or Returned: Fiscal Years 1892 to 2018," Table 39 in the *2018 Yearbook of Immigration Statistics,* last published January 6, 2020, https://www.dhs.gov/immigration-statistics/yearbook/2018/table39.

8 US Department of Transportation Bureau of Transportation Statistics, "Border Crossing Entry Data," last updated January 27, 2021, https://data.bts.gov/Research-and-Statistics/Border-Crossing-Entry-Data/keg4-3bc2/data. In 2019 there were 370 million land border crossings recorded.

9 US Customs and Immigration Service, "INS Records for 1930s Mexican

Repatriations," March 3, 2014, https://www.uscis.gov/history-and-genealogy
/our-history/historians-mailbox/ins-records-1930s-mexican-repatriations.

10   Abraham Hoffman, *Unwanted Mexican Americans in the Great Depression: Repatriation Pressures, 1929–1939* (Tucson: University of Arizona Press, 1974).

11   Wendy Koch, "U.S. Urged to Apologize for 1930s Deportations," *USA Today*, April 5, 2006, https://usatoday30.usatoday.com/news/nation/2006-04-04-19 30s-deportees-cover_x.htm.

12   Immigration Reform and Control Act of 1986, S. 1200, 99th Cong. (1986), https://www.congress.gov/bill/99th-congress/senate-bill/1200.

13   Matthew Freedman, Emily Owens, and Sarah Bohn, "Immigration, Employment Opportunities, and Criminal Behavior," *American Economic Journal: Economic Policy* 10, no. 2 (2018): 117–51.

14   Muzzafar Chishti and Charles Kamasaki, "IRCA in Retrospect: Guideposts for Today's Immigration Reform," Migration Policy Institute policy brief, January 2014, https://www.migrationpolicy.org/research/irca-retrospect-immigration -reform.

15   Peter Brownell, "The Declining Enforcement of Employer Sanctions," *Migration Information Source*, September 1, 2005, https://www.migrationpolicy.org /article/declining-enforcement-employer-sanctions.

16   Richard M. Stana, *Immigration and Naturalization Service: Overview of Management and Program Challenges*, US General Accounting Office: Testimony before the House Committee on the Judiciary, Subcommittee on Immigration and Claims—House of Representatives, July 29, 1999, https://www.gao.gov/assets /110/108056.pdf.

17   Charles A. Bowsher, *Immigration Reform: Employer Sanctions and the Question of Discrimination*, US General Accounting Office: Testimony before the Committee on the Judiciary—US Senate, March 30, 1990, https://www.gao.gov /assets/110/103126.pdf.

18   David Dixon and Julia Gelatt, "Immigration Enforcement Spending Since IRCA," Migration Policy Institute fact sheet, November 2005, https://www .migrationpolicy.org/research/immigration-enforcement-spending-irca.

19   Elizabeth Cascio and Ethan Lewis, "Opening the Door: Migration and Self-Selection in a Restrictive Legal Immigration Regime" (National Bureau of Economic Research Working Paper no. 27874, October 2020), https://www .nber.org/system/files/working_papers/w27874/w27874.pdf.

20   Donald M. Kerwin, "More than IRCA: US Legalization Programs and the Current Policy Debate," Migration Policy Institute policy brief, December 2010, https://www.migrationpolicy.org/research/us-legalization-programs-by-the -numbers.

21   Chishti and Kamasaki, "IRCA in Retrospect: Guideposts for Today's Immigration Reform."

22 Miao Chi, "Improved Legal Status as the Major Source of Earnings Premiums Associated with Intermarriage: Evidence from the 1986 IRCA Amnesty," *Review of Economics of the Household* 15, no. 2 (2017): 691–706.

23 Ying Pan, "The Impact of Legal Status on Immigrants' Earnings and Human Capital: Evidence from the IRCA 1986," *Journal of Labor Research* 33, no. 2 (2012): 119–42.

24 Cynthia Bansak and Steven Raphael, "Immigration Reform and the Earnings of Latino Workers: Do Employer Sanctions Cause Discrimination?," *Industrial and Labor Relations Review* 54, no. 2 (2001): 275–95.

25 Julie A. Phillips and Douglas S. Massey, "The New Labor Market: Immigrants and Wages after IRCA," *Demography* 36, no. 2 (1999): 233–46.

26 Bowsher, *Immigration Reform: Employer Sanctions and the Question of Discrimination.*

27 Freedman, Owens, and Bohn, "Immigration, Employment Opportunities, and Criminal Behavior."

28 Taking Back Our Streets Act of 1995, H.R. 3, 104th Cong. (1995–1996), https://www.congress.gov/bill/104th-congress/house-bill/3/text.

29 US Department of Justice Archives, "Immigration and Naturalization Service Budget 1975–2003," accessed August 1, 2019, https://www.justice.gov/archive/jmd/1975_2002/2002/html/page104–108.htm.

30 US Department of Justice Immigration and Naturalization Service, "Deportable Aliens Located by Program, Border Patrol Sector and Investigations District: Fiscal Years 1994–2000," Table 60 in the *2000 Statistical Yearbook of the Immigration and Naturalization Service*, September 2002, https://www.dhs.gov/sites/default/files/publications/Yearbook_Immigration_Statistics_2000.pdf.

31 Donald Kerwin, "From IIRIRA to Trump: Connecting the Dots to the Current U.S. Immigration Policy Crisis," *Journal on Migration and Human Security* 6, no. 3 (2018): 192–204.

32 Blue Chevigny, "Act One: Where Goes the Neighborhood," in episode 170, "Immigration," October 13, 2000, *This American Life*, produced by Blue Chevigny, Ira Glass, Alex Blumberg, and Julie Snyder, podcast, MP3 audio, https://www.thisamericanlife.org/170/immigration.

33 US Department of Homeland Security, "Aliens Removed or Returned: Fiscal Years 1892 to 2018."

34 US Department of Homeland Security, *Budget-in-Brief: Fiscal Year 2006*, accessed August 1, 2019, https://www.dhs.gov/xlibrary/assets/Budget_BIB-FY2006.pdf; and Congressional Research Service, US Department of Homeland Security, *FY 2021 Budget in Brief*, accessed February 15, 2021, https://www.dhs.gov/sites/default/files/publications/fy_2021_dhs_bib_0.pdf.

35 Ted Hesson, "The Border Patrol's recruiting crisis," *Politico*, February 10, 2019,

https://www.politico.com/story/2019/02/10/border-patrol-recruitment-cri sis-1157171.

36 Donald Kerwin and Kristin McCabe, "Arrested on Entry: Operation Stream-line and the Prosecution of Immigration Crimes," Migration Policy Institute feature, April 29, 2010, https://www.migrationpolicy.org/article/arrested-en try-operation-streamline-and-prosecution-immigration-crimes.

37 US Customs and Border Protection, "U.S. Border Patrol Fiscal Year South-west Border Sector Deaths (FY 1998–FY 2019)," last modified January 29, 2020, https://www.cbp.gov/document/stats/us-border-patrol-fiscal-year-southwest -border-sector-deaths-fy-1998-fy-2019.

38 Jens Manuel Krogstad, Jeffrey S. Passel, and D'Vera Cohn, "Fact Tank: 5 Facts about Illegal Immigration in the U.S." Pew Research Center, June 12, 2019, http://www.pewresearch.org/fact-tank/2018/11/28/5-facts-about-illegal-im migration-in-the-u-s/.

39 Robert Warren, "US Undocumented Population Continued to Fall from 2016 to 2017 and Visa Overstays Significantly Exceeded Illegal Crossings for the Seventh Consecutive Year," *Journal on Migration and Human Security* 7, no. 1 (2019): 19–22, https://journals.sagepub.com/doi/pdf/10.1177/23315024198 30339; and Pew Research Center: Hispanic Trends , "Modes of Entry for the Unauthorized Migrant Population," fact sheet, May 22, 2006, https://www .pewhispanic.org/2006/05/22/modes-of-entry-for-the-unauthorized-mi grant-population/.

40 US Department of Homeland Security, *Fiscal Year 2019 Entry/Exit Overstay Re-port*, March 30, 2020, https://www.dhs.gov/sites/default/files/publications/20 _0513_fy19-entry-and-exit-overstay-report.pdf.

41 American Immigration Council, "The 287(g) Program: An Overview," fact sheet, July 2, 2020, https://www.americanimmigrationcouncil.org/research/28 7g-program-immigration.

42 American Immigration Council, "The 287(g) Program: An Overview."

43 US Immigration Customs and Enforcement, "Delegation of Immigration Au-thority Section 287(g) Immigration and Nationality Act," July 1, 2019, https:// www.ice.gov/287g.

44 Randy Capps, Marc R. Rosenblum, Cristina Rodriguez, and Muzaffar Chishti, *Delegation and Divergence: A Study of 287(g) State and Local Immigration En-forcement*, Migration Policy Institute, January 2011, https://www.migration policy.org/pubs/287g-divergence.pdf; and authors' analysis of data on ICE arrests October 2014 through October 2018, from Transitional Records Ac-cess Clearinghouse Immigration, "Immigration and Customs Enforcement Arrests: ICE Data through May 2018," accessed April 2, 2020, https://trac.syr .edu/phptools/immigration/arrest/.

45 See Migration Policy Institute, "Profile of the Unauthorized Population: Gwin-

nett County, GA," accessed February 14, 2021, https://www.migrationpolicy .org/data/unauthorized-immigrant-population/county/13135; and US Census Bureau, "QuickFacts: Gwinnett County, Georgia," accessed February 14, 2021, https://www.census.gov/quickfacts/fact/table/gwinnettcountygeorgia /PST045219.

46 Authors' analysis of data on ICE arrests October 2014 through October 2018, from Transitional Records Access Clearinghouse Immigration, "Immigration and Customs Enforcement Arrests: ICE Data through May 2018," accessed April 2, 2020.

47 Randy Capps, Muzaffar Chishti, Julia Gelatt, Jessica Bolter, and Ariel G. Ruiz Soto, *Revving Up the Deportation Machinery: Enforcement and Pushback Under Trump*, Migration Policy Institute report, May 2018, https://www.migration policy.org/research/revving-deportation-machinery-under-trump-and-push back.

48 Doris Meissner, Donald M. Kerwin, Muzaffar Chishti, and Clare Bergeron, *Immigration Enforcement in the United States: The Rise of a Formidable Machinery*, Migration Policy Institute report, January 2013, https://www.migrationpolicy .org/research/immigration-enforcement-united-states-rise-formidable-ma chinery.

49 US Immigration and Customs Enforcement, "Secure Communities," March 20, 2018, https://www.ice.gov/secure-communities.

50 American Immigration Council, *Immigration Detainers: An Overview*, March 2017, https://www.americanimmigrationcouncil.org/sites/default/files/re search/immigration_detainers_an_overview_0.pdf.

51 Kate Evans, "Immigration Detainers, Local Discretion, and State Law's Historical Constraints," *Brooklyn Law Review* 84, no. 4 (2019): 1085–1140.

52 Community Justice Project, *The Cost of Complicity: A Fiscal Impact Analysis of Immigration Detainers in Miami-Dade County, Florida*, February 2018, https://miami.cbslocal.com/wp-content/uploads/sites/15909786/2018/02 /embargoed-the-cost-of-complicity.pdf.

53 US Department of Homeland Security Homeland Security Advisory Council, "Task Force on Secure Communities: Findings and Recommendations," September 2011, https://www.dhs.gov/xlibrary/assets/hsac-task-force-on-secure -communities.pdf.

54 Elisa Jacome, "The Effect of Immigration Enforcement on Crime Reporting: Evidence from the Priority Enforcement Program," Social Science Research Network, October 8, 2018, https://papers.ssrn.com/sol3/papers.cfm?abstract _id=3263086.

55 US Immigration and Customs Enforcement, "Priority Enforcement Program," June 22, 2017, https://www.ice.gov/pep.

56 Transactional Records Access Clearinghouse Immigration, "Latest Data: Im-

migration and Customs Enforcement Detainers: ICE Data through June 2020," accessed June 14, 2020, https://trac.syr.edu/phptools/immigration/detain/.

57 New York Police Department, "Summary of Statistics on ICE Detainers July 1, 2018 to June 30, 2019," accessed June 14, 2020, https://www1.nyc.gov/site/nypd /stats/reports-analysis/civil-immigration-detainers.page.

58 Kate Evans, "Immigration Detainers, Local Discretion, and State Law's Historical Constraints."

59 Washington Post Staff, "Full Text: Donald Trump Announces a Presidential Bid," *Washington Post*, June 16, 2015, https://www.washingtonpost.com/news /post-politics/wp/2015/06/16/full-text-donald-trump-announces-a-presiden tial-bid/?utm_term=.4dc9621f40fa.

60 Brooke Seipel, "Trump Resumes Calls for Border Wall in Response to Kate Steinle Murder Trial Verdict," *The Hill*, December 1, 2017, https://thehill.com /homenews/administration/362725-trump-resumes-calls-for-border-wall-in -response-to-kate-steinle.

61 Phil Van Stockum, "I Saw the Kate Steinle Murder Trial Up Close. The Jury Didn't Botch It.," *Politico*, December 6, 2017, https://www.politico.com/maga zine/story/2017/12/06/kate-steinle-murder-trial-jury-didnt-botch-216016.

62 Muzaffar Chishti and Faye Hipsman, "Policy Beat: Sanctuary Cities Come Under Scrutiny, As Does Federal-Local Immigration Relationship," *Migration Information Source*, August 20, 2015, https://www.migrationpolicy.org/article /sanctuary-cities-come-under-scrutiny-does-federal-local-immigration-rela tionship.

63 Joel Rubin and Dakota Smith, "Money for Police Cannot be Pegged to Cooperation with ICE, Judge Rules," *Los Angeles Times*, April 12, 2018, https:// www.latimes.com/local/lanow/la-me-police-grant-ice-20180412-story.html.

64 Betsy Guzmán, "The Hispanic Population: Census 2000 Brief," US Census Bureau, May 2001, https://www.census.gov/prod/2001pubs/c2kbr01-3.pdf; and Sharon R. Ennis, Merarys Rios-Vargas, and Nora G. Albert, "The Hispanic Population: 2010: 2010 Census Briefs," US Census Bureau, May 2011, https://www.census.gov/content/dam/Census/library/publications/2011 /dec/c2010br-04.pdf.

65 Michael Hoefer, Nancy Rytina, and Bryan C. Baker, *Estimates of the Unauthorized Immigrant Population Residing in the United States: January 2010*, US Department of Homeland Security Office of Immigration Statistics report, February 2011, https://www.dhs.gov/sites/default/files/publications/Unautho rized%20Immigrant%20Population%20Estimates%20in%20the%20US%20 January%202010_0.pdf.

66 Carli Brosseau, "ACLU Files Lawsuit Precursor in SB 1070 Challenge Case," *Arizona Daily Star*, November 13, 2013, https://tucson.com/news/local/border

/aclu-files-lawsuit-precursor-in-sb-1070-challenge-case/article_24900305
-4cd5-5edb-a408-81a7aa70ea9 f.html.

67 Pew Research Center for People and the Press, "Broad Approval for New Arizona Immigration Law," May 12, 2010, https://www.pewresearch.org/wp-content/uploads/sites/4/legacy-pdf/613.pdf.

68 Nigel Duara, "Arizona's Once-Feared Immigration Law, SB 1070, Loses Most of Its Power in Settlement," *Los Angeles Times*, September 15, 2016, https://www.latimes.com/nation/la-na-arizona-law-20160915-snap-story.html.

69 Mark Hoekstra and Sandra Orozco-Aleman, "Illegal Immigration, State Law, and Deterrence," *American Economic Journal: Economic Policy* 9, no. 2 (2017): 228–52.

70 American Civil Liberties Union, "Know Your Rights: Immigrant's Rights," accessed June 14, 2020, https://www.aclu.org/know-your-rights/immigrants-rights/.

71 Jie Zong, Ariel G. Ruiz Soto, Jeanne Batalova, Julia Gelatt, and Randy Capps, "A Profile of Current DACA Recipients by Education, Industry, and Occupation," Migration Policy Institute fact sheet, November 2017, https://www.migrationpolicy.org/research/profile-current-daca-recipients-education-industry-and-occupation.

72 Gustavo López and Jens Manuel Krogstad, "Fact Tank: Key Facts about Unauthorized Immigrants Enrolled in DACA," Pew Research Center, September 25, 2017, https://www.pewresearch.org/fact-tank/2017/09/25/key-facts-about-unauthorized-immigrants-enrolled-in-daca/.

73 Sylvia Rusin, "Origin and Community: Asian and Latin American Unauthorized Youth and U.S. Deportation Relief," *Migration Information Source*, August 13, 2015, https://www.migrationpolicy.org/article/origin-and-community-asian-and-latin-american-unauthorized-youth-and-us-deportation-relief.

74 Eduardo G. Gonzales and Angie M. Bautista-Chavez, *Two Years and Counting: Assessing the Growing Power of DACA*, American Immigration Council special report, June 16, 2014, https://www.americanimmigrationcouncil.org/research/two-years-and-counting-assessing-growing-power-daca.

75 US Department of Homeland Security, "Aliens Removed or Returned: Fiscal Years 1892 to 2018," Table 39 in the *2018 Yearbook of Immigration Statistics*.

76 Jens Manuel Krogstad, "Fact Tank: Key Facts about Immigrants Eligible for Deportation Relief under Obama's Expanded Executive Actions," Pew Research Center, January 29, 2016, https://www.pewresearch.org/fact-tank/2016/01/19/key-facts-immigrants-obama-action/.

77 Randy Capps, Heather Koball, James D. Bachmeier, Ariel G. Ruiz Soto, Jie Zong, and Julia Gelatt, *Deferred Action for Unauthorized Immigrant Parents: Analysis of DAPA's Potential Effects on Families and Children*, Migration Policy

Institute report, February 2016, https://www.migrationpolicy.org/research/de
ferred-action-unauthorized-immigrant-parents-analysis-dapas-potential-ef
fects-families.

78   Adam Liptak and Michael D. Shear, "Supreme Court Tie Blocks Obama Immigration Plan," *New York Times*, June 23, 2016, https://www.nytimes.com/2016
/06/24/us/supreme-court-immigration-obama-dapa.html.

79   Jie Zong and Jeanne Batalova, "Spotlight: Korean Immigrants in the United
States in 2015," Migration Policy Institute, February 8, 2017, https://www.migra
tionpolicy.org/article/korean-immigrants-united-states-2015#Immigration
_Pathways_and_Naturalization.

80   United States Citizenship and Immigration Services, *Approximate Active
DACA Recipients as of December 31, 2019*, accessed June 18, 2020, https://www
.uscis.gov/sites/default/files/USCIS/Resources/Reports%20and%20Studies
/Immigration%20Forms%20Data/All%20Form%20Types/DACA/DACA
_Population_Receipts_since_Injunction_Dec_31_2019.pdf.

81   Joseph R Biden, Jr., "Preserving and Fortifying Deferred Action for Childhood
Arrivals (DACA)," presidential memorandum, January 20, 2021, https://www
.whitehouse.gov/briefing-room/presidential-actions/2021/01/20/preserving
-and-fortifying-deferred-action-for-childhood-arrivals-daca/.

82   Jose Magaña-Salgado, *Money on the Table: The Economic Cost of Ending DACA*,
Immigrant Legal Resource Center report, December 2016, https://www.ilrc.org
tes/default/files/resources/2016–12–13_ilrc_report_-_money_on_the_table
_economic_costs_of_ending_daca.pdf.

83   Center for American Progress, "Ending DACA Would Wipe Away at Least
$433.4 Billion from U.S. GDP over a Decade, per CAP Calculations," press
release, November 18, 2016, https://www.americanprogress.org/press/release
/2016/11/18/292673/release-ending-daca-would-wipe-away-at-least-433-4
-billion-from-u-s-gdp-over-a-decade-per-cap-calculations/.

84   Muzaffar Chishti and Sarah Pierce, "Policy Beat: Trump's Promise of Millions
of Deportations Is Yet to Be Fulfilled," *Migration Information Source*, October 29, 2020, https://www.migrationpolicy.org/article/trump-deportations
-unfinished-mission.

85   Shoba Sivaprasad Wadhia, *Reading the Morton Memo: Federal Priorities and
Prosecutorial Discretion*, Immigration Policy Center–American Immigration
Council special report, December 2010, Pennsylvania State University Legal
Studies Research Paper no. 46-2010, https://ssrn.com/abstract=1723165.

86   David J. Bier, "60 Percent of Deported 'Criminal Aliens' Committed Only Victimless Crimes," Cato Institute blog post, June 6, 2018, https://www.cato.org
/blog/60-deported-criminal-aliens-committed-only-victimless-crimes-few-vio
lent-crimes.

87   Muzaffar Chishti and Michelle Mittelstadt, "Unauthorized Immigrants with

Criminal Convictions: Who Might Be a Priority for Removal?," Migration Policy Institute commentary, November 2016, https://www.migrationpolicy .org/news/unauthorized-immigrants-criminal-convictions-who-might-be-pri ority-removal.

88 Sarah K. S. Shannon, Christopher Uggen, Jason Schnittker, Melissa Thompson, Sara Wakefield, and Michael Massoglia, "The Growth, Scope, and Spatial Distribution of People with Felony Records in the United States, 1948–2010" *Demography* 54, no. 5 (October 2017): 1795–1818.

89 Donald J. Trump, "Border Security and Immigration Enforcement Improvements," Executive Order no. 13767, *Federal Register* 82, no. 18 (January 25, 2017): 8793–7, https://www.govinfo.gov/content/pkg/FR-2017-01-30/pdf/2 017-02095.pdf.

90 US Immigration and Customs Enforcement, *Fiscal Year 2019 Enforcement and Removal Operations Report*, accessed June 20, 2020, https://www.ice.gov/sites /default/files/documents/Document/2019/eroReportFY2019.pdf; US Immigration and Customs Enforcement, *Fiscal Year 2018 Enforcement and Removal Operations Report*, accessed August 2, 2019, https://www.ice.gov/doclib/about /offices/ero/pdf/eroFY2018Report.pdf; US Immigration and Customs Enforcement, *Fiscal Year 2016 Enforcement and Removal Operations Report*, accessed June 14, 2020, https://www.ice.gov/sites/default/files/documents/Re port/2016/removal-stats-2016.pdf.

91 US Immigration and Customs Enforcement, *Fiscal Year 2019 Enforcement and Removal Operations Report*.

92 Transactional Records Access Clearinghouse Immigration, "New Deportation Proceedings Filed in Immigration Court by Nationality, State, Court, Hearing Location, Year and Type of Charge," accessed August 2, 2019, https://trac.syr .edu/phptools/immigration/charges/deport_filing_charge.php.

93 Migration Policy Institute Data Hub, "Profile of the Unauthorized Population: United States," accessed July 31, 2019, https://www.migrationpolicy.org/data /unauthorized-immigrant-population/state/US#.

94 Kavitha Surana, "How Racial Profiling Goes Unchecked in Immigration Enforcement," *Pro Publica*, June 8, 2018, https://www.propublica.org/article/ra cial-profiling-ice-immigration-enforcement-pennsylvania.

95 J. Rachel Reyes, "Immigration Detention: Recent Trends and Scholarship," Center for Migration Studies virtual brief, March 26, 2018, https://cmsny.org /publications/virtualbrief-detention/; US Immigration and Customs Enforcement, *Fiscal Year 2019 Enforcement and Removal Operations Report*.

96 US Immigration and Customs Enforcement, *Fiscal Year 2019 Enforcement and Removal Operations Report*.

97 Congressional Research Service, *Expedited Removal of Aliens: Legal Framework*, report, October 8, 2019, https://fas.org/sgp/crs/homesec/R45314.pdf.

98 American Immigration Council, "Fact Sheet: A Primer on Expedited Removal," July 22, 2019, https://www.americanimmigrationcouncil.org/research /primer-expedited-removal.

99 Mica Rosenberg, "More Asylum Seekers Sue Trump Administration over Prolonged U.S. Detention," *Reuters*, May 30, 2019, https://www.reuters.com/article /us-usa-immigration-asylum/more-asylum-seekers-sue-trump-administration -over-prolonged-u-s-detention-idUSKCN1T02PR.

100 Katie Sullivan and Jeff Mason, "Immigration Detention in the United States: A Primer," Bipartisan Policy Center blog post, April 24, 2019, https:// bipartisanpolicy.org/blog/immigration-detention-in-the-united-states-a -primer/.

101 Kristina Davis, "U.S. Officials Say They Are Highly Confident to Have Reached Tally on Separated Children: 4368," *Los Angeles Times*, January 18, 2020, https:// www.latimes.com/world-nation/story/2020-01-18/u-s-officials-say-they-are -highly-confident-to-have-reached-tally-on-separated-children-4-368.

102 Caitlin Dickerson, "The Youngest Child Separated from His Family at the Border Was 4 Months Old," *New York Times*, June 16, 2019, https://www.nytimes .com/2019/06/16/us/baby-constantine-romania-migrants.html.

103 Renuka Rayasam and Dan Diamond, "'Kids Are Really Suffering' as Migrant Surge Overwhelms Health Department," *Politico*, June 25, 2019, https://www .politico.com/story/2019/06/25/refugee-resettlement-children-1553738.

104 US Immigration and Customs Enforcement, *Fiscal Year 2019 Enforcement and Removal Operations Report*.

105 US Department of Justice Executive Office for Immigration Review, "Workload and Adjudication Statistics," last updated January 19, 2021, https://www .justice.gov/eoir/workload-and-adjudication-statistics.

106 American Immigration Council, "Practice Advisory: Reinstatement of Removal," May 23, 2019, https://www.americanimmigrationcouncil.org/practice _advisory/reinstatement-removal.

107 Jennifer Racon, "Opinion Analysis: Justices Uphold Broad Interpretation of Immigration Detention Provision," *SCOTUSblog* blog post, March 20, 2019, https://www.scotusblog.com/2019/03/opinion-analysis-justices-uphold -broad-interpretation-of-immigration-detention-provision/.

108 US Department of Justice Executive Office for Immigration Review, "Workload and Adjudication Statistics."

109 US Department of Justice Executive Office for Immigration Review, "Pending Cases" (April 30, 2019), "Immigration Judge Hiring" (July 2019), and "New Cases and Total Completions" (April 23, 2019), all in "Workload and Adjudication Statistics."

110 Eunice Hyunhye Cho, Tara Tidwell Cullen, and Clara Long, *Justice-Free Zones: U.S. Immigration Detention Under the Trump Administration*, American Civil

Liberties Union Research Report, April 30, 2020, https://immigrantjustice.org /research-items/report-justice-free-zones-us-immigration-detention-under -trump-administration.

111 Cho, Cullen, and Long, *Justice-Free Zones: U.S. Immigration Detention Under the Trump Administration.*

112 US Department of Homeland Security Office of Inspector General, *ICE Does Not Fully Use Contracting Tools to Hold Detention Facility Contractors Accountable for Failing to Meet Performance Standards,* report no. OIG-19–18, January 29, 2019, https://www.oig.dhs.gov/reports/2019/ice-does-not-fully-use-contrac ting-tools-hold-detention-facility-contractors-accountable-failing-meet-per formance-standards/oig-19-18.

113 Transactional Records Access Clearinghouse Immigration, "Three-Fold Difference in Bond Amounts by Court Location," July 2, 2018, https://trac.syr.edu /immigration/reports/519/.

114 Transactional Records Access Clearinghouse Immigration, "Representation at Bond Hearings Rising but Outcomes Have Not Improved," June 18, 2020, https://trac.syr.edu/immigration/reports/616.

115 American Civil Liberties Union, "Federal Appeals Court Requires Immigration Authorities to Consider Financial Resources When Setting Bond," October 2, 2017, https://www.aclu.org/press-releases/federal-appeals-court-requires-im migration-authorities-consider-financial-resources.

116 "Immigration and Nationality Act—Mandatory and Prolonged Detention— Access to Bond Hearings—*Jennings v. Rodriguez,*" *Harvard Law Review* 132, no. 1 (November 9, 2018): 417–26, https://harvardlawreview.org/2018/11/jen nings-v-rodriguez/.

117 Pew Research Center: Hispanic Trends, "II. By the Numbers: Trends in Enforcement," in *2007 National Survey of Latinos,* December 13, 2007, https:// www.pewresearch.org/hispanic/2007/12/13/ii-by-the-numbers-trends-in -enforcement/.

118 Randolph Capps, Rosa Maria Castaneda, Ajay Chaudry, and Robert Santos, *Paying the Price: The Impact of Immigration Raids on America's Children,* Urban Institute report, 2007, http://webarchive.urban.org/UploadedPDF/411566 _immigration_raids.pdf.

119 Capps, Castaneda, Chaudry, and Santos, *Paying the Price: The Impact of Immigration Raids on America's Children.*

120 Andorra Bruno, *Immigration-Related Worksite Enforcement: Performance Measures,* Congressional Research Service report, June 23, 2015, https://fas.org/sgp /crs/homesec/R40002.pdf.

121 Bruno, *Immigration-Related Worksite Enforcement: Performance Measures.*

122 US Department of Homeland Security US Immigration and Customs Enforcement, "Worksite Enforcement Investigations Surge in FY18," December

21, 2018, https://www.ice.gov/news/releases/ice-worksite-enforcement-inves tigations-fy18-surge.

123 Ari Shapiro, Gus Contreras, and Dave Blanchard, "Months after Massive ICE Raid, Residents of a Mississippi Town Wait and Worry," National Public Radio broadcast, November 27, 2019, https://www.npr.org/2019/11/17/778611834 /months-after-massive-ice-raid-residents-of-a-mississippi-town-wait-and -worry.

124 National Immigration Forum, "Error Rates in E-Verify," August 14, 2018, https://immigrationforum.org/article/error-rates-in-e-verify/.

125 National Immigration Forum, "Error Rates in E-Verify."

126 Westat, *Evaluation of the Accuracy of the E-Verify Findings*, report submitted to the US Department of Homeland Security, July 2012, https://www.e-verify.gov /sites/default/files/everify/data/FindingsEVerifyAccuracyEval2012.pdf.

127 Magnus Lofstrom, Sarah Bohn, and Steven Raphael, *Lessons from the 2007 Legal Arizona Workers Act*, Public Policy Institute of California, March 2011, https:// www.ppic.org/content/pubs/report/R_311MLR.pdf.

128 US Department of Homeland Security, "E-Verify Usage Statistics," last up-dated January 7, 2021, https://www.e-verify.gov/about-e-verify/e-verify-data /e-verify-usage-statistics.

129 Pia M. Orrenius, Madeline Zavodny, and Sarah Greer, "Who Signs Up for E-Verify? Insights from DHS Enrollment Records," *International Migration Review* 54, no. 4 (February 2020): 1184–1211.

130 Pia Orrenius and Madeline Zavodny, "The Impact of E-Verify Mandates on Labor Market Outcomes," *Southern Economic Journal* 81, no. 4 (2015): 947–59.

131 Magnus Lofstrom, Sarah Bohn, and Steven Raphael, *Lessons from the 2007 Legal Arizona Workers Act*.

132 Nolan G. Pope, "The Effects of DACAmentation: The Impact of Deferred Action for Childhood Arrivals on Unauthorized Immigrants," *Journal of Public Economics* 143 (September 2016): 98–114.

133 Francisca Antman and Catalina Amuedo-Dorantes, "Can Authorization Re-duce Poverty among Undocumented Immigrants? Evidence from the Deferred Action for Childhood Arrivals Program," *Economics Letters* 147 (October 2016): 1–4.

134 Sarah Bohn, Magnus Lofstrom, and Steven Raphael, "Did the 2007 Legal Ari-zona Workers Act Reduce the State's Unauthorized Immigrant Population?," *Review of Economics and Statistics* 96, no. 2 (2014): 258–69.

135 Associated Press, "Joe Arpaio Racial Profiling Trial Begins," *Politico*, July 19, 2012, https://www.politico.com/story/2012/07/joe-arpaio-racial-profiling-tri al-begins-078734.

136 Pia M. Orrenius and Madeline Zavodny, "Do State Work Eligibility Verification

Laws Reduce Unauthorized Immigration?" *IZA Journal of Migration* 5, no. 5 (2016).

137 Tara Watson, "Enforcement and Immigrant Location Choice" (National Bureau of Economic Research Working Paper no. 19626, November 2013), https://www.nber.org/system/files/working_papers/w19626/w19626.pdf.

138 Bryan Roberts, Gordon Hanson, Derekh Cornwell, and Scott Borger, "An Analysis of Migrant Smuggling Costs along the Southwest Border" (US Department of Homeland Security working paper, November 2010), https://www.dhs.gov/xlibrary/assets/statistics/publications/ois-smuggling-wp.pdf.

139 Emily Ryo, "Detention as Deterrence," *Stanford Law Review* 71 (2019): 237–50.

140 Jonathan T. Hiskey, Abby Córdova, Mary Fran Malone, and Diana M. Orcés, "Leaving the Devil You Know: Crime Victimization, US Deterrence Policy, and the Emigration Decision in Central America," *Latin American Research Review* 53, no. 3 (2018): 429–47.

141 Edward Alden, "Is Border Enforcement Effective? What We Know and What It Means," *Journal on Migration and Human Security* 5, no. 2 (2017): 481–90.

142 Daniel Chiquiar and Alejandrina Salcedo, *Mexican Migration to the United States: Underlying Economic Factors and Possible Scenarios for Future Flows*, Migration Policy Institute Regional Migration Study Group report, April 2013, https://www.migrationpolicy.org/pubs/RMSG-MexicoFlows.pdf.

143 Katharine M. Donato, Jorge Durand, and Douglas S. Massey, "Stemming the Tide? Assessing the Deterrent Effects of the Immigration Reform and Control Act," *Demography* 29, no. 2 (May 1992): 139–57.

144 Gordon H. Hanson and Antonio Spilimbergo, "Illegal Immigration, Border Enforcement, and Relative Wages: Evidence from Apprehensions at the U.S.-Mexico Border," *American Economic Review* 89, no. 5 (December 1999): 1337–57.

145 Douglas S. Massey, Jorge Durand, and Karen A. Pren, "Border Enforcement and Return Migration by Documented and Undocumented Mexicans," *Journal of Ethnic and Migration Studies* 41, no. 7 (2015): 1015–40.

146 Brian K. Kovak, and Rebecca Lessem, "How Do U.S. Visa Policies Affect Unauthorized Migration?" (National Bureau of Economic Research Working Paper no. 26790, 2020), https://www.nber.org/system/files/working_papers/w26790/w26790.pdf.

147 Laura Romero, "Marine Veteran Was among US Citizens Detained by ICE, ACLU Says," ABC News, December 12, 2019, https://abcnews.go.com/Politics/marine-veteran-us-citizens-detained-ice-aclu/story?id=67465583.

148 American Civil Liberties Union, "The Constitution in the 100-Mile Border Zone," accessed June 27, 2020, https://www.aclu.org/other/constitution-100-mile-border-zone.

149 Gilles Bissonette, "State Judge Finds New Hampshire Border Patrol Check-

point Unconstitutional," American Civil Liberties Union blog post, May 9, 2018, https://www.aclu.org/blog/immigrants-rights/ice-and-border-patrol-abuses/state-judge-finds-new-hampshire-border-patrol.

150 America's Voice, "Americans Paying A High Cost in Civil Liberties Due to Trump's Extreme Approach on Immigration," press release, February 11, 2020, https://americasvoice.org/press_releases/americans-paying-a-high-cost-in-civil-liberties-due-to-trumps-extreme-approach-on-immigration/.

151 Byron Tau and Michelle Hackman, "Federal Agencies Use Cellphone Location Data for Immigration Enforcement," *Wall Street Journal*, February 7, 2020, https://www.wsj.com/articles/federal-agencies-use-cellphone-location-data-for-immigration-enforcement-11581078600.

152 Drew Harwell and Tony Romm, "ICE Is Tapping into a Huge License-Plate Database, ACLU Says, Raising New Privacy Concerns about Surveillance," *Washington Post*, March 13, 2019,\ https://www.washingtonpost.com/technology/2019/03/13/ice-is-tapping-into-huge-license-plate-database-aclu-says-raising-new-privacy-concerns-about-surveillance/.

Part Three: Afterward

1 Washington Post Staff, "Full Text: Donald Trump Announces a Presidential Bid," *Washington Post*, June 17, 2015, https://www.washingtonpost.com/news/post-politics/wp/2015/06/16/full-text-donald-trump-announces-a-presidential-bid/?utm_term=.4dc9621f40fa.

2 Jens Manuel Krogstad, "Fact Tank: On Views of Immigrants, Americans Largely Split Along Party Lines," Pew Research Center, September 30, 2015, http://www.pewresearch.org/fact-tank/2015/09/30/on-views-of-immigrants-americans-largely-split-along-party-lines/.

3 Rubén G. Rumbaut and Walter A. Ewing, *The Myth of Immigrant Criminality and the Paradox of Assimilation*, Immigration Policy Center Special Report, Spring 2007, https://www.americanimmigrationcouncil.org/sites/default/files/research/Imm%20Criminality%20%28IPC%29.pdf.

4 Robert J. Sampson, "Immigration and America's Urban Revival," July 7, 2015, *American Prospect*, https://prospect.org/article/immigration-and-americas-urban-revival.

5 Michelangelo Landgrave and Alex Nowrasteh, "Criminal Immigrants in 2017: Their Numbers, Demographics, and Countries of Origin," Cato Institute Immigration and Research Policy Brief no. 11, March 4, 2019, https://www.cato.org/publications/immigration-research-policy-brief/criminal-immigrants-2017-their-numbers-demographics.

6 Rubén G. Rumbaut, Roberto G. Gonzales, Golnaz Komaie, and Charlie V. Mor-

gan, "Debunking the Myth of Immigrant Criminality: Imprisonment Among First- and Second-Generation Young Men," *Migration Information Source*, June 1, 2006, https://www.migrationpolicy.org/article/debunking-myth-immigrant-criminality-imprisonment-among-first-and-second-generation-young.

7   John Gramlich, "Fact Tank: Black Imprisonment in the U.S. Has Fallen by a Third Since 2006," Pew Research Center, May 6, 2020, https://www.pewresearch.org/fact-tank/2020/05/06/black-imprisonment-rate-in-the-u-s-has-fallen-by-a-third-since-2006/.

8   Rob Arthur, "Latinos In Three Cities Are Reporting Fewer Crimes Since Trump Took Office," fivethirtyeight.com, May 18, 2017, https://fivethirtyeight.com/features/latinos-report-fewer-crimes-in-three-cities-amid-fears-of-deportation/.

9   Robert J. Sampson, Jeffrey D Morenoff, and Stephen W Raudenbush, "Social Anatomy of Racial and Ethnic Disparities in Violence," *American Journal of Public Health* 95, no. 2 (March 2005): 224–32.

10 Rubén G. Rumbaut, Roberto G. Gonzales, Golnaz Komaie, and Charlie V. Morgan, "Debunking the Myth of Immigrant Criminality: Imprisonment Among First- and Second-Generation Young Men."

11 Kristin F. Butcher and Anne Morrison Piehl, "Why are Immigrants' Incarceration Rates So Low? Evidence on Selective Immigration, Deterrence, and Deportation" (National Bureau of Economic Research Working Paper no. 13229, July 2007), https://www.nber.org/system/files/working_papers/w13229/w13229.pdf.

12 Daniel P. Mears, "Immigration and Crime: What's the Connection?," *Federal Sentencing Reporter* 14, no. 5 (March/April 2002): 284–88.

13 Jörg L. Spenkuch, "Understanding the Impact of Immigration on Crime," *American Law and Economics Review* 16, no. 1 (Spring 2014): 177–219.

14 George J. Borjas, Jeffrey Grogger, and Gordon H. Hanson, "Immigration and the Economic Status of African-American Men," *Economica* 77, no. 306 (April 2010): 255–82.

15 Butcher, Kristin F. and Anne Morrison Piehl, "Why are Immigrants' Incarceration Rates So Low? Evidence on Selective Immigration, Deterrence, and Deportation."

16 Robert J. Sampson, "Immigration and America's Urban Revival."

17 A 2014 Pew religious-landscape survey found that 75 percent of immigrants reported attending religious services at least monthly, compared to 69 percent of third-or-higher-generation Americans. Pew Research Center, "Religious Landscape Survey," accessed July 3, 2020, https://www.pewforum.org/religious-landscape-study/immigrant-status/immigrants/.

18 John Gramlich, "Fact Tank: What the Data Says (and Doesn't Say) about Crime

in the United States," Pew Research Center, November 20, 2020, https://www
.pewresearch.org/fact-tank/2020/11/20/facts-about-crime-in-the-u-s/.

19 Robert J. Sampson, "Open Doors Don't Invite Criminals," *New York Times*
op-ed, March 11, 2006, https://www.nytimes.com/2006/03/11/opinion/open
-doors-dont-invite-criminals.html.

20 Ruben G. Rumbaut and Walter A. Ewing, *The Myth of Immigrant Criminality
and the Paradox of Assimilation.*

21 American Immigration Council, *The Use of Parole Under Immigration Law*, January 24, 2018, https://www.americanimmigrationcouncil.org/sites/default/files
/research/the_use_of_parole_under_immigration_law.pdf.

22 American Immigration Council, "U.S. Citizen Children Impacted by Immigration Enforcement," fact sheet, November 22, 2019, https://www.americanimmi
grationcouncil.org/research/us-citizen-children-impacted-immigration-en
forcement.

23 Madeline Buiano, "ICE Data: Tens of Thousands of Deported Parents Have
U.S. Citizen Kids," Center for Public Integrity, October 12, 2018, https://pub
licintegrity.org/immigration/ice-data-tens-of-thousands-of-deported-parents
-have-u-s-citizen-kids/.

24 Ajay Chaudry, Randy Capps, Juan Manuel Pedroza, Rosa Maria Castaneda,
Robert Santos, and Molly M. Scott, *Facing Our Future: Children in the Aftermath
of Immigration Enforcement*, Urban Institute report, February 2010, https://
www.urban.org/sites/default/files/publication/28331/412020-Facing-Our
-Future.PDF.

25 Immigration Legal Resource Center, *Non-LPR Cancellation of Removal: An
Overview of Eligibility for Immigration Practitioners*, ILRC Practice Advisory,
June 2018, https://www.ilrc.org/sites/default/files/resources/non_lpr_cancel
_remov-20180606.pdf.

26 Pamela L Cruz, *A Vulnerable Population: U.S. Citizen Minors Living in Mexico*,
Rice University's Baker Institute for Public Policy Issue Brief, March 19, 2018,
https://www.bakerinstitute.org/media/files/research-document/3869bc0a
/bi-brief-031918-mex-citizenminors.pdf.

27 Ryan Schulteis and Ariel G. Ruiz Soto, *A Revolving Door No More: A Statistical Portrait of Mexican Adults Repatriated from the United States*, Migration
Policy Institute report, May 2017, https://www.migrationpolicy.org/research
/revolving-door-no-more-statistical-profile-mexican-adults-repatriated-unit
ed-states.

28 Gisela Salomon, "A Mom in Florida Is Caring for 1,250 Children of Illegal Immigrants In Case Their Parents Are Deported," *Business Insider*, January 20,
2018, https://www.businessinsider.com/nora-sandigo-immigration-activist
-cares-for-thousands-of-children-2018-1?r=AU&IR=T.

29 Mattie Quinn, "Planning for Detention: How 2 States Help Immigrant Chil-

dren Stay Out of Foster Care," Governing.com, January 31, 2019, https://www
.governing.com/topics/public-justice-safety/gov-immigration-deportation
-guardianship-children-maryland.html.

30 Randy Capps, Heather Koball, Andrea Campetella, Krista Perreira, Sarah
Hooker, and Juan Manuel Pedroza, *Implications of Immigration Enforcement Activities for the Well-Being of Children in Immigrant Families,* Urban Institute research report, September 2015, https://www.urban.org/sites/default/files/al
fresco/publication-exhibits/2000405/2000405-Implications-of-Immigration
-Enforcement-Activities-for-the-Well-Being-of-Children-in-Immigrant
-Families.pdf.

31 Mark Greenberg, Randy Capps, Andrew Kalweit, Jennifer Grishkin, and Ann
Flagg, *Immigrant Families and Child Welfare Systems: Emerging Needs and Promising Policies,* Migration Policy Institute research report, May 2019, https://www
.migrationpolicy.org/research/immigrant-families-child-welfare-systems.

32 Seth Freed Wessler, "Felipe Montes Departs the United States for Mexico,
With His Children," *Colorlines,* March 22, 2013, https://www.colorlines.com
/articles/felipe-montes-departs-united-states-mexico-his-children.

33 Fox News, "Deportation Often Means Losing Custody of US-Born Children,"
March 12, 2012, https://www.foxnews.com/politics/deportation-often-means
-losing-custody-of-us-born-children.

34 Capps, Koball, Campetella, Perreira, Hooker, and Pedroza, *Implication of Immigration Enforcement Activities for the Well-Being of Children in Immigrant Families.*

35 Center on Budget and Policy Priorities, "Policy Basics: Temporary Assistance
for Needy Families," last updated February 6, 2020, https://www.cbpp.org
/research/policy-basics-an-introduction-to-tanf.

36 Olivia Golden and Amelia Hawkins, *TANF Child-Only Cases,* Urban Institute
policy brief no. 3, November 2011, https://www.urban.org/sites/default/files
/publication/25426/412573-TANF-Child-Only-Cases.PDF.

37 Jane Mauldon, Richard Speiglman, Christina Sogar and Matt Stagner, *TANF
Child-Only Cases: Who Are They? What Policies Affect Them? What Is Being
Done?,* report submitted to the US Department of Health and Human Services,
December 11, 2012, https://cfpic.org/wp-content/uploads/2020/12/TANF
-Child-Only-Cases-The-Report-0113.pdf.

38 Authors' calculations using IPUMS-ACS data. Data obtained from Steven
Ruggles, Sarah Flood, Ronald Goeken, Josiah Grover, Erin Meyer, Jose Pacas,
and Matthew Sobek, *IPUMS USA: Version 10.0* [data set] (Minneapolis, MN:
IPUMS, 2020), http://doi.org/10.18128/D010.V10.0.

39 Authors' calculations using IPUMS-ACS data. Data obtained from Steven
Ruggles, Sarah Flood, Ronald Goeken, Josiah Grover, Erin Meyer, Jose Pacas,
and Matthew Sobek, *IPUMS USA: Version 10.0* [data set] (Minneapolis, MN:
IPUMS, 2020), http://doi.org/10.18128/D010.V10.0.

40 Authors' calculations using IPUMS-ACS data. Data obtained from Steven Ruggles, Sarah Flood, Ronald Goeken, Josiah Grover, Erin Meyer, Jose Pacas, and Matthew Sobek, *IPUMS USA: Version 10.0* [data set] (Minneapolis, MN: IPUMS, 2020), http://doi.org/10.18128/D010.V10.0.

41 Authors' calculations using IPUMS-ACS data. Data obtained from Steven Ruggles, Sarah Flood, Ronald Goeken, Josiah Grover, Erin Meyer, Jose Pacas, and Matthew Sobek, *IPUMS USA: Version 10.0* [data set] (Minneapolis, MN: IPUMS, 2020), http://doi.org/10.18128/D010.V10.0.

42 Daniel T. Griswold, "Immigration and the Welfare State," *Cato Journal* 32, no. 1 (Winter 2012): 159–74.

43 For a brief summary of the literature, see Ole Agersnap, Amalie Sofie Jensen, and Henrik Kleven, "The Welfare Magnet Hypothesis: Evidence from an Immigrant Welfare Scheme in Denmark" (National Bureau of Economic Research Working Paper no. 26454, revised March 2020), https://www.nber.org/system/files/working_papers/w26454/w26454.pdf.

44 George J. Borjas, "Immigration and Welfare Magnets," *Journal of Labor Economics* 17, no. 4 (October 1999): 607–37.

45 Neeraj Kaushal, "New Immigrants' Location Choices: Magnets without Welfare," *Journal of Labor Economics* 23, no. 1 (January 2005): 59–80.

46 Robin Rudowitz, Elizabeth Hinton, Madeline Guth, and Lina Stoylar, *Medicaid Enrollment & Spending Growth: FY 2020 & 2021*, Kaiser Family Foundation, October 14, 2020, https://www.kff.org/medicaid/issue-brief/medicaid-enrollment-spending-growth-fy-2020-2021/.

47 Medicaid and CHIP Payment and Access Commission, "Exhibit 33: CHIP Spending by State, FY 2019," MACStats, accessed February 14, 2021, https://www.macpac.gov/wp-content/uploads/2015/01/EXHIBIT-33.-CHIP-Spending-by-State-FY-2019-millions.pdf; Congressional Budget Office, *Federal Subsidies for Health Insurance Coverage for People Under Age 65: 2018 to 2028*, May 23, 2018, https://www.cbo.gov/publication/53826.

48 Juliette Cubanski and Tricia Neuman, "The Facts on Medicare Spending and Financing," Kaiser Family Foundation issue brief, August 20, 2019, https://www.kff.org/medicare/issue-brief/the-facts-on-medicare-spending-and-financing/.

49 Erica Williams, Eric Figueroa, and Wesley Tharpe, "Inclusive Approach to Immigrants Who Are Undocumented Can Help Families and States Prosper," Center on Budget and Policy Priorities, December 19, 2019, https://www.cbpp.org/research/state-budget-and-tax/inclusive-approach-to-immigrants-who-are-undocumented-can-help.

50 Samantha Artiga and Maria Diaz, "Health Care Coverage and Care of Undocumented Immigrants," Kaiser Family Foundation issue brief, July 15, 2019,

https://www.kff.org/disparities-policy/issue-brief/health-coverage-and-care-of-undocumented-immigrants/.

51 Dhruv Khullar and Dave A. Chokshi, "JAMA Forum: Immigrant Health, Value-Based Care, and Emergency Medicaid Reform," *news@JAMA*, January 23, 2019, https://newsatjama.jama.com/2019/01/23/jama-forum-immigrant-health-value-based-care-and-emergency-medicaid-reform/.

52 Jim P. Stimpson, Fernando A. Wilson, and Leah Zallman, "ED Visits and Spending by Unauthorized Immigrants Compared with Legal Immigrants and US Natives," *American Journal of Emergency Medicine* 32, no. 6 (June 2014): 679–80.

53 Jonas J. Swartz, Jens Hainmueller, Duncan Lawrence, and Maria Rodriguez, "Expanding Prenatal Care to Unauthorized Immigrant Women and the Effects on Infant Health," *Obstetrics and Gynecology* 130, no. 5 (2017): 938–45.

54 James P. Stimpson and F.A. Wilson, "Unauthorized Immigrants Spend Less Than Other Immigrants and US Natives on Health Care," *Health Affairs* 32, no. 7 (July 2013): 1313–18.

55 Chris Conover, "How American Citizens Finance $17.0 Billion in Health Care for Unauthorized Immigrants," *Forbes*, December 30, 2019, https://www.forbes.com/sites/theapothecary/2020/12/30/how-american-citizens-finance-170-billion-in-health-care-for-unauthorized-immigrants/?sh=661a1f7861aa.

56 Rumbaut, Ruben G. and Walter A. Ewing, *The Myth of Immigrant Criminality and the Paradox of Assimilation*.

57 National Academies of Sciences, Engineering, and Medicine, *The Integration of Immigrants into American Society*, consensus study report (Washington, DC: National Academies Press, 2015): ch. 9.

58 Kenneth Dominguez, Ana Penman-Aguilar, Man-Huei Chang, Ramal Moone-singhe, Ted Castellanos, Alfonso Rodriguez-Lainz, and Richard Schieber, "Vital Signs: Leading Causes of Death, Prevalence of Diseases and Risk Factors, and Use of Health Services Among Hispanics in the United States — 2009–2013," *Center for Disease Control and Prevention Morbidity and Mortality Weekly Report* 64, no. 17 (May 8, 2015): 469–78.

59 Francisca Antman, Brian Duncan, and Stephen J. Trejo, "Ethnic Attrition, Assimilation, and the Measured Health Outcomes of Mexican Americans," *Journal of Population Economics* 33, no. 4 (October 2020): 1499–1522.

60 Silvia Helena Barcellos, Dana P. Goldman, and James Smith, "Undiagnosed Disease, Especially Diabetes, Casts Doubt On Some Of Reported Health 'Advantage' Of Recent Mexican Immigrants," *Health Affairs* 31, no. 12 (December 2012): 2727–37.

61 Lauren Blue, "The Ethnic Health Advantage," *Scientific American*, October 1, 2011, https://www.scientificamerican.com/article/the-ethnic-health-advantage/.

62 Karl Eschbach, Glenn V. Ostir, Kushang V. Patel, Kyriakos S. Markides, and James S. Goodwin, "Neighborhood Context and Mortality among Older Mexican Americans: Is There a Barrio Advantage?," *American Journal of Public Health* 94, no. 10 (October 2004): 1807–12.

63 Janet Currie, "The Take Up of Social Benefits" (National Bureau of Economic Research Working Paper no. 10488, 2004), https://www.nber.org/system/files /working_papers/w10488/w10488.pdf.

64 Marianne Bertrand, Erzo F. P. Luttmer, and Sendhil Mullainathan, "Network Effects and Welfare Cultures," *Quarterly Journal of Economics* 115, no. 3 (August 2000): 1019–55.

65 "Statements of National Policy Concerning Welfare and Immigration," 8 US Code § 1601, accessed June 2, 2020, https://www.law.cornell.edu/uscode/text /8/1601.

66 George J. Borjas, "Welfare Reform, Labor Supply, and Health Insurance in the Immigrant Population," *Journal of Health Economics* 22, no. 6 (2003): 933–58.

67 Robert Kaestner and Neeraj Kaushal, "Immigrant and Native Responses to Welfare Reform," *Journal of Population Economics* 18, no. 1 (2005): 69–92.

68 Tara Watson, "Inside the Refrigerator: Immigration Enforcement and Chilling in Immigrant Medicaid Participation," *American Economic Journal: Economic Policy* 6 (2014): 313–38.

69 Karen Hacker, Jocelyn Chu, Carolyn Leung, Robert Marra, Alex Pirie, Mohamed Brahimi, Margaret English, Joshua Beckmann, Dolores Acevedo-Garcia, and Robert P. Marlin, "The Impact of Immigration and Customs Enforcement on Immigrant Health: Perceptions of Immigrants in Everett, Massachusetts, USA," *Social Science and Medicine* 73, no. 4 (August 2011): 586–94.

70 Harris Meyer, "Tougher Immigration Enforcement Is Taking a Toll on Healthcare," *Modern Healthcare*, April 21, 2017, https://www.modernhealthcare.com /article/20170421/NEWS/170429967/tougher-immigration-enforcement-is -taking-a-toll-on-healthcare.

71 US Immigration and Customs Enforcement, "FAQs: Sensitive Locations and Courthouse Arrests," last updated February 2, 2021, https://www.ice.gov/ero /enforcement/sensitive-loc.

72 Jessica Hanson, "School Settings Are Sensitive Locations That Should Be Off-Limits to Immigration Enforcement," *The Torch* blog post, National Immigration Law Center, May 4, 2017, https://www.nilc.org/news/the-torch/5-4-17/.

73 Josiah McC. Heyman, Guillermina Gina Núñez, and Víctor A. Talavera, "Healthcare Access and Barriers for Unauthorized Immigrants in El Paso County, Texas," *Family and Community Health* 32, no. 1 (2009): 4–21.

74 Ibrahim Hirsi, "Trump Administration's 'Public Charge' Provision Has Roots in Colonial US," *The World* (radio program), Public Radio International, Decem-

ber 19, 2018, https://www.pri.org/stories/2018-12-19/trump-administration-s
-public-charge-provision-has-roots-colonial-us.

75 Tara Watson, "Proposed Immigration Rules and the Safety Net," *EconoFact*,
April 3, 2018, https://econofact.org/proposed-immigration-rules-and-the-safe
ty-net.

76 American Immigration Lawyers Association, "Practice Pointer: Biden Administration Announces Limited Immediate Change to Public Charge Rules," AILA
document no. 21020433, February 10, 2021, https://www.aila.org/advo-media
/aila-practice-pointers-and-alerts/practice-pointer-biden-administration-an
nounces.

77 Hacker et al., "The Impact of Immigration and Customs Enforcement on Immigrant Health: Perceptions of Immigrants in Everett, Massachusetts, USA."

78 Jens Hainmuller, Duncan Lawrence, Linna Martén, Bernard Black, Lucila
Figueroa, Michael Hotard, Tomas R. Jiminez, Fernando Mendoza, Maria I.
Rodriguez, Jonas J. Swartz, and David D. Laitin, "Protecting Unauthorized Immigrant Mothers Improves Their Children's Mental Health," *Science* 357, no.
6355 (September 8, 2017): 1041–44.

79 Nicole L. Novak, Arelene T. Geronimus, and Aresha M. Martinez-Cardoso,
"Change in Birth Outcomes among Infants Born to Latina Mothers after a
Major Immigration Raid," *International Journal of Epidemiology* 46, no. 3 (2017):
839–49.

80 Maya Rhodan, "Attorney General Jeff Sessions Says DACA Program Will Be
Phased Out," *Time*, September 5, 2017, http://time.com/4927227/daca-undocu
mented-dreamers-jeff-sessions/.

81 Michael Olivas, *No Undocumented Child Left Behind: Plyer v. Doe and the Education of Undocumented Schoolchildren* (New York: New York University Press,
2012).

82 James Plyler, Superintendent of the Tyler Independent School District and Its
Board of Trustees et al., Appellants, v. J. and R. Doe et al. Texas, et al., Appellants, v. Certain Named and Unnamed Undocumented Alien Children et al.,
457 US 202 (1982), https://www.law.cornell.edu/supremecourt/text/457/202
#writing-USSC_CR_0457_0202_ZO.

83 US Census Bureau, "Historical Table 6: Women 15 to 44 Years Old Who Had
a Child in the Last 12 Months and Children Ever Born per 1,000 Women, by
Nativity Status, Region of Birth, Citizenship Status, Race, Hispanic Origin, and
Age: CPS, Selected Years, 1994–2010," accessed August 6, 2019, https://www
.census.gov/data/tables/time-series/demo/fertility/his-cps.html#par_list_6.

84 Steven A. Camarota, Bryan Griffith, and Karen Zeigler, *Mapping the Impact of
Immigration on Public Schools*, Center for Immigration Studies report, March
2017, https://cis.org/Report/Mapping-Impact-Immigration-Public-Schools.

85 Jeffrey S. Passel and D'Vera Cohn, "Fact Tank: Children of Unauthorized Immigrants Represent Rising Share of K-12 Students," Pew Research Center, November 17, 2016, http://www.pewresearch.org/fact-tank/2016/11/17/children-of-unauthorized-immigrants-represent-rising-share-of-k-12-students/.

86 Authors' analysis of 2017–2019 Current Population Survey data. Data obtained from Sarah Flood, Miriam King, Renae Rodgers, Steven Ruggles and J. Robert Warren, *IPUMS USA: Version 8.0* [data set] (Minneapolis, MN: IPUMS, 2020), https://doi.org/10.18128/D030.V8.0.

87 National Center for Education Statistics, "English Language Learner (ELL) Students Enrolled in Public Elementary and Secondary Schools, by State: Selected Years, Fall 2000 through Fall 2017," Table 204.20 in *Digest of Education Statistics 2019*, accessed June 27, 2020, https://nces.ed.gov/programs/digest/d19/tables/dt19_204.20.asp.

88 Aimee Chin, N. Meltem Daysal, and Scott A. Imberman, "Impact of Bilingual Education Programs on Limited English Proficient Students and Their Peers: Regression Discontinuity Evidence from Texas," *Journal of Public Economics* 107 (November 2013): 63–78.

89 James M. Poterba, "Demographic Structure and the Political Economy of Public Education," *Journal of Policy Analysis and Management* 16, no. 1 (December 1998): 48–66.

90 Elizabeth U. Cascio and Ethan G. Lewis, "Cracks in the Melting Pot: Immigration, School Choice, and Segregation," *American Economic Journal: Economic Policy* 4, no. 3 (2012): 91–117.

91 Wayne Riddle, *Implications of Community Eligibility for the Education of Disadvantaged Students Under Title I*, Center on Budget and Policy Priorities report, July 20, 2015, https://www.cbpp.org/research/food-assistance/implications-of-community-eligibility-for-the-education-of-disadvantaged.

92 Massachusetts Department of Elementary and Secondary Education, *Low-Income Student Calculation Study*, February 2017, http://www.doe.mass.edu/bese/docs/fy2017/2017-02/item9-study.pdf.

93 Chaudry, Capps, Pedroza, Castaneda, Santos, and Scott, *Facing Our Future: Children in the Aftermath of Immigration Enforcement*.

94 Jie Zong and Jeanne Batalova, "How Many Unauthorized Immigrants Graduate from U.S. High Schools Annually?," Migration Policy Institute fact sheet, April 2019, https://www.migrationpolicy.org/research/unauthorized-immigrants-graduate-us-high-schools.

95 National Center for Education Statistics, "The Condition of Education: Immediate College Enrollment Rate," last updated April 2020, https://nces.ed.gov/programs/coe/indicator_cpa.asp.

96 Zaidee Staveley, "University of California Will Support Undocumented Students, Even If DACA Ends," EdSource, November 12, 2019, https://edsource.org

/2019/university-of-california-will-support-undocumented-students-even-if
-daca-ends/619844.

97 US Department of Education, "Financial Aid and Undocumented Students:
Questions and Answers," February 2019, https://studentaid.ed.gov/sa/sites
/default/files/financial-aid-and-undocumented-students.pdf.

98 Catalina Amuedo-Dorantes and Chad Sparber, "In-State Tuition for Undocumented Immigrants and Its Impact on College Enrollment, Tuition Costs, Student Financial Aid, and Indebtedness," *Regional Science and Urban Economics*
49 (November 2014): 11–24.

99 National Conference of State Legislatures, "Undocumented Student Tuition:
Overview," September 19, 2019, https://www.ncsl.org/research/education/un
documented-student-tuition-overview.aspx.

100 Robert Bozick and Trey Miller, "In-State College Tuition Policies for Undocumented Immigrants: Implications for High School Enrollment among Non-
Citizen Mexican Youth," *Population Research and Policy Review* 33, no. 1 (February 2014): 13–30.

101 Neeraj Kaushal, "In-State Tuition for the Undocumented: Education Effects
on Mexican Young Adults," *Journal of Policy Analysis and Management* 27, no. 4
(2008): 771–92.

102 Lisa Christensen Gee, Matthew Gardner, Misha E. Hill, and Meg Wiehe, *Undocumented Immigrants' State and Local Tax Contributions*, Institute on Taxation and Economic Policy report, last updated March 2017, https://itep.org/wp
-content/uploads/immigration2017.pdf.

103 Migration Policy Institute Data Hub, "Profile of the Unauthorized Population:
United States," accessed July 31, 2019, https://www.migrationpolicy.org/data
/unauthorized-immigrant-population/state/US#.

104 Gee et al., *Undocumented Immigrants' State and Local Tax Contributions*.

105 Sean G. Hanagan, "Social Security Administration 'No Match' Letters to Employers Make Another Comeback," *National Law Review*, December 14, 2018,
https://www.natlawreview.com/article/social-security-administration-no
-match-letters-to-employers-make-another-comeback.

106 Social Security Administration Office of the Inspector General, *Status of the
Social Security Administration's Earnings Suspense File*, Informational Report
A-03-15-50058, September 2015, https://oig.ssa.gov/sites/default/files/audit
/full/pdf/A-03-15-50058.pdf.

107 Stephen Goss, Alice Wade, J. Patrick Skirvin, Michael Morris, K. Mark Bye,
and Danielle Huston, *Effects of Unauthorized Immigration on the Actuarial Status
of the Social Security Trust Funds*, Actuarial Note no. 151, Social Security Administration Office of the Chief Actuary, April 2013, https://www.ssa.gov/oact
/NOTES/pdf_notes/note151.pdf.

108 Board of Trustees, Federal Old-Age and Survivors Insurance and Federal Dis-

ability Insurance Trust Funds, *2018 Annual Report of the Board of Trustees of the Federal Old-Age and Survivors Insurance and Federal Disability Insurance Trust Funds*, June 5, 2018, https://www.ssa.gov/OACT/TR/2018/tr2018.pdf.

109 Goss et al., *Effects of Unauthorized Immigration on the Actuarial Status of the Social Security Trust Funds*.

110 Hunter Hallman, "How do Undocumented Immigrants Pay Federal Taxes? An Explainer," Bipartisan Policy Center blog post, March 28, 2018, https://bipartisanpolicy.org/blog/how-do-undocumented-immigrants-pay-federal-taxes-an-explainer/.

111 Alexia Fernández Campbell, "Undocumented Immigrants Pay Taxes Too. Here's How They Do It.," *Vox.com*, April 17, 2017, https://www.vox.com/policy-and-politics/2017/4/17/15290950/undocumented-immigrants-file-tax-returns.

112 Internal Revenue Service, "Individual Taxpayer Identification Number (ITIN) Reminders for Tax Professionals," accessed August 6, 2019, https://www.irs.gov/individuals/international-taxpayers/individual-taxpayer-identification-number-itin-reminders-for-tax-professionals.

113 Treasury Inspector General for Tax Administration, *Recovery Act: Individuals Who Are Not Authorized to Work in the United States Were Paid $4.2 Billion in Refundable Credits*, report no. 2011–41–061, https://www.treasury.gov/tigta/auditreports/2011reports/201141061fr.pdf.

114 David North, "Congress Takes a Step against Paying Illegal Aliens to Stay in the U.S.," Center for Immigration Studies, December 19, 2017, https://cis.org/North/Congress-Takes-Step-Against-Paying-Illegal-Aliens-Stay-US.

115 David North, "Congress Takes a Step against Paying Illegal Aliens to Stay in the U.S."

116 David North, "Congress Takes a Step against Paying Illegal Aliens to Stay in the U.S."

117 Internal Revenue Service, "IRS: Refunds Worth $1.1 Billion Waiting to Be Claimed by Those Who Have Not Filed 2014 Federal Income Tax Returns," news release, March 8, 2018, https://www.irs.gov/newsroom/irs-refunds-worth-one-point-one-billion-dollars-waiting-to-be-claimed-by-those-who-have-not-filed-2014-federal-income-tax-returns.

118 National Academies of Sciences, Engineering, and Medicine, *The Economic and Fiscal Consequences of Immigration*, consensus study report, (Washington, DC: National Academies Press, 2017), https://doi.org/10.17226/23550.

119 Carol Keeton Strayhorn, *Undocumented Immigrants in Texas: A Financial Analysis of the Impact to the State Budget and Economy*, Texas Office of the Comptroller special report, December 2006, http://www.fosterglobal.com/policy_papers/TexasAnalysisCost-BenefitOfUndocdWorkers.pdf.

120 Stephen Appold and James H. Johnson, "The New North Carolinians: The Economic Impact of the Hispanic and Immigrant Population in North Carolina," *Social Science Research Network* (February 10, 2014), https://papers.ssrn.com/sol3/papers.cfm?abstract_id=2434374.

121 Congressional Budget Office, "Cost Estimate: S.6211 Comprehensive Immigration Reform Act of 2006," August 18, 2006, https://www.cbo.gov/sites/default/files/cbofiles/ftpdocs/75xx/doc7501/s2611spass.pdf.

122 Congressional Budget Office, *The Economic Impact of S. 744, the Border Security, Economic Opportunity, and Immigration Modernization Act*, report, June 18, 2013, https://www.cbo.gov/publication/44346.

123 US Citizenship and Immigration Services, "Historical National Average Processing Time (in Months) for All USCIS Offices for Select Forms by Fiscal Year," accessed August 6, 2019, https://egov.uscis.gov/processing-times/historic-pt.

Conclusions

1 Joshua Partlow and David A. Farenhold, "'If You're a Good Worker, Papers Don't Matter': How a Trump Construction Crew Has Relied on Immigrants without Legal Status," *Washington Post*, August 9, 2019, https://www.washingtonpost.com/politics/if-youre-a-good-worker-papers-dont-matter-how-a-trump-construction-crew-has-relied-on-immigrants-without-legal-status/2019/08/09/cf59014a-b3ab-11e9-8e94-71a35969e4d8_story.html.

2 In FY 2019, there were 267,258 ICE removals (with 85,958 originating from interior arrests). Dividing the total ICE budget of $7.6 billion by all ICE removals yields a dollars-per-removal number of $28,000. US Immigration and Customs Enforcement, *Fiscal Year 2019 Enforcement and Removal Operations Report*, accessed June 20, 2020, https://www.ice.gov/sites/default/files/documents/Document/2019/eroReportFY2019.pdf; US Department of Homeland Security, *Budget-in-Brief: Fiscal Year 2020*, accessed July 31, 2019, https://www.dhs.gov/sites/default/files/publications/19_0318_MGMT_FY-2020-Budget-In-Brief.pdf.

3 Border Security, Economic Opportunity, and Immigration Modernization Act, S. 744, 113th Congress (2013–2014), accessed October 25, 2020, https://www.congress.gov/bill/113th-congress/senate-bill/744.

4 Congressional Budget Office, *The Economic Impact of S. 744, the Border Security, Economic Opportunity, and Immigration Modernization Act*, report, June 18, 2013, https://www.cbo.gov/publication/44346.

5 Sarah Stillman, "The Race to Dismantle Trump's Immigration Policies," *New Yorker*, February 1, 2021, https://www.newyorker.com/magazine/2021/02/08/the-race-to-dismantle-trumps-immigration-policies.

INDEX

Page numbers in italics refer to figures and tables.